Jekyll Island's Early Years

A Wormsloe
FOUNDATION
PUBLICATION

Jekyll Island's Early Years

From Prehistory through Reconstruction

JUNE HALL McCASH

The University of Georgia Press | *Athens and London*

Paperback edition published in 2014 by
The University of Georgia Press
Athens, Georgia 30602
www.ugapress.org
© 2005 by June Hall McCash
All rights reserved
Designed by Kathi Dailey Morgan
Set in Adobe Caslon by BookComp Inc.
Printed and bound by Sheridan Books
The paper in this book meets the guidelines for
permanence and durability of the Committee on
Production Guidelines for Book Longevity of the
Council on Library Resources.

Most University of Georgia Press titles are
available from popular e-book vendors.

Printed in the United States of America
18   17   16   15   14   P   5   4   3   2   1

The Library of Congress has cataloged the
hardcover edition of this book as follows:
McCash, June Hall.
Jekyll Island's early years :
from prehistory through Reconstruction /
June Hall McCash.
xv, 280 p. : ill., maps ; 25 cm. —
(Wormsloe Foundation publications ; no. 25)
Includes bibliographical references (p. 253–261) and index.
ISBN 0-8203-2447-7 (alk. paper)
1. Jekyll Island (Ga.)—History. I. Title.
II. Publications (Wormsloe Foundation) ; no. 25.
F292.G58M385 2005
975.8'742—dc22   2005001134

British Library Cataloging-in-Publication Data available

Paperback ISBN 978-0-8203-4738-7

FOR RICHARD,

who led me back to the feast

Contents

Preface

Surely Prospero, waving anew his magic wand,

could never summon from the vasty deep an

island more historically picturesque.

FRANKLIN HARVEY HEAD

HE STATEMENT quoted above was one of the few truths that Franklin Head stated in his charming spoof, "The Legends of Jekyl Island," written to entertain his friends at the Chicago Literary Club in December 1892.[1] He first presented the narrative as a light diversion for this group of congenial intellectuals who gathered regularly to hear each other's literary productions. Since that time it has been published on several occasions. First printed in May 1893 in the *New England Magazine*, it was privately printed a year or so later as a pamphlet for the pleasure of Head's friends under the title of *Studies in Early American History: The Legends of Jekyl Island*. These "homegrown legends," as the editor of a still later printing calls them in a postscript, soon took on a life of their own and had by 1894 already begun to be taken seriously by occasional authors in earnest publications such as the *Christian Advocate*.[2] The last version was privately published in 1902 as a little booklet that Head distributed among club members and friends. To the later versions he added a few additional historical "facts" and photographs of "General Oglethorpe" and other distinguished figures—in reality, photographs of Chicago men who were members of both the Jekyll Island Club and the Chicago Literary Club. To any observant reader, the photographs would even more clearly underscore the parodic intent of the work. For example, the photograph labeled "Rev. George Whitefield," a well-known English

In 1892 Franklin Harvey Head
wrote a spoof of Jekyll Island's history
for the Chicago Literary Club. When
later writers took it seriously, it became
the source of much misinformation about
Jekyll Island's early years.
(*Men of Illinois*, 1902)

clergyman who came to Georgia in 1738, is, in fact, an image of the popular
club member Nathaniel K. Fairbank. A leather-bound copy of this booklet,
personally signed by Franklin Head with the words "For the Jekyl Island
Club with the best wishes of its consiencious [*sic*] historian," is included in
the collection of the Georgia Historical Society.[3] From this delightful and
evidently successful hoax, written to amuse his clever friends, come many of
the inaccuracies and much of the misinformation that circulated for decades
about Jekyll Island's early history. Even though Head had never intended
his version of Jekyll "history" as a serious interpretation and no doubt would
have been surprised that anyone could mistake it for truth, he was nevertheless quite right about one important point. The island is "historically
picturesque."

A more serious attempt to capture the island's history was undertaken
by the club member Charles Stewart Maurice and his wife, Charlotte. Together, sometime before her death in 1909, they wrote a small booklet in
which Charlotte collected historical notes and legends, while her husband
penned a brief outline of the early days of the elite Jekyll Island Club, which
had been organized on the coast of Georgia in 1886.[4] Charlotte's notes,
though brief, had been carefully researched and she sought, unlike Franklin
Head, to present an accurate account. For the most part, with only occasional errors derived from anecdotal accounts, she achieved her goal. The
primary importance of the little book for our purposes, however, is that it

Charlotte Holbrooke Maurice made
the first serious attempt to retell Jekyll
Island's early history. (From the collection
of the Tioga Point Museum, Athens, Pa.)

points to the interest of Jekyll Island Club members in the early history of the island. The division of labor for the Maurice booklet also suggests that the island's history is justifiably viewed and accurately told in two fundamentally different parts: the early history of the island and the club history.

Like most of those who come to Jekyll Island today and seek to learn about its past, I first became interested in the Jekyll Island Club era, with its amazing array of members with names like Gould, Rockefeller, Vanderbilt, and Pulitzer. An exhibit of archival materials from the collection of the Jekyll Island Museum happened to be on display during one of my first visits to the island. The exhibit, which included the original membership list, the clubhouse register, and the map drawn by Horace W. S. Cleveland, identifying the owners of the various lots, had an amazing impact on both me and my coauthor, my late husband, Bart McCash. Thus, it was the club, not the island's earlier history, that became the subject of our book together, *The Jekyll Island Club: Southern Haven for America's Millionaires* (University of Georgia Press, 1989). The second volume, *The Jekyll Island Cottage Colony* (University of Georgia Press, 1998), which we had just begun before his untimely death in 1991, is an expansion of that club history and tells the stories of the various families who owned cottages in the club compound at Jekyll.

The present volume represents a completely new departure, an effort to capture, with as much accuracy as modern research allows and with greater access to archival materials than Charlotte Maurice had, the period of Jekyll history that has never been told in any detail, the preclub era. I depict the time when Native Americans occupied or seasonally used the island until the period that shook our nation and changed the South forever—the Civil War and its aftermath during Reconstruction.

Readers who wish to continue the story beyond this era are encouraged to see the earlier two volumes mentioned above, on the history of the Jekyll Island Club, for which this current work is, essentially, a "prequel." Those two books continue the story of Jekyll Island that was begun so many thousands of years ago in an age that has no recorded history. For information on the state era of the island, which began in 1947, five years after the closing of the club during World War II, readers are encouraged to examine an article that I recently coauthored with my son and university colleague C. Brenden Martin, "From Millionaires to the Masses: Tourism at Jekyll Island, Georgia," in a volume titled *Southern Journeys: Tourism, History, and Culture in the Modern South* (University of Alabama Press, 2003), edited by Richard Starnes. Perhaps one day we can jointly write the fascinating history of the state era in greater detail and thereby complete the story of this Georgia Golden Isle.

Acknowledgments

I N PREPARING this present volume, I have, as always, had the full support and help of the staff at the Jekyll Island Museum. I would especially like to thank Warren Murphey, whose ongoing enthusiasm for my projects and tirelessness in answering my endless questions are invaluable. John Hunter as well has contributed in countless ways, particularly in helping me to locate and obtain photographs of items from the collection of Native American artifacts found on Jekyll Island and contained in the museum. Both have assisted my work in the Jekyll archives and collections with willingness and enduring patience. At the Museum of Coastal History on St. Simons, I appreciate the assistance of Pat Morrison, Deborah Thomas, and Marilyn Marsh. And at the Georgia Historical Society, where I became a virtual fixture for several weeks, I would like to express my appreciation to all the staff members who cheerfully helped me to locate materials and answered my stream of questions, especially Susan Dick and Jewell Anderson Dalrymple. The staff at the Georgia Department of Archives and History, particularly Dale Couch and Sandy Boling, has also provided invaluable resources and assistance, as has the staff in special collections at Emory University, the University of Georgia, and especially Alan Boehm at the Walker Library of Middle Tennessee State University. I would like to add a particular word of thanks to Carey Knapp and Diane Jackson at the Three Rivers Regional Library in Brunswick, Georgia; to Lola Jamsky, clerk of the Superior Court of Glynn County; and to Mary Evelyn Tomlin, archivist at the National Archives Southeastern Region at East Point, Georgia. Many other curators and staff members have been helpful in sharing their materials, including those at Duke University; the University of North Carolina's Southern Historical Collection; the Winterthur Museum; the National Archives of St. Kitts, Basseterre, West

Indies; and the British Public Records Office. Amy Hedrick and Chris Chapman have also provided assistance and enthusiasm for helping ferret out obscure materials in Brunswick.

I am particularly indebted to descendents of the remarkable people whose lives are told in this book. Patrick Demere shared with me his typescript and collection of documentary evidence on his ancestor Raymond Demeré and his brother Paul. Irene Cordell made available to me invaluable information on the Horton family. Henry Howell was helpful with information about and photographs of both the Lamar and du Bignon families. Robert Cronk provided genealogical information he had collected on the family of Clement Martin. Doris Liebrecht has through the years and on all my Jekyll projects generously helped me piece together the story of the du Bignon family. The late Mrs. Malcolm Kitchens shared her information as well on the du Bignons. E. Lynn McLarty (with whom I spent a productive day of research in the Glynn County Courthouse) provided much information on Henri du Bignon's second and third families, and the image of William Turner, which had been preserved by his mother-in-law, Charlotte Granberry Gillespie. Mary Elizabeth Dubignon also added details on Henri du Bignon's second and third families. Marian Payne, the granddaughter of William du Bignon of Jekyll Island, helped with many of my questions and provided me with photographs and helpful information about her family, descendents of John Couper du Bignon. All of these people and many others, too numerous to mention, have provided assistance along the way.

Recent works on Georgia history have also been very helpful, notably that of Martha Keber, whose friendship, support, and suggestions have added substantially to my book. Her book *Seas of Gold, Seas of Cotton: Christophe Poulain DuBignon of Jekyll Island* (University of Georgia Press, 2000) is the result of years of meticulous research and fills many gaps, especially on the early years of Christophe before he arrived in Georgia. The many publications of Buddy Sullivan, whom I also claim as a friend, have also been invaluable. Needless to say, I have frequently relied on the works of other historians as well, too many to enumerate, whom I have never had the pleasure of knowing. I would particularly like to mention Charles Hudson's work and helpful suggestions, which have been much appreciated, as well as Mary Bullard's books, especially *Cumberland Island: A History*, which has been a useful resource.

The wonderful university at which I spent most of my academic career—

Middle Tennessee State University—has provided resources and assistance without which I could never have completed this task. First and foremost, the efficient staff members in the Interlibrary Loan Office of Walker Library, where no work is too obscure for them to pursue, have been critical in gathering information for this task. The Division of Photographic Services has been invaluable in helping to provide many of the images the book contains, and the Division of Publications and Graphics (with special thanks to Lawanda Baker) prepared the map of the Guale and Timucua regions (see p. 9). Perhaps most important of all, I would like to thank the University Research Committee for grants along the way that have allowed me the time to work on this book.

A special word of gratitude goes to my historian son (and coauthor mentioned above), Bren Martin, for reading with a keen eye several of the chapters and providing useful and constructive criticism, and to Selby McCash, for his helpful photo search at the Library of Congress. I would like to express my deepest appreciation as well to my friend D. Michelle Adkerson for her many helpful stylistic suggestions and her true appreciation for Jekyll Island and its history. Above all, I am grateful for the constant love and support of my husband, Richard Gleaves, for listening to or reading various versions of every chapter with patience and interest, for occasionally being a second set of eyes and hands in archives when time was short, and for reminding me to eat when I was too engrossed in my work to remember.

My heartfelt thanks goes to all of these people for their help and support at various stages of the project, and a special word of gratitude to Nicole Mitchell, director of the University of Georgia Press, and Nancy Grayson, associate director and editor in chief, for their enthusiasm for this project even before we had met, and especially for the three-month deadline extension that was a godsend at a critical time. Finally, I would like to express my appreciation to Sarah McKee and Jon Davies, who so capably shepherded this project through the publication process, and to my extraordinary copyeditor, Jeanée Ledoux, for her meticulous scrutiny and helpful suggestions in preparing the final manuscript for publication.

It has given me a particular sense of satisfaction to see the evolution of these early years flow into a complete story, rather than remain a series of sequential (and seemingly unrelated) events, as they are so often perceived. I can only hope the reader finds as much pleasure in reading the book as I have had in writing it.

Introduction

On all these shores there are echoes of past and future:

of the flow of time, obliterating yet containing all that has gone

before; of the sea's eternal rhythms—the tides, the beat of surf,

the pressing rivers of the currents—shaping, changing,

dominating; of the stream of life, flowing as inexorably as any

ocean current, from the past to an unknown future.

RACHEL CARSON, *Edge of the Sea*

EKYLL ISLAND is the smallest of Georgia's Golden Isles, one of a chain of barrier islands that stretch like a string of pearls along the coast. Located toward the southern end of the state's shoreline and better protected than most coastal areas from storms by a series of great barrier reefs, Jekyll is situated in the innermost part of what geologists call the Georgia bight. The area sustained plant and animal life for millions of years before its first human residents arrived. During that time prehistoric animals—mastodons and mammoths—roamed the area, and the land that is now an island lay many miles inland. Sea levels of the Pleistocene Era were approximately 350 feet lower than they are at present, and the land area of Jekyll Island was still part of the mainland. Some two thousand years later, during the Miocene and Pliocene geological epochs, the glaciers began to melt, and sea levels began to rise, eating away at the land areas to form the barrier islands along the coast of present-day Georgia. Thus, Jekyll Island was born.

Only nine miles long and two miles wide, it lies at a latitude of 31° north and a longitude of 81°41´ west, separated from the mainland and Brunswick, Georgia, by a magnificent six-mile stretch of marshland, which Sidney

Lanier extolled in his well-known poem "The Marshes of Glynn." Though the island is protected to some extent by its favored location, Jekyll has nonetheless experienced occasional hurricanes that roar in from the coast of Africa to slam into the eastern shores of America, wreaking havoc in their path. Although it has been buffeted by major deadly storms like those recorded in 1804 and 1898, Jekyll has suffered less than coastal areas of other states like Florida and North Carolina that jut farther eastward, and the island's appeal has far outweighed the seasonal dangers of coastal life. As a consequence, countless generations of humans for thousands of years have been drawn to its usually calm waters, maritime forest, salt marshes, and tidal streams, which provide food and nurture to sea creatures, animals, and people alike.

Two primary factors have shaped the course of human life on Jekyll: the natural environment and human conflict. In spite of them, the men and women who have claimed the right to live on Jekyll have used it, much as we still do today, primarily as a place of refuge and tranquility, an escape from or defense against the world's turmoil, a natural haven where one seeks to find peace from the harried life that besets us elsewhere. Yet its history reminds us again and again that there is no true escape, for the forces of nature and the conflicts of humanity have repeatedly disrupted the tranquility of island life and left their marks throughout Jekyll's recorded history.

The island's journey in time is unique, and though its history is at times interwoven with that of its neighboring islands, its unfolding narrative is ultimately unlike that of any other Sea Island along the coast of Georgia. Its residents have been without exception noteworthy people who have played significant or representative roles in the history of Georgia and whose lives have often reflected some of the most important events of our developing nation. It is the intent of this volume to explore their lives and their use of the island, from the earliest inhabitants through the Civil War and its aftermath.

The first residents we can identify with any certainty are the Native peoples, the Timucua, who were using the island as a seasonal home and hunting ground at the time the first Europeans arrived. Native groups did not long survive the invasions and exploitation of their lands or the attempts by the Spaniards to convert them to the Catholic faith. When the English came and drove the Spanish definitively from the area, Jekyll became the home of Major William Horton, who found there both a refuge from the incessant squabbles of the colonists living at Frederica on neighboring St. Simons Island and a respite from his military duties. Horton was a courageous and reliable aide to General James Edward Oglethorpe, Georgia's founder, and served as military commander in his absence during the period of the English trustees' colony. But even though Horton may have on occasion avoided the colonists' petty quarrels by taking refuge on Jekyll, he could not, even there, escape the impact of military conflict with the Spaniards.

At the time Georgia became a royal colony in the period preceding the American Revolution, Jekyll was owned by the family of one of only twelve members of the King's Council, Clement Martin, whose father settled on the island in an effort to escape the threat of slave uprisings and economic competition in the Leeward Islands of the West Indies. Following the American Revolution, when the Martin family, which had been loyal to the Crown, was banished by the victorious colonists, Jekyll became the property of the first large-scale Sea Island cotton planter in the new state of Georgia, Richard Leake. Finally, a few years later, when revolution broke out in France, inspired in part by the success of the Americans against the English king, Jekyll would become the refuge of another family of royalists, the du Bignons, who came to America in the early 1790s to preserve their fortune and their lives. They had first settled with other French émigrés on Sapelo but soon moved to Jekyll to escape the irreconcilable quarrels that broke out among the émigré settlers. Like Horton, even at Jekyll the du Bignons could not totally escape human conflicts, and the island was twice invaded and pillaged during and just after the War of 1812. Jekyll Island remained in the hands of the du Bignon family for nearly a century, until the Civil War, which disrupted their plantation life, compelling them to evacuate the island for use first by Confederate and then by Union troops and freed slaves. When members of the family returned, Jekyll briefly became a refuge for an unconventional interracial relationship that would likely not have been tolerated on the mainland. Thus, throughout these early years the lives of the island's residents reflect the tribulations and struggles of our emerging country. This volume focuses on these stories.

Of course, the history of Jekyll does not end there, though the later years have been explored in other volumes. Briefly stated, when the greatest civil and military conflict of the new nation seemed to be behind us, the island was purchased in 1886 by the Jekyll Island Club, an elite family-oriented organization that survived until World War II. Club members were among the best known and wealthiest financiers and industrialists in an America just beginning to flex its muscle in the modern world. People like J. P. Morgan, William Rockefeller, Marshall Field, and Joseph Pulitzer, to mention only a few of the club's remarkable members, came to Jekyll Island annually from January to early April to find respite from the northern winters and the stressful business environments of cities like New York and Chicago. There they enjoyed the gentle climate, the natural setting, and a life of relative simplicity that evaded them in their everyday lives in the North. But even at Jekyll, once again our national conflicts found them, and it was the coming of World War II that put an end to the club. When the Jekyll Island Club closed in April 1942, only four months after the bombing of Pearl Harbor, the island became an outpost for the military, as it had been for the British before the American Revolution and for Confederate forces in the early years of the Civil War. Army, navy, and coast guard troops patrolled the island during the war years to protect the mainland from enemy attack. Such patrols were deemed necessary since, only a short time after the closing of the Jekyll Island Club in 1942, German submarines found their way into the Brunswick harbor waters.

When World War II ended, although a few remaining loyal club members made halfhearted efforts to reorganize and reopen the elite Jekyll Island Club, it became clear that it was a concept whose time had passed. Few had the wealth in postwar America to belong to such an exclusive club, which rarely broke even, much less made a profit. The war had led to a democratization of society that rendered such exclusivity almost "un-American." The coup de grâce came when the final member who had the funds to back such a project, Frank Miller Gould, the grandson of the financier and railroad magnate Jay Gould, died suddenly of a heart attack in 1945. Any further attempts to reopen the Jekyll Island Club seemed useless, and club officers began to consider selling the island to investors.

The state of Georgia in the person of Melvin E. Thompson, who became governor in one of the most controversial elections the state has ever seen, stepped in and rescued the island from almost certain disaster at the hands of commercial investors, whose only goal was to make a profit. Thompson, despite criticism and political controversy over the purchase of the island, was determined to turn Jekyll into a state park for the people of Georgia, whatever it took. In spite of opposition from political opponents like

Herman Talmadge, he accomplished his goal through a process of condemnation in which Jekyll Island Club officers cooperated, balking only briefly at the mere $675,000 the state paid for the island and all its improvements.

In 1947 the state of Georgia took over the stewardship of the island for use as a state park. The extraordinary foresight of its planners on the newly formed Jekyll Island State Park Authority left approximately two-thirds of the island undeveloped. The Georgia legislature finally wrote that ratio of undeveloped land into law in the early 1970s.[1] Thus, Jekyll has not become, like so many coastal areas, particularly in Florida, a desert of concrete shadowed by high-rise condominiums. It has remained instead a protected haven that allows humans and animals to coexist, where children can delight in the deer that emerge from their palmetto shelters at dusk, where wild turkeys can sometimes be spotted along the roadways, and where families of raccoons roam and forage freely. Jekyll Island today remains unique among the Georgia barrier isles, one of only three islands accessible by a causeway, yet the only one of the three where development is strictly controlled and where humans enjoy a predominantly natural environment that will continue to be preserved as long as the state remains faithful to its stewardship.

The story of the Jekyll Island Club, which became a legend in its own time, has been told and retold.[2] The part of the island's past that is the least known is that prior to the club era.[3] Thus, the purpose of this book is to fill that gap and take the reader back to the beginnings of human history on the island, to see how these factors—the environment, human conflict, and a desire for refuge—have shaped Jekyll's history. The island's journey in time from the earliest Native American residents through the Civil War and its aftermath is an important part of Jekyll's unfolding saga. It is a story that reflects in microcosm many of the early struggles of our country in its infancy, and it deserves to be remembered.

CHAPTER ONE

In the Beginning

Go where we will on the surface of things,

men have been there before us.

HENRY DAVID THOREAU

HE HUMAN STORY of the Georgia barrier isle that today we call Jekyll Island began more than eleven thousand years ago, long before our recorded histories. We know little of the earliest settlers along these shores, for the rising sea levels have long since covered all traces of their existence. Most archaeologists contend that they were probably nomadic Paleo-Indians whose ancestors reached North America by way of a land bridge across the Bering Strait during the Pleistocene era and eventually made their way to the Atlantic Ocean. Other recent theories suggest that the first inhabitants may have arrived by coastal navigation of a more southerly route.[1] If that were the case, then Jekyll Island's first residents may have been Paleolithic ocean travelers, well familiar with coastal regions.

Certainly, these earliest settlers must have hunted and fished, as did their descendents, enjoying the increasingly mild seasons in the area that is today coastal Georgia. Although we have scant knowledge of these first residents, later inhabitants of the island left us more direct evidence of their material culture in the form of shards of pottery, primitive tools, and shell middens that date back at least forty-five hundred years. These remains, recovered by archaeologists, provide irrefutable evidence of human activity on Jekyll as early as 2500 BC, and by 1000 BC, during a time archaeologists call the Deptford Period, sites of human habitation and use were common on the island.[2] The first inhabitants of Jekyll were most likely small family units, though later residents developed villages and a more complex social structure. The archaeological findings, valuable as they are, are but fragments of a distant and now-lost past that whisper to us of the island's secrets, of the first residents' life and death on Jekyll's shores, of the feasts of oysters that they enjoyed, and of the many footprints they left behind, now erased by winds and tides.

Jekyll's early story is an intriguing one, perhaps even more shadowed in mystery and misinformation than that of some of the larger Georgia islands. Much of what we thought we knew about Jekyll's earliest years has proven to be false, and although our knowledge has dramatically increased in recent years, much of Jekyll's aboriginal history still remains incomplete and imprecise.[3] The archaeological record makes clear that, in these early years, no single culture or tribe can be said to have laid claim to Jekyll. It was, as one report describes it, a "crossroad of cultural interaction."[4] It no doubt changed hands many times before our recorded histories. Even in the historical era, it was occupied at various times by Native American groups known as the Timucua and the Guale (pronounced Wali) before it became a hunting ground for a Creek people known as the Yamacraw.

For many decades historians gave Jekyll's Native name as *Ospo*. So firmly set in the popular mind was this "fact" that Walter Jennings, who built a cottage at the Jekyll Island Club in 1927, named his new home after the island itself, or so he thought, calling it "Villa Ospo." However, Native American names for both the Timucua and Guale were not tied to the place but rather to the people, and as the people moved, the name moved with them. It is not impossible that the island may once have been known as Ospo, even though the name was later associated with another site, but no reliable documentary evidence supports this claim. Whatever the Native peoples may have called the island that we know today as Jekyll is lost in the mists of unrecorded time.

For many years scholars believed that the Native Americans who populated Jekyll Island at the time the first Europeans arrived in the New World were a Muskogean-speaking people known as the Guale, described by the Georgia historian E. Merton Coulter as "a loose federation" of Creek peoples who lived in coastal Georgia.[5] Historians and anthropologists believed that the Guale territory extended "from approximately the lower Satilla River in southern Georgia [just south of Jekyll Island] to a point at least as far up the Atlantic coast as the North Edisto River in South Carolina."[6]

Today, however, we know that when the first Europeans reached Jekyll's shores, its residents belonged to an entirely different Native group known as the Timucua, who spoke a coastal dialect called Mocama, from which the Spanish derived the name they gave to the coastal Timucuan area.[7] Scholars writing today place the boundary between Guale and Mocama at the time of the first European arrival in *La Florida* (which included much of the southeastern United States and certainly all of the Georgia coast) to the north of Jekyll Island at the northern branch of the Altamaha River, thus including in Timucua-held lands the islands of Jekyll and St. Simons. Over time, as a consequence of the impact of European colonists, those boundaries changed significantly, as eventually the Guale would be forced to migrate farther south to escape slave raids along the coast. By 1726, not long before the founding of the colony of Georgia, the civilization that existed when the first Europeans arrived had been clearly altered by that same alien culture. According to a Spanish *auto*, or deposition, given that year by residents of *La Florida*, the Timucua were no longer in the area of Jekyll at all. By then the dividing line between Timucuan and Guale territories was San Juan del Puerto at the mouth of the St. Johns River (which divides Georgia from Florida today).[8]

For many years scholars also placed the mission town of San Buenaventura de Guadalquini on Jekyll Island, but subsequent evidence provided by both documents and maps of the sixteenth century has established conclusively that Guadalquini was, in fact, on the southern tip of St. Simons Island, though its residents may well have used Jekyll as a hunting ground.

Our earliest documentary record of Jekyll's indigenous people we owe to the first Europeans—Spaniards and Frenchmen—who began to explore the region in the sixteenth century, leaving behind a picture of the highly structured civilization they found there. Thus, what we know of these Native people is based largely on the reactions of the alien Europeans, who observed them, drew their pictures, and wrote down their impressions. We are fortunate that these first encounters were so thoroughly documented, for they give us our only glimpses, however imperfect they might be, into what the Native culture was like before the Europeans changed it irrevocably.

Although the Spanish were the first Europeans to reach North America, the first to set foot on Jekyll Island or interact with its inhabitants were French Huguenots (Protestants) who came to the New World with Jean Ribault in 1562 to establish the claim of France to what they called *La Floride Françoise*.[9] More than thirty years earlier, in 1526, Native Americans on Jekyll may have spotted Spanish galleons—a little fleet of six ships—

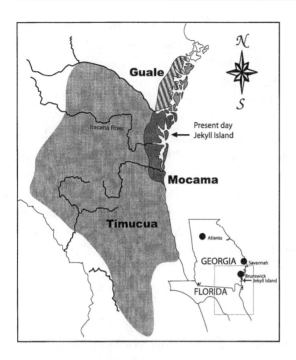

Approximate locations of Timucua (including those who spoke the coastal dialect the Spanish called Mocama) and Guale peoples at the time of their first contact with Europeans.

led by Lucas Vásquez de Ayllón, in search of a verdant and utopian region called Chicora.[10] But the Spanish colonists did not stop at Jekyll and instead sought their utopia farther to the north. Their stay in the region lasted only three months and was beset by starvation, illness, unseasonably cold weather, dissension in the ranks, and, finally, the death of their leader, Ayllón, before they finally returned to Santo Domingo.[11]

Nevertheless, the legend of Chicora lived on, feeding the imaginations of people for years to come. The mapmaker Diego Ribero praised it in the legend of one of his maps: "The country of Ayllón [Chicora] . . . is well suited to yield breadstuff, wine, and all things of Spain."[12] But more than thirty-five years passed, and the Spanish did not return, though their king, Philip II, continued to claim all of *La Florida* among his possessions in the New World.[13] In the absence of Spanish occupation, the French sent their own colonists into the region.

Accompanied by René Laudonnière and about 175 men, Ribault's two ships left Le Havre, France, on February 18, 1562, following a route that carefully avoided passing through the waters of any Spanish-occupied territory.[14] When the French expedition landed near what they called the River of May (the St. Johns River), which they named for the month of their arrival (on May 1), Timucuan peoples lined the north and south shores of the river. Those on the north shore greeted the travelers cordially, and the chief spoke at length to Ribault, who "could not understand the language, much less the meaning." The chief then gave him gifts of "a plume of egret feathers, dyed red, and a basket made from palm fiber, very artfully constructed, together with a great skin drawn upon and painted with pictures of various wild beasts, so vividly represented that they seemed almost alive."[15]

Those on the south bank of the river, led by the great chief Saturiwa, seemed equally friendly, though Saturiwa himself remained aloof and somewhat wary, arriving without women and children and accompanied by a band of armed men and his two sons. The people waded out to meet the newcomers with baskets of mulberries and corn and received the Frenchmen hospitably. Little could the Native people know of what these contacts would mean to them in the years to come.

Ribault's first official act was to erect a stone column carved with the French coat of arms on the riverbank to claim the territory for France in order to mark "the first boundary and limit of his majesty."[16] He would do the same at the northernmost end of the expedition at a spot the Frenchmen would name Port Royal (on the southern part of the South Carolina coast), thus claiming for France all of the coast of present-day Georgia.

As all eyewitnesses attest, everywhere the Frenchmen went the Timucua were predisposed to be friendly toward them, receiving them with "gentleness and kindness" and "signs of friendship and good will."[17] They seem to have been a people who were by nature generous and trusting until they were given a reason not to be.[18] Ribault's own account of this first voyage perhaps best captures the sense of enthusiasm and optimism the explorers had for this land at the outset:

> [We] entered and viewed the country thereabout, which is the fairest, most fruitful, and most pleasant in all the world, abounding in honey, venison, wild fowl, forests and woods of all sorts, palm trees, cypress, cedars, bay trees, and the highest, greatest, and fairest vines in all the world with grapes accordingly, which naturally and without man's help and trimming grow to the top of oaks and other trees that are of wonderful greatness and height. And the sight of the fair meadows is a pleasure not able to be expressed with tongue, full of herons, curlews, bitterns, mallards, egrets, woodcocks, and of all other kinds of small birds, with harts, hinds, bucks, wild swans and sundry other wild beasts. . . .

in short, it is indescribable, the commodities that are seen there and shall be found more and more in this incomparable land, never as yet broken with plow irons, bringing forth all things according to its first nature, whereof the eternal God endowed it.

Ribault thought that he, too, had found the legendary utopia: "This is the land of Chicore, whereof some have written, and which many have gone about to find, for the great riches they perceived by some Indians to be found there."[19]

Two days after their arrival, Ribault's crews set sail with enthusiasm to explore the coastline to the north, naming the various rivers and islands they discovered along the way. When they reached what the Natives called the Iracana River (today the Satilla), at the south end of Jekyll Island, they paused to take notice of the area. Laudonnière notes, "We had not gone far when we discovered another beautiful river, and we dropped anchor to investigate it. Trimming out two boats for the reconnaissance, we discovered an island and a king, as affable as the others. We named this river the Somme River."[20] To Jekyll Island Ribault gave the name *Ile de la Somme*, which was used on subsequent French maps and is the first name of Jekyll that we can document with certainty. Ribault describes the area that included Jekyll as "a country full of havens, rivers and islands of such fruitfulness as cannot be expressed, and where in [a] short time great and precious commodities might be found." He tells of both "great islands and small, goodly meadow grounds and pastures, and everywhere such abundance of fish as is incredible."[21]

The French would return twice more to the area during their three years of coastal exploration. On their first visit they encountered in the area a "great king," most likely Tacatacuru, an ally of Saturiwa, the powerful chief befriended earlier by the French. Tacatacuru's village was on what is known today as Cumberland Island but which then bore the name of its chieftain. He would remain loyal thereafter to the French, a decision that would later incur for him the wrath of the region's first Spanish governor.

In the summer of 1564 the French once again "arrived at the mouth of the Somme River[,] . . . dropped anchor and landed so that we could explore the place just as we had done at other locations." There they again met the "chief of the area, who was one of the tallest and best proportioned men that I have ever seen," and his queen. Laudonnière described the "Indian

Eaxona Iracana

This engraving, based on the work of Jacques Le Moyne, shows vessels entering the Iracana River (which the French renamed the Somme). The island to the right is probably the earliest representation of what is today Jekyll Island. (Theodor de Bry, 1591)

René Laudonnière strikes a gallant pose in this portrait. (Taken from Léon Guérin, *Les Navigateurs français*, 1847)

beauty" of the queen, who "had such a virtuous countenance and modest gravity that there was not one among us who did not greatly praise her. At her side were five of her daughters. All of these were well formed, and so polite that I easily concluded that their mother had been their teacher and had shown them what was right and how to develop their character."[22]

In 1565 the French were for the third time in the area around Jekyll. Laudonnière, then in command of the remaining sailors, "sent out toward the river which the Indians call Iracana, named the Somme River by Captain Ribault." This time they encountered "a great assembly of the principal leaders of the area." The French captain commented, "They had come together to have a good time, because that is the place where the prettiest girls and women of the countryside are," undoubtedly remembering his meeting with the beautiful queen and her daughters the year before.[23] On each of their visits to the area, the French explorers encountered significant numbers of Natives. The coastal area on and around Jekyll apparently teemed not only with animal life but with human life as well.

Accounts of the first French settlers, most notably René Goulaine de Laudonnière and Jacques Le Moyne de Morgues, provide some of our richest sources of information on these earliest known residents of the area.

Both left verbal descriptions, colored to some extent by their own cultural bias, of the Native peoples and their way of life before it was altered by almost daily contact with the Spanish. Le Moyne, an artist by trade, accompanied Laudonnière on his second voyage to *La Florida* in 1564. He came to the New World with the "precise role . . . to chart the seacoast, and observe the situation of the towns and the depth and course of the rivers, and also the harbour, the houses of the people, and anything new that might be in that province."[24] Le Moyne's drawings of Timucuan life are fortunately preserved in copies made by a German engraver, Theodor de Bry, who in 1591 published Le Moyne's account, translated into Latin, along with etchings of Native American life based on his work. Only one of Le Moyne's original Timucuan works, a miniature from his voyage to America, survives and is now in the New York Public Library. But the existence of that one work allows us to compare the artist's original work with a de Bry engraving of the same scene. They are virtually identical in detail. De Bry has made no essential changes in composition, depicting figures, artifacts, costumes, and so on exactly as they are in Le Moyne's work (see pp. 16–17).[25]

We also have two other well-known drawings by John White (later the leader of the famed "Lost Colony" on Roanoke Island in North Carolina), which were also supposedly "copied directly from Le Moyne."[26] They depict a man and woman of *La Florida* who appear to be Timucua and who are drawn in details of dress, artifacts, and hairstyles in a manner similar to the de Bry engravings (see p. 19).

Whatever inaccuracies or misinterpretations the images or the texts may contain, these descriptions are the only ones we have that predate the Spanish occupation. They represent a valuable record, filtered through Le Moyne's eyes, of a way of life now vanished.

At the time of European arrival, the coastal region of what we know today as Georgia was populated with tens of thousands of Natives living in the area. Population density at the time has been estimated at 10.4 persons per square mile, which, though sparse by today's standards, represents a significant number of people in these precolonial lands. If that population estimate is reasonably accurate for Jekyll Island, it would suggest that as many as 180 people could have been living on the island.[27] They seem to have been living peaceably with their neighbors to the north, the Guale. Although the two groups did not share a common language, it appears that they were able to trade effectively with one another and even influence each

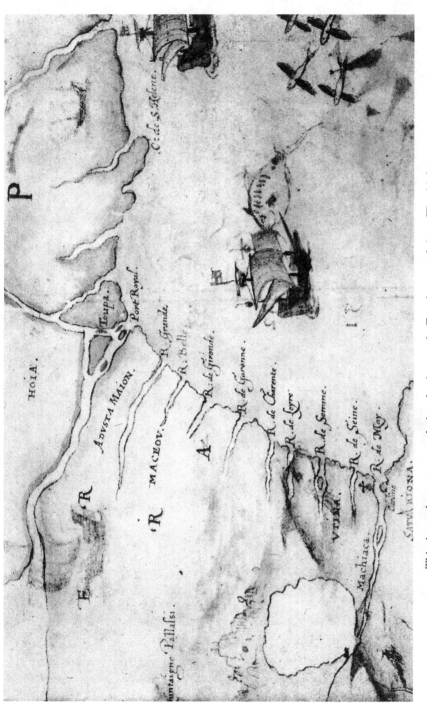

This sixteenth-century map depicts the rivers as the French renamed them. The third river to the north, Rivière de Somme, as it is depicted here, was the Iracana (today the Satilla), the entrance to which is south of Jekyll Island. (Theodor de Bry, 1591)

This drawing of a Native chief showing Laudonnière the column erected by Ribault is the only original Timucuan drawing by Jacques Le Moyne that survives. It reveals, however, that de Bry's engraving of the same scene is identical in detail to Le Moyne's drawing. (Print Collection, Miriam and Ira D. Wallach Division of Art, Prints and Photographs, The New York Public Library, Astor, Lenox and Tilden Foundations)

other's way of life to some extent. Our only direct evidence of one tribe making war on the other occurred during the so-called Juanillo Rebellion, which was the direct result of Spanish interference in their cultures and would not take place until 1597.

The Timucua-speaking peoples, however, were never united among themselves. They were divided into a variety of chiefdoms that were often at war with one another. In fact, the word "Timucua" is apparently derived from the word "Timogua," which the French interpreted to mean "enemy."[28] Their society was essentially matrilineal, ruled by hereditary chieftains, who could be either male or female, but who inherited the title through the female lineage. Thus, instead of a male chief's child being his heir, it was his sister's son or daughter. In other respects, their political structure appeared to Laudonnière to be similar to a feudal system, in which the lesser chiefs were united under a greater leader. Theirs was indeed a hierarchical society wherein a chief (or *holata*) of a small village would pay tribute to a higher chief, sometimes called a *paracusi*. These high chiefs sometimes formed alliances against others. At the time of the first French visit, Saturiwa and Tacatucuru were in a confederation against a holata named Outina, whose lands lay inland, away from the coastal area.[29]

Warfare among the Timucua could be brutal, and warriors commonly brought home the scalps, arms, or legs of their enemies to be displayed as trophies. Their primary weapons were spears, darts, and bows and arrows. They made "the string for their bows from the gut of a stag or from stag skin" and their "arrowheads from the teeth of fish and from stones which they cleverly fashion."[30] An arrowhead (see illustration on p. 20), found on the north end of Jekyll Island, is made of a flintlike mineral called "chert" and was most likely obtained by bartering with inland tribes.

The Timucua made no decisions, and certainly none so serious as to go to war, without careful deliberation. The chiefs were counseled and supported by other high-ranking persons in the tribe, whom the Spanish would later refer to as *principales*. As one Franciscan friar remarked, "They have their natural lords among them. These govern . . . with the assistance of counselors, who are such by birth and inheritance. [The chief] determines and reaches decisions on everything that is appropriate for the village and the common good with their accord and counsels."[31]

Two other figures essential to the tribal ruling class were the *isucu* (doctor) and the *yaba* (shaman). Both performed necessary functions within the

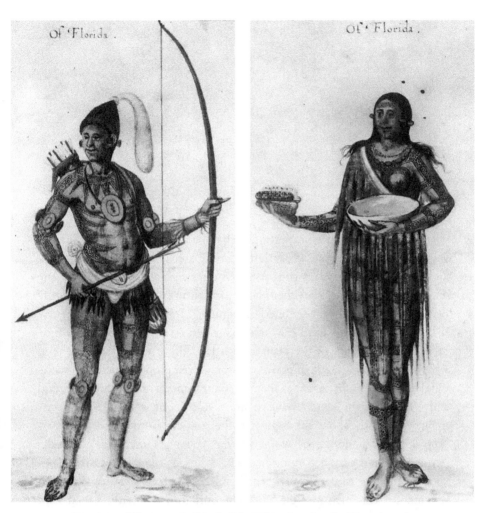

Drawings of Timucuan Indians by John White, based on Le Moyne's work.

Arrowhead (or projectile point) found on Jekyll Island. (Courtesy of the Jekyll Island Museum archives)

village. The isucu was an expert on herbal medicines and cures, while the yaba performed the role of a priest, casting spells, foretelling the future, and carrying out religious rites. We know little about the religion of the Timucua, except that, like other Native American cultures, they apparently held spiritual beliefs that centered on nature and the environment.

Both Laudonnière and Le Moyne expressed an appreciation and admiration for the beauty of the people, with Le Moyne noting that the men were "olive in color, large of body, handsome, well proportioned, and without deformities." He describes them as "handsome, strong, well-made, and active fellows" who were "Brave in spirit" and "fight well." He also comments frequently about the beauty of the women. Both sexes wore their "very black" hair long, the women letting it hang loose, while the men "truss it up in a very becoming manner," where it served as a convenient spot for tucking their arrows when they were hunting or at war.[32] When unbound, it extended to their hips. The only time women cut their hair, according to Le Moyne, was in mourning for their dead husbands, when they cut it "below the ears and [scattered] it on the grave," along with the husband's weapons and the shell cup he drank from. Even those Le Moyne calls "hermaphrodites," actually biological males who wore women's clothes and hairstyles, he describes as "strongly built and vigorous." The "hermaphrodites" were used to do the work of "draught animals," and in his drawings he depicts them carrying provisions or serving as stretcher bearers in time of war.[33]

Men's clothing consisted primarily of breechcloths made of softened deerskin or roots. Most of the women, however, made their garments, worn below their waists, from Spanish moss, which the Timucua called *guano,* no doubt well smoked to remove the chiggers that must have lurked inside then as they still do today. Women's garments of deerskin, softened and painted, were usually reserved for the wives of chieftains or for female holatas.

The Timucua painted their deerskins with lifelike representations of animals and other images and decorated their own "bodies, arms, and thighs with handsome designs," pricking the color into the skin, a process that sometimes caused them to fall sick from infection. They also adorned themselves with paint, which they could change from day to day, black, red, or sometimes blue, depending on the group and the person. They wore "feathers of various sorts, necklaces of a special sort of shell, bracelets of fishes' teeth, girdles consisting of silvery balls, both long and rounded, and many pearls fastened to their legs."[34] Both men and women fashioned earrings, which they "fasten[ed] to their perforated ear lobes." These were made of "small but longish fish bladders which when blown up shine like pearls, and when stained red resemble rather pale carbuncles." Le Moyne expressed astonishment that "such uncivilized people should be provided with such delightful devices."[35]

Often their artistry was practical as well. They made long-handled reed fans to shade the holata's wife from the sun and shorter-handled fans for other purposes, such as fanning a fire, cooling themselves, or coyly hiding their faces. Le Moyne describes the marriage ceremony of a chief whose wife, the new queen, holds "a small fan in her hand with a kind of bashful dignity."[36] In addition to such fans, they wove baskets in many sizes and shapes, large and small, to carry their produce and store their food. The archaeological record tells us that they also made pottery of various sorts and sizes, some of it plain, some decorated with patterns.

The Timucua loved music and dancing and celebrated their victories in battle with musical accompaniment. They played an instrument made from thick reeds, "discordantly and raggedly, merely blowing the pipes as hard as they could."[37] They did not use drums as we know them. Instead they had gourd rattles and flat stones, which they pounded with clubs for percussion. They also used a tambourine-like instrument called an *atavel* to accompany their singing and dancing. Le Moyne attended the marriage of a chief and described the ritual dance performed by girls, who formed a circle without holding hands. They wore "a broad girdle from the front of which a wide pouch hangs down to cover their private parts. Then along the rest of the girdle little oval decorations of gold and silver are attached, dangling on

This engraving suggests how the Native Americans used their crafts—pottery as well as baskets and fans made from the local palmettos and reeds. (Theodor de Bry, 1591)

Young Timucuan men enjoy their sporting activities. (Theodor de Bry, 1591)

their hips, so that in dancing they can make them jingle when they sing the praises of the chief and his wife."[38] Later Spanish missionaries sought to take advantage of the Timucua's love of music to engage them in the singing of the mass.[39]

Dancing was not their only recreation. They also played games and sports, with running and archery primary among them. Le Moyne has recorded a ball game, where a goal (a "tree trunk . . . about fifty to fifty-five feet high, supporting at the top a sort of square frame woven from twigs") was set up in the middle of a cleared area. The object apparently was to hit the square frame in order to win.[40] He also mentioned hunting and fishing in the context of sports. However, considering that these activities were essential to their subsistence, it is probable that the Timucua did not view hunting and fishing as "sport" in the way the Europeans did.

Each man had one wife, according to Laudonnière, except for the king, who was "permitted to have two or three wives," but "his first wife is the only one recognized as queen, and only her children inherit the property and authority of the father."[41] This polygamous practice, also typical of the Guale, would bring the latter into conflict with the Spanish missionaries, who adamantly opposed the practice. Children are rarely mentioned in the Le Moyne or Laudonnière accounts, perhaps because little in their treatment or behavior seemed remarkable. One exception, however, is Le Moyne's claim that he witnessed the "custom" of the sacrifice to the chief of firstborn sons, and he left us a drawing to record the event. As the mother bemoans her son's death, women surround her in a circle "singing with joy but without joining hands." A group of six males stands apart, and one of them takes the infant. When the ritual is finished, the "executioner" takes the child and "slaughters him on [a] wooden [tree]trunk in front of the chief and all present."[42] In the drawing the Frenchman, seated beside a Timucuan man who seems to be explaining the ritual, appears to draw back in horror at the scene, but the French do not interfere. They merely record the event. The different approaches of the French and the Spanish, as their later attempts at colonization will bear out, are worth noting here. Simply put, the French sought to live in greater harmony with the Native Americans, trying to understand their culture to some extent (no doubt for their own economic gain and to facilitate trading), while the Spanish were much more intent on saving their souls and molding the Natives in ways consistent with their own European standards.

In this image, the Frenchman seems to draw back in horror as he watches the
ritual sacrifice of a newborn baby. (Theodor de Bry, 1591)

The focal point of Timucuan villages was what Laudonnière referred to
as "the great public house" or council house, which "symbolized the bond of
community for villages where dwellings were often widely scattered."[43] It
was the center of village life, where the chief met with his people to discuss
whatever affairs might be placed before them at any given moment. It was
a large round structure with an open space in the center that could contain
the entire village population. An inner ring of benches around the perimeter
walls provided seating. There was a center opening in the roof, permitting
smoke to escape when ceremonial fires were built. According to one later
source, the council house was used not only for serious meetings but also as
"a community house where the Indians came together to hold their dances
and assemblies and to drink a brew of cacina."[44] Cacina (or cassina) was a
strong tea made from the leaves of the yaupon holly or *ilex vomitoria* and
containing caffeine in amounts comparable to coffee and Asian tea. Often
used for ceremonial functions, it was drunk very hot, usually from a whelk
shell easily found along the island shores.[45]

Individual shelters were also round and built to withstand rain and wind.
Jean Ribault, captain of the first and third French expeditions, wrote that
they were "constructed of pieces of wood placed vertically and generally

covered with reed after the fashion of a tent."[46] Le Challeux, a ship's carpenter who left his own account, pointed out that they were covered with palm fronds, which were certainly plentiful on Jekyll. A later Spanish visitor marveled that, though they were constructed without nails, the dwellings were "built so well that they last for many years, because in being spherical, their shape forms a pyramid figure. And thus the water flows down without penetrating the straw, which is placed all around and thickly."[47] Most were relatively small and intended only for shelter. Only the holata's house was larger and sometimes divided into several rooms.

The coastal Timucua, who spoke the Mocama dialect, had adapted the rhythm of their lives to the climate and seasons along the coast. Their life seems to have been highly structured as a combination of agriculture, on the one hand, and hunting and gathering on the other. They lived during the spring and summer months in villages around which they planted foods such as corn, pumpkins, various types of beans, and gourds. Just like farmers today, they sowed in the spring, hoed and tended their plants in the summer, and harvested in the late summer and fall, except for corn, which they planted twice a year, in March and June, harvesting after three months. Men and women alike participated in the planting, with men breaking the ground with hoes that were constructed from shells or large fish bones and attached to wooden handles, while women actually sowed the seed. In the winter months, however, most of the people abandoned their villages and took to the woods, building shelters only of palm fronds, and hunting deer, alligators, and turkeys (which Laudonnière called "Indian chickens"). They fished the waters of the estuaries and rivers, especially for oysters and other shellfish, and gathered acorns and nuts to sustain them through the cooler months. All were available in abundance on Jekyll Island. According to Laudonnière, they smoked their meat and fish "thoroughly and meticulously, so that they can more easily be kept from going bad." They roasted whole ears of corn, as well as "lizards and wild animals, which are delicacies with them, and also roots of various sort, some of which are edible and others having medicinal properties." Le Moyne writes that the Timucua were "temperate in their eating as a result of which they live a very long time. . . . They certainly put Christians to shame who reduce their span of life by holding immoderate feasts and drinking parties, and who deserve to be handed over for training to these base uncivilized people and brutish creatures in order to learn restraint."[48]

The Native Americans of the region dug small boats from hollow logs,
creating vessels that are similar to the piraguas used during the plantation era
for travel among the islands. (Theodor de Bry, 1591)

Despite Le Moyne's prejudicial language, his description contains a
strong element of admiration for the Native culture, and he painted a picture
of Timucuan society as well developed, with clear social stratification and
customs; an appreciation for beauty; a healthy population, both in numbers
and well-being; and a rhythm of life that allowed them to provide for their
needs and still enjoy some leisure. They appeared to have been a happy
people, for the most part open, generous, and hospitable.

The Guale, their neighbors to the north, who would later also occupy
Jekyll Island, shared many of these same characteristics. At the time of
European arrival, they were still living on the northernmost islands of the
Georgia coast, from Sapelo to St. Catherines. John R. Swanton has suggested that the name Guale may come from the Muskogean word *wahali*,
meaning "the south."[49] They were strictly a Georgia coastal people, and
most of the village sites were close to salt water, where they enjoyed a plentiful diet of seafood, especially oysters, whelks, crabs, and various types of
fish. Like the coastal Timucua, they ate roasted fish and oysters; hunted
deer and wild turkeys; grew corn, beans, squash, and pumpkins; and gathered acorns, which they roasted and ground for various dishes. They ground

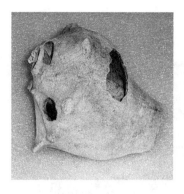

Native American shell tool found on Jekyll Island. (Courtesy of the Jekyll Island Museum archives)

their corn "in deep and narrow wooden mortars," presumably for the purpose of making bread and corn cakes.[50]

The Guale were a smaller group than the Timucua and lived at the time of the first European contact in a much smaller region. Like the Timucua, they were a matrilineal society, and their chiefs, called *micos,* could be either male or female. Although there was certainly a ruling group, they seem to have been less strictly hierarchical in structure than their neighbors to the south. They made all their village decisions as a group. As Laudonnière described the process, "The men do nothing without assembling and counseling together thoroughly before arriving at a decision."[51] The mico's advisers were referred to in Spanish documents as *mandadores* and *aliaguitas* and seemed sometimes to function as subchiefs.[52] Many men of the ruling ranks, not just the chief, were often polygamous, maintaining their wives (who were sometimes sisters to each other) in separate households.

Unlike the Timucua, they did not always live in villages, though a council house similar to that of their neighbors was still an important part of their lives. The houses were more spread out, with a shell midden (a pile of discarded seashells, in essence their garbage dump) beside most of the individual dwellings. One of the major differences between the two cultures was the construction of these dwellings. Guale houses were not round like those of the Timucua, but rather rectangular and of a "wattle-and-daub" structure. They set posts, usually of yellow pine, into trenches and crosshatched them with cane, spaced at least fifteen centimeters apart. To this they applied clay fortified with Spanish moss to keep out the cold and drafts. Laudonnière commented on the industriousness of the women in contrast to the idleness of the men. As one European noted, "The little

The Guale used the wattle-and-daub construction method in building their dwellings. (Taken from Mark F. Boyd, John W. Griffin, and Hale G. Smith, *Here They Once Stood: The Tragic End of the Apalachee Missions* [University Press of Florida, 1951]. Reprinted with permission of the University Press of Florida)

work that is done among the Indians is done by the poor Women, while the men are quite idle, or at most employed only in the Gentlemanly diversions of Hunting and Fishing."[53] The statement reflects a significantly different cultural perspective from that of the Native Americans, for whom hunting and fishing were far more than "Gentlemanly diversions." They were a matter of survival. We know that the Guale men, like the Timucua, also helped with the planting, hoeing the ground while the women sowed.

The Guale also enjoyed games and sports, though not always the same ones as the Timucua. One eyewitness account from 1595 describes a game that sounds very much like an early version of field hockey and even more like a Cherokee game called "chunkee." The Guale game was played "with a rod or piece of sharp pointed antler" for sticks. One of the chiefs rolled a stone "the size and shape of a bread cake" while the players pursued it with their sticks. The observer noted, "it seemed to me that he who ran the fastest and arrived first with his rod and the stone" was the winner.[54]

Their life seemed relatively balanced between play and practicality, as their artifacts reflect. They made various types of pottery for practical use but often ornamented it using a stamped cross, swirl, or check design. In later years their pottery would be influenced by Spanish ceramics, and archaeologists have found remains of plates and pitchers with handles. They also sometimes applied paint to the Spanish-type designs.[55] Like the Timucua, they also liked to adorn their bodies with paint, decorating their faces, chests, thighs, and arms, and to wear shell beads on their upper arms or wrists.[56] One Spanish friar complained that "the pagans," as he referred to them, "go about smeared and painted with a bright reddish color, and when this is lacking they paint themselves with soot and charcoal."[57] There is, however, no mention of their tattooing their bodies, as the Timucua did.

The most important thing that set the Guale and the Timucua apart from one another, however, was their respective languages. Guale was a dialect of Muskogean, the most widely spoken language group in Georgia, while Timucua was more limited in scope and has no clear linguistic relatives in North America.[58] Scholars are still debating the possible relationship of Timucua to other languages, though with no conclusive results. In fact, we know a good deal about the language, for nine documents in Timucua survive. A Spanish friar, Francisco Pareja, wrote a grammar, a confessionario, and three catechisms in the Timucuan language, while another friar, Gregorio de Morvilla, added two more religious works. Two letters survive that were actually written by Timucuan leaders in their Native tongue.[59] While the Guale dialect has not been so extensively recorded as the Timucuan language, one of the earliest Spanish friars, a Jesuit missionary, did compose a Guale grammar.[60]

Although the two Native groups may have influenced each other's cultures, they did not intermarry until a century or so after the first European contact. By this time the populations were becoming so small that it was difficult to find appropriate mates within the group, thus accelerating the loss of group lines and distinctions.

Thousands of artifacts have been unearthed on Jekyll Island (primarily at the north end) that bear testimony to the Timucuan and Guale presence, and one archaeologist has even discovered near the midpoint of the island the location of a Native village and a large structure that may prove to be a council house. However, little remains on the surface for the average visitor to see.[61] Only fragments of pottery, shell tools, and kitchen middens of oyster shells, buried for the most part in centuries of sand and silt, still bear testimony to the feasts once held on Jekyll's shores. But archaeologists have identified many promising aboriginal sites, most of which remain to be explored. Many of these, though not all, are at the north end of the island not far from where the ruins of the Horton house stand today. Some of them have been disturbed by subsequent development. Nonetheless, the artifacts testify to the various activities, from agriculture to oyster feasts, once enjoyed by the various Native communities that lived or hunted there.

Legend and lore of later years contend that in the Jekyll Island Club compound, in front of the cottage once owned by William Rockefeller, stood a Native burial mound, from which the cottage (Indian Mound) took its name. Allegedly, when it obstructed the Rockefellers' view of the Marshes of Glynn, the cottage owner had the mound lowered. After the closing of the club in 1942, children of Jekyll Island Club workers told stories of finding skulls in the mound area. The truth of this assertion remains unsubstantiated, for no archaeological dig has ever been undertaken at this site. If it could be proven, however, it would represent the only known burial mound on Jekyll Island.

THE SPANISH OCCUPATION of the coastal region that began in 1565 would completely alter and ultimately destroy Jekyll's Native cultures. When news of the first two French expeditions reached the ears of the Spanish king who had already claimed the area, although his explorers had left no enduring colony behind, he reacted quickly. Philip II, a staunch Catholic, ordered Pedro Menéndez de Avilés to sail to the area (at his own expense and for whatever profit he might earn thereby), drive out the French Huguenots, explore the coastline, and establish a new Spanish settlement. At the same time Menéndez was preparing for his voyage, Ribault was in Dieppe, France, outfitting his own new expedition, intending to bring provisions and reinforcements back to Fort Caroline, the little colony he had left behind under Laudonnière's command, near what is today the border of Florida and Georgia. The race was on. The outcome must surely be one of the most dramatic and decisive moments in American history.

The French colonists, weary and discontent, thinking that Ribault was not going to return, were preparing to abandon the fort and sail back to France when, on August 28, Ribault's seven ships came into sight. Four of the vessels paused outside the sandbar off the coast, while the three smaller ships made their way up the river to unload and ferry the passengers and their cargo to land, a process that took several days. Before the unloading was finished, however, the Spanish galleons of Menéndez sailed into view. Although the French vessels had superior strength, the rival groups were to learn about the force of the coastal environment on the ways of humans. The four vessels outside the bar sought to elude the Spanish, but winds began to blow, and an unexpected hurricane drove the French ships to the south, changing the course of events and giving the final victory to the Spaniards, who attacked Fort Caroline and killed every Huguenot they could find. Jean Ribault's son, Jacques, whose ship still lay at anchor in the channel, eventually rescued those few who had managed to escape into the woods, among them both Laudonnière and Le Moyne.[62] The French ships that had eluded the Spanish and been driven south by the hurricane foundered on the beach at what the Spanish later named Matanzas (which means "slaughter") Inlet. There the stranded Frenchmen were discovered by the Spanish, who brutally and mercilessly killed all the Huguenots who had survived the hurricane, save musicians and craftsmen who could be of use to them. Among the dead was Jean Ribault.

La Florida and Jekyll Island were now in the undisputed hands of the Spanish, who took over Fort Caroline and renamed it San Mateo. Only one further French expedition sought revenge for the massacre at Fort Caroline. Disappointed at the indifference of the French (and Catholic) king to the brutal acts of the Spanish, in 1568 one Captain Dominique de Gourgues, a Gascon by birth and himself Catholic, "resolved to go to Florida to see if he could avenge the insult done to the King and to all France."[63] He undertook the voyage at his own expense and arrived with two small sailing ships and a *patache*, propelled by oars and suitable for navigating the rivers. He sailed to the River Seine (the St. Marys), where his crew met the people of Saturiwa. According to the sixteenth-century account of the voyage, when the Natives recognized the visitors as Frenchmen, they "began to dance, which is an ordinary sign of joy among them."[64] The following day Saturiwa assembled his allies, among them his son, Atore, and Tacatacuru. Together the French and the Timucua captured and destroyed three Spanish forts, including San Mateo. They slaughtered the captives in vengeance for the victims of Fort Caroline. Then, promising to return a year later—a promise he did not keep—Gourgues and his men sailed back to France, leaving the Timucua to accept whatever retribution the vengeful Spanish chose to mete out.[65] The French never followed up on this successful attack, abandoning the area and the inhabitants to Spanish domination.

The Spaniards soon rebuilt their forts and renewed with vigor their determined goal of converting the Natives to the Catholic faith. The Jesuits whom Menénedez sent out at first made little headway among the coastal population and finally abandoned what one scholar has called "laboring in the fields of the Lord" to return to Spain.[66] But Menéndez quickly replaced the Jesuits with Franciscans.

At first the Spanish priests met with amazing success at converting the peoples of the coastal area to Christianity, despite some reports of discontent and the fleeing of some Natives into the woods. In the years to come the Spanish would establish an entire chain of missions along the Georgia coast, including one on the island south of Jekyll that they named San Pedro de Mocama (Cumberland) and eventually two on the island to the north called San Buenaventura de Guadalquini (St. Simons).[67]

The Spaniards renamed Jekyll Island *Isla de Ballenas* (the Island of Whales), and a map drawn by Antonio de Arredondo in 1737 and published in 1925 by Herbert Bolton confirms the name of the island.[68] No evidence, either archaeological or documentary, has been found thus far to support conclusively the existence of a mission on Jekyll. However, one recently discovered document dating from 1726 refers to an intriguing island mission named *Peraban*, the location of which is still undetermined, but which, one scholar suggests, may have been the Native name for Jekyll.[69] The name appears in a very orderly list of the "islands" (in reality, missions) from the north of the Georgia territory to the Florida border, and in that list the name Peraban comes between Guadalquini (on St. Simons) and San Phelipe (a second mission on the north end of Cumberland)—in short, the exact location of Jekyll Island. In the document in question, an infantry captain named Juan Ruíz de Mexia listed the islands "which owed obedience to this government," including the following: "the Island of Sapola [Sapelo], that of Azago, that of Guadalquina [both on St. Simons], that of Peraban [on Jekyll?], that of San Phelipe, that of San Pedro [both on Cumberland], Turpiqui, San Felipe, Santa Maria [all on Amelia Island], and the Island of San Juan [Fort George Island], and that on all the islands referred to were settled Christian Indians with missionaries of San Francisco who administered them the sacred sacraments."[70] His list moves in a completely logical way down the coast. Thus, although no archaeological evidence has yet been found to substantiate the presence of a mission on Jekyll, we cannot rule out the possibility.[71] The fact that Peraban was not included in a 1681 census of Guale and Mocama ordered by the governor of *La Florida,* Juan Márquez Cabrera, may suggest that it was either too small and unimportant to be included or that it was a late-developing mission (postdating 1681) and thus one of relatively short duration. Reconciling the two names used in Spanish sources would not be difficult if the Isla de Ballenas was a newly minted Spanish name, while Peraban was perhaps an older Mocaman name in current use. Or it may simply have been the name of a mission on the Isla de Ballenas. Whether or not it contained a small mission, Jekyll Island certainly possessed all that was needed to provide a comfortable life for Native and Spaniard alike—ample game and fish, fresh water, and plenty of palmettos for constructing suitable dwellings.

Although we know that the Timucua resisted the new religion even as late at 1579, the Franciscans made significant inroads among the Native population. By 1600 many of the Timucuan chiefs and consequently their people, influenced by gifts or threats from the friars and the Spanish soldiers, had allowed themselves to be baptized.[72] There is no question that the new *cacique* (as the Spanish referred to the Native rulers) of San Pedro (Cumberland Island) had accepted Catholicism by 1597 and had begun to receive instruction from a missionary called Fray López. The cacique had a Spanish name, Don Juan, and a wife named Doña María. They spoke Castilian Spanish, dressed in Spanish clothes, and seemed comfortable with their acculturation by the Spanish and their religion.[73] The Timucuan residents of Jekyll Island, in all likelihood, had also adopted the Christian religion by this time.

Though the Guale to the north had begun to accept Christianity as well, many were, like some of the Timucua, reluctant to abandon their old customs. One of their micos, whose name was also Juan, became enraged when a Franciscan friar told him that he would have to give up all but one of his wives. He organized a revolt, known today as the Juanillo Rebellion, in which his warriors attacked not only the Guale missions, brutally killing five Franciscan friars, but also Spanish-friendly Timucuan villages. On the feast day of St. Francis, 1597, the four hundred warriors came in twenty-six canoes, bypassing Jekyll, to attack the Timucuan village and mission of San Pedro on Cumberland Island. When the Guale rose up against both the Spanish and the Timucua, the latter, whose previous loyalty to Spain may have been dubious, became the allies of the Spanish. One scholar has described this incident as "the earliest documented anticolonial rebellion in North America."[74]

After the Guale attack, the governor evacuated the friars from San Pedro and suggested to Don Juan that he and his people move to locations closer to St. Augustine. They did so briefly, though by Ascension Day in the spring of the following year, they had all returned to the island. The rebellious Guale attacked again in October, torching at least three villages and killing some inhabitants. Don Juan asked for help from the Spanish governor, who sent only sixteen soldiers, but then, as the danger continued, he reinforced the troops with fifty more.

Although the Guale revolt was a painful shock to the friars, it was but a brief setback for the Spanish missions, which were soon in operation again. Not long after these attacks, the determined Spanish established a new Timucuan mission, this time north of Jekyll on the south end of St. Simons Island, a mission named Guadalquini. Its proximity to Jekyll, an easy canoe ride from the north shore (much easier than it would be today after erosion and the dredging of the channel have taken their toll on both islands), makes it almost certain that there was interaction between the groups that lived on Jekyll and those in Guadalquini. In fact, archaeological evidence supports the greatest activity at the north end of Jekyll, nearest Guadalquini. The new mission on St. Simons grew in importance as San Pedro on Cumberland began to diminish. In 1616 it would be the site of a special assembly, the Franciscans' provincial chapter meeting.[75]

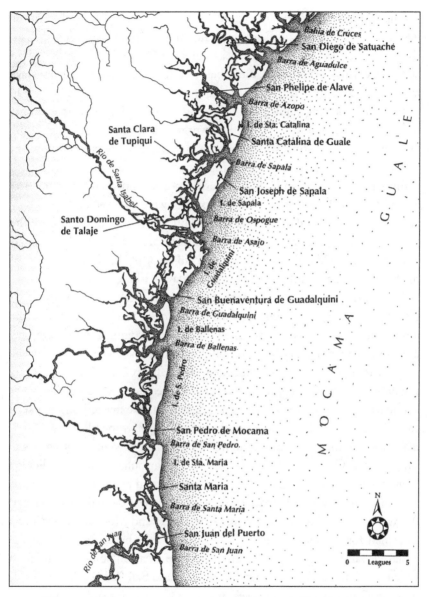

This map, based on the mission era, shows the location of San Buenaventura
de Guadalquini at the south end of what is today St. Simons Island, just north
of the Isla de Ballenas, the name the Spaniards gave to Jekyll Island.
(Courtesy of John Worth, from *The Struggle for the Georgia Coast:
An Eighteenth-Century Spanish Retrospective on Guale
and Mocama*)

Guadalquini would remain vital for more than half a century. But in the 1680s raids by French and English pirates and by colonists from Carolina, which had been established in 1670, as well as by hostile Natives encouraged by the new English colonists, took their toll. Increasing pressure from slave raids and attacks from the north caused the beginning of a Guale migration to the south, putting pressure in turn on the coastal Timucua and forcing them even farther south. The Spanish urged them to move closer to the presidio at St. Augustine, where they not only could better protect them but also, even more important from their perspective, could better count on the Natives for their own protection. Guadalquini remained an active mission only until 1684, when the church and convent were attacked and burned by pirates.[76] Gradually all of the coastal mission towns were deserted, and the Spanish, though they continued to make territorial claims to the Georgia coastal area, would effectively abandon it in favor of the territory south of the St. Johns River in the area we know today as Florida.

Although these were the events that finally caused the coastal Native peoples to abandon the Georgia Sea Islands, their real troubles had begun the moment the first Europeans touched their shores, bringing with them new diseases to which the Natives were completely vulnerable. Not long after the mission at Guadalquini was established, especially from 1614 to 1617, plague, smallpox, and measles epidemics decimated the Natives, killing thousands and leaving behind a weakened population. To make matters still worse, a cultural divide developed between the older people, who still clung to Native ways, and the younger acculturated Timucua, who were adopting Spanish practices. One writer noted in 1616 that "the younger Indians ridiculed their elders who still maintained the old beliefs and practices."[77]

In 1618 a new and unsympathetic governor, Juan de Salinas, arrived in St. Augustine to administer the territories of Guale and Mocama. Conditions worsened for the Natives under his rule, and they began to feel virtually enslaved. According to the testimony of one Spanish soldier, "Christian Indians . . . fled to the woods in both Guale and San Pedro [Cumberland] provinces" during Salinas's six-year term of office (1618–24).[78] Though conditions under Salinas were intolerable, they grew even worse under a later governor, Diego de Rebolledo, whose insensitivity and indifference to Native culture finally forced the western Timucua to rise up in organized rebellion in 1656.

Anticipating the arrival of the ships of Oliver Cromwell to attack St.

Augustine, Rebolledo summoned the inland Timucua, who had been organized into a militia on call to aid the Spanish. He sent a demeaning message
to the caciques, ordering them all, even the highest ranking among them,
to come to St. Augustine, carrying on their backs "at least three arrobas
[seventy-five pounds] of maize."[79] He sent the message by Captain Agustín
Pérez, who made matters worse by carrying out his duty in an imperious
manner.[80] The Spanish had used the Timucua for generations as unpaid
labor whenever they were needed, always excepting the caciques, of course.
Previous governors had courted the Native rulers, flattering them with gifts
and inviting them to share their hospitality and their table whenever they
were in the area. Rebolledo, however, did neither, and this last insult was
too much. The caciques, enraged at his insolence, took up arms against the
Spanish. Although the revolt was short lived and unsuccessful, and relatively few lives were lost, it resulted in a brutal retaliation by Rebolledo and
the hanging of the rebel leaders, their bodies left conspicuously on display
for other Timucua to see.[81]

Coastal Natives, those who occupied Jekyll and adjacent islands, already
diminished in number and destabilized by illness, had not joined in the
rebellion. By the mid-1680s the islands no longer teemed with the presence
of the Timucua and the Guale as they once had. They were weaker now,
less proud, and less able to resist the Spanish demands. The peoples were no
longer strong in their confederations and no longer lived in clearly defined
lands that they called their own. The islands belonged to the Spanish now,
and the Timucuan villages were interspersed with those of the Guale and
Yamasee. Sometimes various groups lived together in a single village, as
Guale and Yamasee did in San Pedro by 1675.[82] Thus, like the adjacent
islands, Jekyll may have briefly been home to Guale and Timucua alike, as
both groups began to lose their distinct identities. Their decline had been
rapid because disease, overwork, slave raids, and discouragement decimated
their ranks.

Although the Spaniards had not set out on a deliberate program of geno-
cide, the effect over the long term was the same. Within two hundred years
of the first European encounter, which began for Jekyll Island residents in
1562, the Native cultures would be destroyed and the thousands of apparently healthy, happy people on the Georgia coast would be no more. Both
these hapless peoples, the Timucua and the Guale, had greeted the newcomers initially with friendliness and gifts: baskets brimming with food,

deerskins that kept them warm in winter, and other items of value. Over time the Natives' attitudes would change, but their resistance came too late and would no doubt have been futile even at the outset. As a direct consequence of European encroachment into their territory, by 1765 both the Timucua and the Guale were extinct, never again to walk the shores of Jekyll or any other island along the Georgia coast.

A list of five Native settlements by Franciscan friars in 1752 gives the name of only one remaining Timucuan village—Palica. It contained but twelve men, seven women, and ten children. Their cacique, who, if he was even still alive, would have been seventy-six years old, bore the thoroughly Spanish name Juan Ximénez.[83] The Timucua were not the only ones affected by these changing conditions. The Guale tribe was similarly diminished, and in their remaining village of Tolomato, only twelve men and fourteen women were left. The lack of children tells the tale.[84] Within seven years, the five Native villages had dwindled to only two, which no longer had any tribal distinctions.

Before the end of the eighteenth century, when the Spaniards finally surrendered Florida to the British, the few surviving Timucua left the American mainland for Cuba, along with the Spanish. They lived out their remaining years in a foreign land, where once again, disease and discouragement took their toll. With the death of these final remnants of a once-proud people, the collective past of the Timucua was lost and almost forgotten. Like the other barrier islands, Jekyll was left emptied of its people, awaiting what might come next.

CHAPTER TWO

William Horton
and the Trustees' Colony

Has heaven reserved, in pity for the poor,

No pathless waste, or undiscovered shore?

No secret island in the boundless main?

No peaceful desert yet unclaimed by Spain?

SAMUEL JOHNSON, 1738

 HOUGH Jekyll lay empty for a time, populated only by deer, raccoons, and other wild creatures, it did not lack for nations—both European and Native American—that laid claim to it. The Spanish continued to consider it part of their New World holdings, though they had essentially abandoned it, creating a buffer zone or what has been called a "debatable land" between themselves and the Carolina colony of the English.[1] The English had first made claim to Jekyll Island and the entire Georgia coast in 1629, during the very height of the Spanish mission era, when King Charles I bestowed on Sir Robert Heath a land grant that encompassed all territory from the southern tip of Virginia to the northern tip of Cumberland Island, thus including Jekyll Island as its southernmost coastal land area. The land grant amounted to nothing, for Heath never visited the area and took no interest in it, and eventually it was restored to the crown.

In 1663 King Charles II granted the same territory to a group known as the Eight Lords Proprietors and named it Carolina in honor of Charles I. He later extended the grant southward as far as St. Augustine. A treaty signed between France and Spain on July 18, 1670, sought to establish peace and set the geographical limits of their respective interests in the New World. It reconfirmed Spanish claims to Georgia, though it allowed for previous English settlements, including the recently established Charles Towne. But the treaty had little effect, and the coastal area of the future colony of Georgia, claimed by Spain as part of *La Florida* while the British claimed it as well as a part of Carolina, was destined to be disputed for the next sixty-two years.

Although the English made frequent raids against Spanish missions on the Georgia coast in the 1680s, their first serious attack against the Spanish came in 1702, when the governor of Carolina, James Moore, personally led a failed siege against St. Augustine. When the king of France, Louis XIV, sought to place his grandson on the throne of Spain, he provoked the War of Spanish Succession (known in America as Queen Anne's War). The English were wary of any alliance between Spain and France that might bring the French back to the region and threaten the very existence of Carolina. They feared France, now the most powerful country in Europe, far more than Spain, and Moore wanted to head off any French occupation of the coastal area by a preemptive strike against the Spanish stronghold "before it be strengthened with French forses [*sic*]."[2]

In anticipation of just such an attack, the Spanish had begun construction at St. Augustine in 1672 on a mighty fort that, when completed, was said to be "the strongest and largest on the continent this side of Veracruz."[3] The Spanish governor had received a warning about the impending attack and had about two weeks to get ready. He called for help from Havana, gathered all the residents of St. Augustine inside the fort, and made preparations for a long siege. In fact, the siege lasted less than two months. On December 26, 1702, four powerful warships flying the Spanish flag appeared on the horizon. The English, trapped in the inlet, set fire to their own ships as well as to the town and retreated north on foot. It would be more than thirty years before they would again challenge the Spanish in *La Florida*. England and Spain, however, were not the only nations that laid claim to the Georgia coast and the island we know today as Jekyll.

The Creeks, who aided the English in 1702, would later fight against them in the so-called Yamasee War of 1715, asserting their own territorial rights to the islands between the St. Johns River and Savannah. In late November 1717 the English and the Creeks concluded a treaty establishing trade and peace agreements. In talks leading to the treaty, English negotiators made a verbal commitment that "the English would not settle south and west of the Savannah River" without the Creeks' consent.[4] Though few Creeks seemed interested in the coastal area, a small group of Lower Creeks known as the Yamacraw moved near what would become Savannah and laid claim to the islands.

In June 1732 King George II granted a charter to a board of trustees to establish and administer the colony of Georgia. The major force behind the project was General James Edward Oglethorpe. England's prime minister, Sir Robert Walpole, opposed the plan, fearing another confrontation with the Spanish. Despite objections from Walpole, whom Oglethorpe characterized as "a parvenu and a grubby politician," the colony "caught the imagination of the English people."[5] One of the stated purposes for the colony was for "settling poor persons of London," a handful of whom had been liberated from debtors' prisons to start a new life in America. Although not more than a dozen of Georgia's settlers had ever been in jail for debt and the scope of the project was soon broadened to include other settlers as well, it was still viewed by the British largely as a charity colony.

Oglethorpe came to the New World in January 1733 and, in recognition of the treaty with the Creeks, established the first settlement in the new colony at the extreme northern limit of Georgia, as far away from the Spanish stronghold of St. Augustine as he could get. In February he founded the town of Savannah at Yamacraw Bluff on the banks of the Savannah River and set to work to obtain permission from the Creeks to occupy lands farther south.

The Treaty of Savannah, signed on May 21, 1733, between the trustees and the "Chief Men of the nation of the Lower Creeks," gave the consent that Oglethorpe needed. In that document the Creeks agreed to convey to the English colonists "all those Lands which our Nation hath not occasion for to use." These lands included most of the Georgia Sea Islands, among them Jekyll, which the Creeks had for the most part left deserted, except for hunting purposes. They reserved for their own use only the islands of Sapelo, Ossabaw, and St. Catherines. The terms of the treaty were to apply "as long as the Sun shall shine or the waters run in the Rivers." In exchange for their lands, the Creeks received a variety of agreed-upon goods, among them doeskins, buckskins, blankets, guns of various types, powder and bullets, fabric, tools, brass wire, buttons, a brass kettle, a hat, a white shirt, and a looking glass.[6]

General James Edward Oglethorpe, founder of the colony of Georgia.
(Courtesy of the Georgia Historical Society)

In the wake of the signing of the agreement, General Oglethorpe returned to England, taking with him his new friend and supporter Tomochichi, chief of the Yamacraw, as well as the chief's nephew and heir, Toonahowi. The visitors were presented not only to the trustees but also at the court of George II. Upon the trio's return in 1736, Tomochichi escorted the general southward "to show Mr. Oglethorpe how far their possessions reached" and presumably how much land the English were now entitled to occupy. He conducted the English party past Jekyll Island and all the way to the St. Johns River, noting, "that is the Spanish guard. All on this side [of] that river we hunt; it is our ground. On the other side they hunt, but as they have lately hurt some of our people, we will now drive them away."[7]

The treaty with the Creeks allowed Oglethorpe to recruit new colonists and develop a plan to establish the town of Frederica on St. Simons Island. Oglethorpe knew that this move to a position farther south and closer to St. Augustine would be provocative to the Spanish, as the short-lived Fort King George in Darien (1721–36) had been. Anticipating possible attacks from the outset, he selected a site on the leeward side of the island that would be relatively easy to defend. Although he brought no regular soldiers with him, he planned to train the colonists to defend themselves, should the Spanish attack come.

Jekyll remained unoccupied by English settlers until almost four years after the chartering of the colony of Georgia in 1732. In 1734 Oglethorpe gave to the island the name of his benefactor, Sir Joseph Jekyll, who contributed the then-princely sum of six hundred pounds to support the colony. Oglethorpe wrote to Sir Joseph from his ship on September 19, 1738, the day after his arrival at Frederica for his third visit to the colony, to tell him that he was anchored "in a harbour and near an island that bears your name. God has given us the greatest marks of his visible protection to this colony."[8] Sir Joseph never received the letter, for he had died on August 19, though the news had not yet reached the colony. Despite the fact that Sir Joseph Jekyll spelled his name with two *l*'s, the name of the island for almost two hundred years would be spelled "Jekyl." It was not until 1929 that the Georgia legislature officially corrected the spelling.

Jekyll Island's first English resident would be a remarkable man named William Horton, who joined Oglethorpe's colonists during the general's second voyage to Georgia. Horton's service to the colony was considerable and, in military terms, perhaps second only to that of Oglethorpe himself.

Sir Joseph Jekyll, for whom Jekyll Island is named.
(Courtesy of the Jekyll Island Museum Archives)

Over twelve years he rose from the modest position he had formerly held as subsheriff of Herefordshire to that of major in the British Army, and his commitment to the new colony was unwavering.[9]

William Horton was the second son of William Horton of Hereford and his wife, Philipp (possibly an abbreviation of a more common English female name, Philippa).[10] William's elder brother, Thomas, died in infancy, leaving him as the only remaining son, though he had an older sister, Catherine, and a younger sister, Mary, all born within four years of one another. William himself was baptized in the Hereford St. Nicholas Parish in Herefordshire on December 21, 1708, and, given the practice of infant baptism in the Church of England, was probably born that same year.[11] If so, his father died when he was only six years old, in June 1714, leaving to his son, William, in his will "all my Books of what kind of nature soever, and also my Fowling pieces."[12] (A gentleman, after all, should be educated and equipped for the manly art of hunting.) The will had been drawn up seventeen months before the older William's death, when he was probably already ill, for he refers to himself as "being weak in Body but of perfect mind, memory and understanding." The children's mother, Philipp, still a young woman, a few years later married a man named Richard Butler, the second son of Lord Viscount Mountgarrett, from the parish of Hereford St. Owen.[13] The family apparently moved into the parish of their stepfather, for when young William married in his early twenties, he and his wife, Rebecca, had their own firstborn son, William Aldworth Horton, baptized in the Hereford St. Owen Parish on February 2, 1731. During the course of their marriage, the couple would have at least one more son, Thomas.[14]

Another early settler of Georgia, Levi Sheftall of Savannah, remembered Horton as a tall man with red hair. From all appearances, Horton had the fiery temperament that went with it. He arrived in Georgia with a group of colonists who sailed with Oglethorpe in late 1735. The ship on which he came, the 220-ton *Symond,* under the command of Captain Joseph Cornish, was one of two—the other being the *London Merchant* commanded by Captain John Thomas—that were fully loaded by mid-October with provisions and passengers and waiting at the port of Gravesend, England, to set sail. Leaving behind his wife and young children until he could provide a home for them, Horton set out with anticipation to discover what kind of life they might have in the colony of Georgia, which to many was still a wilderness but to others, like himself, held great promise.

English colonists preparing to depart from Gravesend.

The two ships left Gravesend on October 20, planning to rendezvous on November 1 with an escort vessel, the *Hawk*, commanded by Captain James Gascoigne. However, fog, unfavorable winds, and the failure of the *Hawk* to arrive at the appointed place on time forced the ships to idle at anchor at the port of Cowes for several weeks. Supplies that were supposed to sustain the colonists during their first winter in Georgia were being gobbled up at an alarming rate. Even worse, they were about to lose the "useful season" for cultivating land.[15]

Many of those aboard, Oglethorpe's so-called worthy poor, had been given free passage, fifty acres of land, and maintenance for one year, in exchange for which they were expected to plant crops, build homes, and engage in "all other works for the common good and public weal" of the colony.[16] William Horton, however, was not among them. Instead, he was one of a group of "adventurers" who could well afford to pay their own passage. In exchange for his passage, he was granted five hundred acres of land, the maximum permitted under the trustees' regulations. The trustees required these "adventurers" to bring to Georgia no fewer than one indentured servant for each fifty acres of land and to cultivate at least one hundred acres of their grant within ten years.

Horton had petitioned the trustees for approval of his grant on September 17, 1735. Judging him to be a man of good character and, more important perhaps, "worth 3000 pounds," a week later they readily approved his grant of five hundred acres on Jekyll Island, the southernmost point of land grants to date. By October 14 he had boarded the *Symond* with his ten servants and was as eager as the others to reach his destination.[17] But a month later they were still waiting for fair winds.

Among the other passengers were the Anglican brothers, Charles and John Wesley, who were setting out for Georgia, Charles as secretary for the colony, and John with the pious intent of converting the Native Americans to Christianity. They held prayer services twice a day on the ship, while another group, mainly German "Dissenters," worshipped in their own way. The Wesleys watched the behavior of the other passengers with growing disapproval, and finally, when they felt things were getting out of hand, they complained to General Oglethorpe. As a result, one of Horton's female servants was put ashore "for Drinking and indecent behaviour."[18] Although Oglethorpe was willing to find a replacement for the woman, Horton was furious with the Wesleys and fed up with their pious ways. To show his contempt he awakened them late one night, according to John Wesley, "by dancing [on the deck] over our heads." However, Horton, a gentleman both in rank and at heart, acknowledged his rude conduct and "begged . . . pardon the next day."[19]

The Wesleys recognized the fact that Horton would "in the colony have great influence," and John Wesley acknowledged in his diary that he "must, if possible, be won." With this in mind, John Wesley tried to patch up their differences, but a residue of ill will clearly remained between them. In the years to come Wesley would openly side with Horton's enemies, while Horton, in turn, would come to view the clergyman as a troublesome meddler whose opinions he held in contempt. Well aware of Horton's coldness toward him, Wesley finally asked Horton directly why he acted in such a manner. Horton made this reply with equal directness: "All your sermons are satires upon particular persons, therefore I will never hear you more; and all the people are of my mind, for we wont [*sic*] hear ourselves abused. Besides, they say they are Protestants. But as for you," he went on, "they cannot tell what religion you are of. They never heard of such a religion before. They do not know what to make of it." (It would later be given the name of Methodism.) Horton blamed on Wesley "all the quarrels that have been here since you came. . . . Indeed there is neither man nor woman in the town, who minds a word you say. And so you may preach long enough; but nobody will come to hear you."[20]

As tensions mounted on the *Symond,* even though the *Hawk* had finally arrived, the contrary winds continued to blow. Finally on December 10, "a moderate gale" notwithstanding, the three ships began the eight-week voyage to the New World.[21] Ironically, after the long wait for the *Hawk,* only two days out of port heavy winds separated the escort vessel from the rest of the fleet, and she was not seen again until long after they reached Georgia. Otherwise, at sea all went well, with no deaths, four births, and very few disciplinary infractions during the voyage. Horton took his meals with General Oglethorpe and ten other gentlemen, including the Wesley brothers.[22]

The colonists sighted land on February 4, 1736, and the next day the *Symond* and *London Merchant* dropped anchor off Tybee Island at the mouth of the Savannah River. Oglethorpe immediately departed for Savannah. Perhaps hoping they would patch up their differences, he left Horton, John Wesley, and a factor named John Brownfield in charge, with strict instructions to allow the colonists to come ashore to bathe and do laundry but otherwise to keep them isolated. Above all, they were forbidden to drink rum, which the trustees had prohibited to the colonists. The thirsty sailors evidently did not think the rule applied to them. But when Horton and his associates found rum in their possession, they followed orders, smashing bottles and staving in a cask. The sailors were disappointed and no doubt grumbled among themselves, but, according to official records, they "bore the liquor's being spilt with great submission."[23]

Oglethorpe wanted to keep the passengers close to the ships mainly because their voyage was not yet over. Their ultimate destination was not Savannah but St. Simons Island, situated below the Altamaha River on the southern reaches of the Georgia frontier. Here Oglethorpe planned to establish a new fort to serve as a military bastion against the Spaniards in St. Augustine. But once again, the trip was delayed. The captains of the *Symond* and *London Merchant* refused to sail to Jekyll Sound (now called St. Simons Sound), arguing that, without the *Hawk* to lead them, navigation around St. Simons was too risky for large ships. Oglethorpe worried that the colonists "were losing the best season both for building and improving."[24] But the arrival from New York of another sloop, the *Midnight,* which landed at Tybee Island on February 14 carrying a cargo of assorted

John Wesley proved to be a thorn in the side of William Horton, both during and after their voyage to Georgia aboard the *Symond*. (National Portrait Gallery, London)

The *Symond* and the *London Merchant* pass by the Isle of Wight as they set sail for Georgia in 1735. This drawing was made by a twenty-five-year-old Salzburger named Philip Georg Friedrich von Reck, who sailed on the *London Merchant*. (Courtesy of the Royal Library, Copenhagen)

provisions, would save the day. Desperate for a solution, Oglethorpe bought the ship's entire cargo of goods, "on condition that she should . . . deliver them on St. Simons," taking with them all unmarried men, under William Horton's command; weapons; ammunition; and tools. The *Midnight*'s captain, delighted to unload his cargo so easily, agreed, setting sail for Jekyll Sound the following day.[25] As the ship approached its destination, Horton could see his land grant on Jekyll, green and alluring. No doubt he felt a sense of excitement and opportunity as he gazed on the island for the first time. But there was much to do at Frederica before he would have a chance to explore it.

Horton and his men worked tirelessly for the next several weeks unloading the ships, constructing a fort, and building shelters and a storehouse. It was an entirely new way of life for most of the men. Although they had some provisions, if they wanted fresh meat they were required to hunt it themselves. Horton's fowling pieces, inherited from his father, may have come in handy, though he no doubt needed larger weapons for the five alligators he killed in a single day. One evening a party of friendly Natives brought some game for the colonists and "all made merry . . . having a plentiful meal."[26]

In the meantime, Oglethorpe made arrangements to transfer as much of the cargo and as many passengers as possible from the original ships to two smaller vessels, the *James* and the *Peter and James*. The remaining settlers made the trip, which took them six days, in piraguas, long flat-bottom boats outfitted with both oars and sails. It was the end of a journey that had begun in England five and a half months before.

One of the last to arrive was Francis Moore, who had stayed behind on Tybee to oversee the unloading of the *Symond* and *London Merchant*. He sailed aboard the *Peter and James*, which reached "the opening between Jekyl Island and St Simons" on the evening of March 22. When he went ashore at Frederica the following morning, Moore was amazed at how much work the men had accomplished in so short a time: "There was a battery of cannon mounted, which commanded the river, and the fort almost built. . . . The town was building, the streets were all laid out." Horton and his men had accomplished their task with efficiency and speed. In addition, each family had constructed a bower of palmetto leaves, a task in which they had no doubt been assisted by friendly Natives, who were experienced in constructing such temporary shelters, for they were "tight in the hardest rains, . . . the palmetto leaves lying smooth and handsome." The entire town, Moore declared, looked "something like a camp." Contributing to that camplike appearance were three large tents, "two belonging to Mr. Oglethorpe, and one to Mr. Horton, pitched upon the parade [ground] near the river."[27]

Despite their excitement at finally reaching their destination, the settlers were also quick to realize the dangers of their frontier community, which virtually taunted the Spaniards in their own backyard. Certainly Oglethorpe knew the risk, and he delayed barely a day after his arrival before launching an expedition to the St. Johns River, the very doorstep of the massive fort at St. Augustine, "to see where His Majesty's dominions and the Spaniard's join."[28] He was accompanied by Horton, a band of Natives, and a detachment of Scottish Highlanders from Darien. Although they passed by the full length of Jekyll Island, Horton could only gaze at its greenness and imagine his future there. He could see the great oaks and the wide, sandy beaches, and yet, for the moment it must have seemed as far away as England. The expedition delivered the Scotsmen to the northeast end of Cumberland Island to erect a new outpost, Fort St. Andrews. When they returned to St. Simons toward the end of the month, Oglethorpe had nothing but praise for the Native Americans, the Highlanders, and in particular, "Mr. Horton who has not undressed himself since he came here, though he has a tent and bed standing, which he has given to the sick and has been with me in an open boat all the Southward expedition."[29] It was evident from the outset that the general viewed Horton as a valuable and courageous aide. As time went on he would come to rely on him more and more for important and often perilous assignments.

At long last, at the end of April, having worked ceaselessly to build the fort at Frederica, Horton finally had an opportunity to explore his own five-hundred-acre grant on Jekyll Island. A scout boat took him across Jekyll Sound to the north end of the island. Unfortunately, his first visit to the site resulted in tragedy. When the vessel landed, Horton ordered that a swivel gun be fired to signal the arrival and let those on St. Simons know "how the lands bore from the town." The young gunner, zealous but evidently inexperienced, fired the cannon again and again, reloading exuberantly with increasing amounts of powder. On the third shot the cannon exploded, mortally wounding the young soldier. Although Horton rushed him back to St. Simons for medical attention, the young man died of his head wounds the next day, achieving the distinction of "being the first man that died at Frederica."[30] The accident on Jekyll was but the first incident in a history that would inextricably link the two islands throughout the Frederica era.

Although Horton's first visit to Jekyll was cut short, he evidently had enough time to quickly examine the soil and vegetation. From his first impressions, he concluded that "the land was exceedingly rich." But his assessment was, at best, superficial, and he still had much to learn about agricultural life on the coast of Georgia. The sandy soil, though blackened on the surface from years of accumulated and undisturbed organic matter as the island lay empty of its human inhabitants, would provide crop nourishment for only a few seasons before it would have to be repeatedly enriched by some type of fertilizer or manure. Although at first sight it looked suitable for planting, he would eventually find it to be something of a disappointment.[31] Nonetheless, at the time Horton looked forward to his Jekyll venture with high hopes. For the moment, however, he had little time to supervise any planting on the island, though he may have left some of his servants there to begin the task.

The Jekyll property stood without defense, unquestionably the most vulnerable homestead on the Georgia coast, south of Fort Frederica, with only the fledgling Fort St. Andrews as a defense between his land and the Spaniards. Horton was understandably eager to assist General Oglethorpe with his plans to further fortify the lands to the south. On May 2 the general ordered Horton to take a boatload of ammunition, weapons, and supplies to the Highlanders at Fort St. Andrews.[32] Oglethorpe also established a second fort garrisoned by a company of regular British troops on the southern tip of St. Simons, Fort Delegal, which stood just across the sound from Horton's Jekyll Island land grant. The general was also in the process of initiating plans for still another fortification (Fort St. George) on the St. Johns River under the very noses of the Spanish. He planned to put patrol boats on the river, ostensibly to prevent Natives friendly to the English from attacking the Spanish but in reality as part of a defense scheme to secure the Georgia coast from enemy invasion. All these provisions no doubt gave Horton greater peace of mind about the safety of his own holdings on Jekyll.

When the plan was implemented in May, Horton and a Major Richards undertook a dangerous and delicate diplomatic mission to the Spaniards. They set out on the thirteenth on a long and arduous pull toward St. Augustine, carrying letters from Oglethorpe to the Spanish authorities that sought to explain away the presence of patrol boats on the St. Johns as a peaceful measure and disclaiming any hostile intent. Reaching the St. Johns, the English officers in charge of the expedition found the Spanish outposts deserted. Horton volunteered to walk the forty miles to St. Augustine to inform the governor of their presence and to carry out his mission. Departing with only two servants, he set such a stiff pace that one of the men fell exhausted by the wayside. According to an account told later to Francis Moore, by then keeper of stores in Frederica, Horton "arrived at the river within sight of the castle [at St. Augustine] about four in the evening, and fired his gun several times for a boat to come. . . . at last one came, and carrying him over, he was conducted to the governor, who received him very civilly." The governor sent riders to rescue the abandoned servant and to conduct Major Richards, bearing Oglethorpe's dispatches, to St. Augustine. Spanish hospitality continued for several days, and Horton and Richards were even invited to a dance. But suddenly they were placed under house arrest and accused of spying. Interrogated and even threatened by the governor, Horton refused to divulge any information about the strength of Frederica and retorted, with a certain arrogance, that "he was a subject of Great Britain, and his sovereign was powerful enough to do him justice."[33]

Oglethorpe was enraged when he heard the news of his emissaries' arrest, denouncing it as a "flagrant breach of the laws of nations," and he began preparations for combat, viewing Horton's arrest as the opening of hostilities between England and Spain.[34] But the Spanish soon released both Horton and Richards, with a request for them to negotiate with Oglethorpe on behalf of Spain. Oglethorpe met the returning party on the Spanish frontier, where he had arrived to take charge of operations. It was there that Horton delivered the request from the Spanish, and Oglethorpe agreed to talk with Spanish representatives, but only in his own territory. By mid-June Horton had returned to Frederica to the "great joy" of the inhabitants.[35]

When the Spanish vessels bringing their ambassadors arrived in the area only a few days later, Oglethorpe took precautions to keep them away from Frederica so that they could not "make any discovery of our strength." Instead, he met with them on board the *Hawk,* which had finally arrived and was anchored in Jekyll Sound. He arranged for Horton, who had no doubt met them when he was in St. Augustine, to provide them hospitality for several days on Jekyll Island during their visit from June 19 to 22. They would, in fact, be his first guests there. Since Horton had as yet constructed no house in which to lodge them, the English provided for their sleeping quarters "two handsome tents lined with Chinese, with marquises [marquisette] and walls of canvass, to be set down and pitched upon Jekyl Island, and also a present of refreshments."[36] Oglethorpe knew that his fledgling community was still extremely vulnerable to the superior strength of the Spanish, and he had no intent of exposing its weakness to the ambassadors by housing them in Frederica. But Jekyll Island, always vulnerable to attack, exposed the Spaniards to another danger. During one night of their stay, hostile Natives crept onto the island, intending to attack the Spanish in retaliation for an earlier attack against their people. However, they were prevented from doing so, presumably by their host, and the Spaniards retired in safety.

Despite the diplomatic negotiations and the intentions of the English to keep their guests safe, the meeting did not achieve any guarantee of peace with the Spanish. Both sides remained wary of the other. Though the Spanish ambassadors could not see Fort Frederica, they could hear the cannons and perhaps glimpse with spyglasses whatever show of strength the English could muster at Fort Delegal, across the sound from Jekyll. Certainly, during the three nights they spent on the island, they could clearly see the weakness of Jekyll, where, though fortifications were planned, none were ever built.[37] The negotiations did little to help the tense situation. Neither group trusted the other, and, following the meetings, both sides took additional steps to prepare for hostilities. The Spanish governor requested and received a reinforcement of fifteen hundred regular troops in order to prepare for military action against the English colonists at some future date. Oglethorpe rushed back to England as soon as possible to raise a regiment of troops that he felt certain would be needed at some point to defend the colony against the Spanish. In 1740, after his return, he would further strengthen the Georgia coastal defenses with the construction of Fort Prince William at the south end of Cumberland Island. Only Jekyll remained completely defenseless.

During his trip back to England in 1736, Oglethorpe left Horton, a man he knew to be of courage and fortitude, in charge of a very nervous population at Frederica.[38] Rumors of an imminent Spanish invasion frequently ran rampant through Georgia and were reported as far north as South Carolina and even as far away as London. The "people resolv'd to defend themselves against the Spaniards if attack'd," Horton informed the Earl of Egmont in March 1737, adding also that "they were industrious, but wanted corn."[39]

The lack of corn was the source of festering discontent that had surfaced barely a month after Oglethorpe's departure. "There is and has been for near 2 months since a great want of provision and great complaining amongst the people so that we dread the consequence," wrote Thomas Hawkins, a bailiff and the surgeon in Frederica.[40] These were precisely the same problems that had beset the earlier Spanish and French colonies in the nearby areas—hunger, friction among the colonists, fear of hostile forces, and even the threat of mutiny against their leader. No doubt the danger of their situation made them all edgy, and quarrels broke out over trivial matters, some of them directed toward Horton himself. Despite Horton's every effort to mollify the disgruntled settlers, the situation remained volatile. He reported to Thomas Causton, first bailiff and keeper of the stores in Savannah, "that some of the freeholders have threatened to nail up the guns, to seize the Pettiquas, to put the storekeepers in chains," and hardly a day had gone by without his personally enduring "the greatest abuses."[41]

By late April, during a rare moment of respite, Horton was on Jekyll seeing to the planting of his own crops when, during his absence, a man named Wilson accused him of stealing his boat. The truth of the matter was that Horton had agreed to lend a boat to James Gascoigne, captain of the *Hawk,* and had borrowed one from a Mr. Lawley, who was a co-owner of the vessel in question. Gascoigne used the boat for two days on official business and returned it in better condition than it was in when he got it. Nevertheless, Wilson, the other owner, was enraged. He pressured Bailiff Hawkins to call a court into session and subjected Horton to "a great deal of Billingsgate language."[42] Each man pleaded his own case, for as Francis Moore noted about the colony, "there are no lawyers allowed to plead for hire, nor no attorneys to take money."[43] After Lawley testified that the boat was a loan, not a theft, and that Wilson well knew it, the verdict was, of course, not guilty. But such incidents made life at Frederica difficult, and Horton was undoubtedly relieved to be able to escape the bickering colonists from time to time and take refuge on his own quiet lands on Jekyll, where no such political problems existed. He was convinced that at least some of the problem arose from subversive letters to the colonists from his old enemy, John Wesley, which were poisoning the atmosphere.[44]

By December 1737 Horton had regained full control in Frederica, and his orders were allegedly being obeyed "with pleasure."[45] Nonetheless, the bitterness over this affair lingered for years and resurged in 1744 with a new charge of usurpation of power against Horton. According to an account in the colonial records, Horton threatened "to have Mr. Thomas Hawkins, (first bailiff) shot thro the head[,] to chain Mr. Saml. Perkins (second bailiff) to an oar in a scout boat and to starve Mr. John Calwell (third bailiff) to Death."[46] Such threats clearly reveal that Horton was near the end of his patience.

In December 1737 he traveled to Savannah for an extended series of conversations with William Stephens, the recently appointed and newly arrived secretary of the trustees. They struck up a "frank and easy" relationship, and Horton characteristically tried to paint a positive picture of the situation at Frederica, minimizing the frictions of the recent past. Discontent in the colony arose mainly from the colonists' complaints that they could not satisfactorily meet their requirements without slave labor, which was still forbidden by the trustees. The prohibition against slavery did not stem from any altruistic sentiments on the part of the English gentlemen who oversaw the colony, but rather from the belief that the importation of slaves would create idleness and luxury among the colonists. Horton sought to convince Stephens that "the people were orderly and industrious on their lands."[47] In spite of his usually positive attitude, Horton did complain to Stephens about one man, Thomas Causton, who, as keeper of the Savannah stores, he believed, could have done much to relieve the situation. But his disagreements with Causton spurred Horton on to harder work in developing his own land grant, where success with agriculture and cattle could make him less dependent on Causton's goodwill. He had begun to realize by this time that the land on Jekyll was not as rich as he had at first thought, and he had no doubt had the same failure as the other colonists with the trustees' requirement that each settler plant mulberry trees, in an effort to produce silk. The combination that seemed to work best on Jekyll was grazing cattle, which helped to renew the land with a steady supply of manure, and growing corn. It was a fortuitous combination, for the settlers desperately needed both corn and beef, and Horton had his servants hard at work to supply these needs from his Jekyll lands.

By the end of 1736 he had somehow found time to build a two-story house on Jekyll Island at a location later identified by archaeologists as a prehistoric Native American site dating back perhaps a thousand years.[48] It was not elegant but was nonetheless a serviceable wooden structure with a parlor and a hall on the main floor, a fireplace at each end, and two bed-

Conjectural drawing of the Horton house during the colonial era. (From J. Everett Fauber, "A Comprehensive Report and Proposal for the Restoration of Captain Horton's House on Jekyll Island." Courtesy of the Jekyll Island Museum Archives)

rooms upstairs. The facade of the house, which faced north toward Jekyll Sound, probably had a veranda and an upstairs balcony. Horton also constructed servants' quarters, a barn, and various other outbuildings nearby.[49] Within two years, by January 1738, he had more than twenty acres fenced in and under cultivation, still less than the one hundred acres the trustees required, but the best he could do, even with ten servants. Although he was interested in experimenting with crops besides corn, his military duties came first.

Later that same month the new colonial secretary, William Stephens, arrived to inspect the southern part of the Georgia colony. A signal gun summoned Horton on January 28 from Jekyll Island to Frederica upon Stephens's arrival. The two men met on St. Simons about 3:00 p.m. For the next several days Horton escorted the secretary proudly on a tour of the area, through the town and fort of Frederica, to Fort Delegal, to Fort St. Andrews on Cumberland, and finally to his own plantation on Jekyll. Stephens was duly impressed and noted that Horton's plantation flourished "with a good Number of Servants, and considerable Improvements made." He spent two nights on the island as Horton's guest in his new house, which Horton was proud to show off, providing hospitality as best he could without his wife on hand. On February 2, 1738, Lieutenant Delegal joined them there. Stephens, who viewed Horton as a hospitable man, wrote that he "would not allow us to part without dining with him, which I perceived he had made some Provision for, and we fared well."[50]

Despite its flourishing appearance in February, Horton's plantation, like those of the other settlers, would not thrive throughout the year. A late frost the following month took its toll, followed by a severe drought for the second year in a row. Horton informed the trustees of his worries: "The crops of corn . . . are very bad," he wrote. "The seed was far from being good, and, the season proving very dry, it is generally parched up."[51] To make matters worse, repeated false alarms warning of a Spanish invasion frayed the nerves of the colonists and took them away from their work. Each time the alarm sounded, men rushed needlessly from their fields to take up their arms, and Horton was compelled to abandon his fields as well and hasten across the sound by boat to Frederica. It was a costly disruption, for most of the colonists had only themselves and their families to depend on for labor. On one occasion when a Spanish attack was expected, Horton ordered the men to stay in sight of the town, though their fields may have been miles away. Though the men "readily obeyed," one of them claimed that it set back his labor four months.[52] Horton's greatest advantage on Jekyll was the group of servants he had brought with him from England, who could keep up the work in his absence. As a consequence, his crops were doing better than most.

Nevertheless, serious food shortages were beginning to set in and supplies were still slow in coming from the storehouse in Savannah. Oglethorpe later informed the trustees that the people would "have starved or abandoned the place had not Mr Horton given his own cattle and corn to eat."[53] Despite the hardships, in his report to the trustees on August 26, 1738, Horton himself tried as always to present the situation in Frederica in a positive light: "The people of Frederica have and, I thank God, still do enjoy an uncommon share of health, and I have taken pains to keep a good harmony amongst them and therein have succeeded to my wishes. For no set of people in their circumstances live in a more peaceable manner than they have done for many months past. They have cultivated as much land as they can take care of themselves but for want of servants have not been able to clear as much as their neighbors at Darien."[54] He concluded his report with a comment that reflected his deep commitment to the welfare of the colony and his loyalty to the trustees: "If I can in any shape be serviceable to this colony I shall ever think it my duty to be so and shall esteem it the greatest honour to receive commands and will to the utmost of my abilities execute them."[55]

Horton had seen the town of Frederica as well as his own land grant on Jekyll through a difficult time of adjustment, but he must have anticipated with pleasure the return of Oglethorpe and the arrival of the new regiment the general had recruited in England. In early May advance units of that regiment reached Savannah. One company continued on to Frederica, where Horton, recently commissioned an ensign in the Forty-second Regiment of Foot, would take command of it. He welcomed the reinforcements with open arms and began preparing for those still on their way. Oglethorpe, with the rest of his regiment aboard five transports, finally arrived at St. Simons on September 18, 1738. To his relief, they had reached the island before the long-dreaded Spanish attack. The Spaniards had missed the moment. Oglethorpe wrote jubilantly, "though they had 1500 men at Augustine and there was nothing in Georgia but the militia of the country, [they] delayed attacking them 'till the regular troops arrived."[56] The presence of regulars who now manned the various forts set the settlers' minds at rest. The new assistance also relieved them of their chronic military duties, provided them with a greater sense of security, and gave them more freedom to tend their crops.[57]

One of Oglethorpe's first duties upon his return was to promote William Horton once again in October 1738, this time to lieutenant in the Fifth Company. He clearly understood Horton's importance and generosity to the little colony, and he knew his reputation for honesty, practicality, courage, efficiency, and devotion to duty. He was well aware that without Horton there during his absence, the little community might not have survived at all.[58] With the general back in the colony, Horton was freed from his daily administration of the town and fort of Frederica, only to take on other important duties. Oglethorpe sent him on a trip up the Savannah River to find Mary Musgrove Matthews, a famed Native American interpreter, and summon her to Frederica, where she lived for a time. Another excursion took him to South Carolina to obtain supplies for the soldiers.[59] But he found some time for his own work on Jekyll Island. A report titled "State of the Province of Georgia in the Year 1740" submitted by colonists on November 10 acknowledged that "Upon Jekyl Island there is but little good Land, not above 300 or 400 acres, the rest being Sandy Sea Beach. Mr. Horton has his Lot upon this Island and has made great improvements there."[60] He seems to have done his best to make the most of his situation.

He did not hesitate, however, to abandon his land to accept an assignment from Oglethorpe that sent him on a mission back to England to deliver dispatches, render an accounting to the trustees, and, above all, recruit thirty additional troops for the new regiment. Reinforcements were especially critical, for in October 1739, the friction with Spain had finally broken out in a conflict known as the War of Jenkins' Ear. Clashes along the Georgia-Florida border began in November.[61] On December 29, 1739, Oglethorpe penned a letter to the trustees and soon afterward handed it to Horton for delivery: "I send this by Mr. Horton whom there is no need of recommending to you. You know his behavior when he commanded the Southern Division of the Province in my Absence. I could not think of a way more likely to acquaint you with the whole particulars of the province, than by sending him home, who can explain every thing."[62]

Horton must have looked forward to the trip back to England with exceptional anticipation. His family was still there, and he had not seen them for almost four years. His eagerness is evident by the fact that he hastened to Savannah, arriving late on the night of January 27, 1740, to await the departure of his ship. This time the wait must have seemed even more interminable than it had when he first left England. Once again, ill winds were the primary problem, and it was not until March 22 that favorable winds finally allowed Horton to set sail for England. One can only imagine the happy reunion, upon his arrival in early May, between William and Rebecca Horton. His children, still very young, must have grown almost beyond recognition during his long absence.[63]

Nevertheless, Horton had duties he did not intend to neglect. He went about them as briskly and efficiently as possible, dining on May 9 with John Percival, the Earl of Egmont, and giving him his usual bright picture of affairs in Georgia. Throughout the month he called on various British noblemen and officials, including the Duke of Newcastle and Sir Robert Walpole, pleading for funds for scout boats and explaining repeatedly the dangers posed by the Spanish and the need for a new grenadier company and more officers to reinforce Oglethorpe's regiment.[64]

During his stay in England, Horton was caught up in an important debate between the trustees and a Georgia planters' lobby represented by

Thomas Stephens, the "wayward son" of Horton's friend, William Stephens. Thomas Stephens had returned to London in 1739 to inform all who would listen of the "deplorable conditions" that existed in Georgia; he presented complaints from landowners who opposed the trustees' land tenure policies and the law prohibiting Negro slavery. Horton, by contrast, spoke in favor of the trustees' policies and denounced Stephens's statements as "full of slander and lies." He accosted Stephens personally and tried in vain to convince him of "his folly & vanity in attempting to set himself up against the trustees." But Stephens persisted, even going so far as to suggest to the Earl of Egmont that Horton himself had belittled the future of the colony. "I readily promis'd not to repeat the allegation," wrote Egmont, "as knowing should Lt Horton hear of it, he would break his bones."[65]

Although Horton defended the trustees vigorously, both in Georgia and in England, as was his duty, he was not totally unsympathetic to some of the planters' grievances and had, in fact, already spoken out for a few changes in the tenure policies. According to Secretary Stephens, Horton made it quite plain in a report to the trustees that the regulations requiring land to be forfeited unless a certain number of acres was cleared within a specified time were "Impossible . . . to fulfill" (even by him) and had "so discourage[d] the people, that the best of them were determining to quit the Colony."[66] He also stressed that the five-hundred-acre limitation on land grants "was a great Error." On the issue of slavery, however, he was still firmly opposed and believed that its introduction into the colony would be a grave mistake. In later years as Horton himself needed additional labor, he would have a change of heart and allow himself to be finally persuaded of the benefits of slavery, but only under carefully controlled conditions to ensure humanitarian treatment. At this time, though, he still believed that the introduction of slavery would be the ruin of the colony. As a direct consequence of Horton's (not Stephens's) testimony, the trustees finally agreed to relax the land tenure regulations, but they staunchly retained the prohibition against slavery. Horton was gratified and assured the trustees that "all reasonable people in the Colony would be satisfied."[67]

Equally successful in convincing the trustees of the need for the new grenadier company, he began to recruit the necessary troops. On Christmas Day in 1740 he was once again promoted, this time to captain. Given command of the new grenadier company of thirty men, he readied the troops for the voyage to Georgia to be made in February 1742. To everyone's delight, he also received permission to transport women and children with the soldiers free of charge as an inducement for the latter to remain permanently as settlers in Georgia.[68] It was undoubtedly on this occasion that Horton brought his own wife and children with him to Georgia, as there is no mention of them in earlier documents.[69] We do know, however, that after this trip to England his wife, Rebecca, and his sons, William and Thomas, were living with him in the colony. Their arrival on June 17, 1742, could not have come at a more dangerous time. The Spanish were expected at any moment, and, unfortunately, some of the soldiers and sailors whom Horton had brought with him had fallen sick during the voyage, and his mate, Mr. Montgomery, was dead.[70]

Horton must have been eager to show to his wife and sons his own private island and the home he had constructed for them there, but he had little or no time to settle his family on Jekyll, for four days later, on June 21, the long-expected Spanish offensive against the Georgia colony began in earnest. While Horton was still in England, the general had unsuccessfully besieged St. Augustine, provoking the Spanish to retaliate. Now Spanish ships bombarded Fort William, the fortification on the southern tip of Cumberland Island and close to the Spanish frontier, which Oglethorpe had erected during Horton's absence.

When news of the Spanish bombardment reached St. Simons, Horton left his family, who no doubt took refuge in Frederica, and rushed his newly organized grenadier company, along with a band of Native Americans, to the aid of Fort William. The English were further reinforced by troops from Fort St. Andrews, which Oglethorpe decided to abandon in order to reinforce Fort William and engage the Spanish farther south.[71] But they accomplished little more than slowing down the Spanish attack, for Cumberland Island was never the primary target of the Spanish armada. They were headed for Frederica.

On July 5, 1742, the fleet, under the command of General Manuel de Montiano, sailed into Jekyll Sound, landed troops at Gascoigne's Bluff, and seized Fort St. Simons on the south end of the island. Two days later a Spanish advanced guard marching toward Frederica encountered Oglethorpe and his troops in their path. Two skirmishes followed, the best known of which was the battle of Bloody Marsh. Although the outnumbered English drove back the Spaniards, their victory did not seem decisive, for Montiano's losses were relatively slight. According to exaggerated

Escutcheon of William Horton.
(Plate is part of the collection
at Ft. Frederica National
Monument, printed with
the permission of the
National Park Service)

British estimates, Montiano lost about two hundred soldiers in the battle. In reality, casualties were much fewer, and he still had an estimated three thousand men on the island in full possession of Fort St. Simons. Oglethorpe, recognizing the vulnerability of his forces, fell back to mass all his troops for the protection of Frederica and wait for the attack. He knew that he was greatly outnumbered, but he did not realize the degree to which the battle at Bloody Marsh had demoralized the Spaniards. Then, at a propitious moment in the lull, William Horton arrived with his garrison from Fort William, sailing boldly across Jekyll Sound in broad daylight and in plain view of the Spanish.[72]

The tenacity of the British at Bloody Marsh, coupled with the audacious arrival of Horton and the additional prospect of reinforcements from Carolina, gave the Spaniards pause as they considered the possibility of further attacks. They sent a galley and two smaller vessels up the river toward Frederica on July 11, but, according to Oglethorpe, "We fired at them with the few guns we had so warmly that they retired."[73] Evidently the Spanish were convinced that the British troops were stronger than they actually were, and Montiano was concerned that an attack by the British fleet might cut off all hope of escape. His anxiety increased when the sails of five British ships from South Carolina came into view from the north. Thus, to the surprise of Oglethorpe, on July 12, 1742, General Montiano began withdrawing his army.

Late in the afternoon Spanish troops razed Fort St. Simons, then boarded their vessels and sailed across the sound directly to Jekyll Island, which they knew to be defenseless. In a final gesture of defiance toward the English, toward Horton in particular, and in frustration with their failure on St. Simons, they swarmed over the island, torching Captain Horton's house and outbuildings and destroying his crops and livestock before turning their ships in retreat back to Florida.[74] The destruction wreaked on Jekyll Island would prove to be the last hostile action of the Spanish army in Georgia.

The following March, Oglethorpe led a retaliatory raid on St. Augustine. Perhaps recognizing that the Spanish had been definitively driven from his colony, he made this his final military action on behalf of Georgia. In July he departed for England, this time for good. Once more, he appointed Horton military commander at Frederica and sent notification of that fact to Secretary William Stephens on July 12, 1743—one year to the day after the Spanish had destroyed Horton's Jekyll Island home.[75] When two of Frederica's civil magistrates left the town for England, Horton was compelled to assume greater civil authority as well, a "usurpation" of power that brought complaints from the remaining magistrates.[76]

Saddled yet again with the responsibility of leadership, Horton knew that he also still had his own home to reconstruct on Jekyll and his family to care for. He began as well to prepare his own sons for leadership. One of the boys, probably Thomas, the second son, who was said to be "promising" and would later play the greater role in the colony and the Revolution, left Jekyll for Purrysburg, South Carolina, in August 1743 to be educated under the tutelage of a "French Minister."[77]

Before his family's arrival, rumors had circulated that Horton himself was a discouraged planter. Thomas Causton, whose opinion my be viewed with skepticism, had written to the trustees as early as 1741 that, although Horton had "built himself a house, kept a stock of cattle and had ten servants," he had become discouraged about prospects on Jekyll, declaring that "the labour was vain" and that he had "set his servants to hire."[78] Whether or not the rumor was true, with Rebecca at his side, Horton seems to have taken on a renewed vigor and determination to make his grant on Jekyll into a true home and to try again for a successful cultivation.

Rebecca Horton's first clear view of Jekyll may have been a visit to look over the ruins of her husband's burned-out plantation house. But together they would rebuild, and this time it would be a home not so easily destroyed. It would not be a wooden structure, as the first one had been, but rather a sturdier house of tabby, a local and durable mixture of lime, sand, and crushed seashells, its outside glazed to perfection. Shell middens, left

The remains of the Horton house on Jekyll Island.
(Courtesy of the Jekyll Island Museum Archives)

by the island's earlier Native residents, abounded at the island's north end, and Horton took advantage of them as building materials for his new house. Indeed, it is a tribute to Horton's determination that the tabby house is still standing today—one of only two surviving two-story colonial plantation houses made of tabby in the state of Georgia. Although Rebecca may never have had the opportunity to see the first house, her tastes must have influenced the plan of the new house, erected over the charred foundations of the earlier structure and completed most likely in 1743. Like the first house, the new one had chimneys at both ends; the downstairs had a tabby floor and was divided into two rooms by a tabby wall. Upstairs were two bedrooms, one for William and Rebecca and one for their sons.[79] The home had "a red-hipped roof and a back verandah that opened out from both floors."[80] A great cooking hearth filled the kitchen with warm smells that permeated the entire house. The family planted a vegetable garden, an orange grove, and a kitchen garden where Rebecca grew herbs for her cooking. She could see her boys playing outside from the kitchen window or as she mended their clothes before the fire in the parlor or shelled peas on the verandah. Not far from the house, alongside a navigable stream (subsequently called du Bignon Creek), Horton built other tabby outbuildings, a dock, and a well.

By 1745 Horton's land grant seemed to be flourishing once again. With the dangers of Spanish attack in abeyance, Horton had more time to devote to his own estate, and he was more eager than ever to improve the land. He had indicated to William Stephens his intention to make a fresh start. Stephens, always an admirer of Horton, wished him well in his endeavors. "I well know he is a gentleman that wants neither a Genius to attempt, nor a Resolution to carry on, any purpose that he takes in hand," he wrote. He did wonder, however, whether Horton had sufficient servants "to accomplish his good Intent."[81] In fact, Horton had already encountered some problems along these lines, having suffered the loss of four of his servants, who had stolen his boat and run away.[82] But he was determined to branch out in his cultivation endeavors in an effort to provide more variety in and perhaps more income from his crops. Wanting to help Horton make the most of his plantation, Stephens, in 1745, sent him three thousand grapevine cuttings, including white and black muscadine grapes, from his own vineyards. Stephens himself had little success with his experimental vineyards, and it is probable that Horton fared little better.[83] But he also planted barley, which thrived. In 1747 he ordered a "Great Copper" pot for the purpose of brewing beer on Jekyll, which he made available to the soldiers at Frederica.

In October of that year William and Rebecca Horton entertained the Philadelphia merchants William Logan and James Pemberton. On October 14 the visitors took "Capt Kerrs Boat with six Oars" to Jekyll, arriving about 3:00 p.m. Logan clearly enjoyed the visit, professing to find Horton "very much the gentleman" and "very fine in conversation." Unlike earlier visitors, who had merely "fared well," Logan claimed that they were "handsomely Entertained & spent ye remandr of the Day in walking abt the plantation, which is a tolerable good piece of Land and has many Savannahs."

Jekyll was ideal, because of the open areas, to graze cattle, which was its salvation. Horton's good luck with cattle may also have benefited from previous experience in his native Herefordshire, where cattle raising was one of the most important factors of the economy. In any case, it proved to be a significant part not only of his Jekyll plantation but also of the entire food supply of Frederica, for, as Logan noted, Horton "supplies all Frederica with Fresh Meat." Before their departure Logan and his party also took advantage of Horton's cattle, sending over "five of Our best hands last night late to Jekyl for a Couple of Beefs which we got killed for Our provisions." The visitors were deeply impressed with Horton's hospitality and generosity, and before their departure from the area, Logan recorded, the captain "was So kind that he would not let us go without presentg us with two fine sheep & a fresh Quarter of Beef, which I believe he had killed on purpose and was the Best I have seen on the Island. He also sent on board [our vessel] a Variety of pott-herbs & wanted us only to mention anything he had that We might think would be serviceable to us on Our Voyage." The herbs were most likely Rebecca's contribution from her own kitchen garden, for she no doubt made every effort alongside her husband to make Jekyll seem like a true home.

Ever since their arrival, Logan noted, Horton had done everything he could to oblige them, "with the utmost Chearfulness [*sic*] & readiness." They had enjoyed Captain Horton's generous hospitality on more than one occasion. In fact, even as they were awaiting fair winds for sailing on December 3, he invited them over once more to Jekyll for dinner, "Where We Were Entertained as usual, . . . with the utmost Civility." After dinner they walked over to the barley field, "which Captain Horton has With the utmost Industry got into fine Ordr and sowed and was just come up & looked Well."[84]

One of Horton's enemies, John Terry, whom Horton had convicted of a crime and who was trying to ingratiate himself with the trustees, contradicted Logan's assessment. "It is true," he averred, "that Capt Horton has Sewd Barley at Jeekel, But what he Reapd was Little better than Chaff, And Not fit for the purpose For wch the Copper is Intended."[85] Terry's motives were clearly to undermine Horton in any way he could, for, in fact, the barley did quite well that year. The following August, another of Horton's guests, a man named John Pye, reported to the trustees on the state of the plantation, noting particularly the harvested barley: "While I was at ye Southward I had ye Pleasure to see Major Hortons Improvements on the Island of Jeykill.—He has a very Large Barnfull of Barley not inferior to ye Barley in England, about 20 Ton of Hay in one Stack, a Spacious House & fine Garden, a plow was going wth Eight Horses." Horton also had a new crop, which impressed Pye even more, for it was still rare in Georgia. "[A]bove all," he wrote, "I saw Eight Acres of Indigo of which he has made a good Quantity & two Men are now at Work (a Spaniard

& English Man) they told me the Indigo was as good as that made in the Spanish West India's."[86]

Whether two men were sufficient to work eight acres of indigo and whether they truly had the knowledge to follow through with the complex series of fermentation processes, straining, bagging, drying, and cutting that it entailed remained to be seen. Horton had been inspired perhaps by hearing of the efforts of Eliza Lucas Pinckney in South Carolina, whose success with the crop had begun in the mid 1740s. In 1744 she had reserved all her seed for sharing with others, and Horton had perhaps even benefited from her generosity.[87] But indigo production was labor-intensive and highly technical, and the crop was easily damaged by cold and insects. William Stephens was no doubt right to wonder whether Horton had sufficient servants for all the tasks he was undertaking.

The barley that the visitors noted was intended, as Terry's letter makes clear, "for brewing of Beer at Jekyl." A historical sign on Jekyll today indicates what purports to be the site of Georgia's first brewery alongside du Bignon Creek. Later archaeological findings suggest that the structures in question may not have been used for that purpose but rather as a dwelling, for wine storage, or as a loading platform. However, we know for certain that Horton did brew beer in large quantities on Jekyll Island.[88] In 1753 the South Carolina planter Jonathan Bryan reported seeing both a large "Malt House" of at least eighty to one hundred feet long by thirty feet and "a large Brew-house of wood with all Conveniences for Brewing."[89] Given the size of his facilities, it seems clear that Horton was brewing for more than his own personal use.

Horton may, however, have been overzealous in trying to take on too much too quickly, and his last good year on Jekyll Island seems to have been 1747. His ill health at the end of the year must have contributed to his discouragement as well as his growing need for a larger labor force. Whatever the reason, whether he was sick of the constant battles with the heat, the unbidden storms, the sandy soil, and the insects of his island plantation, or whether he was merely seeking to make a case for his son to receive other land, he announced in June 1748 that Jekyll Island was "at length found totally unfit for cultivation." For that reason he requested that his young son Thomas be granted five hundred acres of land on the Great Ogeechee River.[90] The trustees approved the petition on behalf of the younger Horton, who went to seek his fortune in present-day Greene County, which he

This image purports to show the ruins of Horton's brewery, though archaeologists
have suggested that it is more likely the ruins of a dwelling or a storehouse.
(Courtesy of the Margaret Davis Cate Collection, Fort Frederica
National Monument, Georgia Historical Society)

would later represent at the convention that created the constitution of the
state of Georgia in 1788.[91]

Even during the time he had been trying to get his plantation back on
its feet, William Horton still had military duties to perform as commander
of the southern division of Georgia with headquarters at Frederica. He had
received his final promotion to major in Oglethorpe's regiment of regulars
in the summer of 1745 and could never afford the luxury of concentrating
his attention on farm and family. The War of Jenkins' Ear had merged
in 1744 into a much broader conflict, King George's War (1744–48), which
would involve the French as antagonists as well as the Spanish. Once again,
daily expecting an attack from St. Augustine, Horton published the official
declaration of war in Frederica in July and began taking aggressive action
against the Florida frontier.[92] In any given month in 1744 and 1745, he could
be found along the Savannah River attempting to intercept illegal South
Carolina trade with the enemy, in the upcountry parleying with Native

Americans to retain their friendship, or in Savannah consulting about colonial affairs with William Stephens, who had by now been appointed president in overall charge of Georgia.[93]

In October 1747 Horton fell ill, succumbing to an epidemic that swept through Frederica.[94] Even though he recovered under the watchful care of his wife, he was still weak. Nonetheless, he continued to work diligently to try to balance the interests of the colonists and the trustees as well as his own interests on Jekyll. The growing pressure from colonists and his own need for more workers changed his mind, albeit grudgingly, about the restrictions against slavery in the colony. In an effort to convince the trustees to lift the prohibition against the importation of slaves into Georgia, he went to Savannah in late 1748 for a meeting to discuss the issues. Once again, he was struck down by "a malignant fever." This time he could not shake it off, and "to the universal sorrow of all his acquaintance," he died, still in his forties, and was buried in Christ Church in Savannah.

In a letter to Oglethorpe, telling him of Horton's death, James Habersham made it clear how hard Horton had worked for the colony and how much he would be missed: "Major Horton's unwearied and generous exertions in the service of this colony have perhaps contributed not a little, to abridge the number of his days." He had insisted on coming to Savannah "to meet the president, assistants and other representatives, to consult on an affair of the greatest importance to the colony." Habersham paid what was perhaps his finest tribute when he concluded that Horton's "conduct and opinions, gave renewed specimens of his wisdom and prudence. . . . he shined in war and peace, in public and in private stations."[95]

Rebecca Horton never married again. In recognition of her husband's service to the colony, she received a widow's pension of thirty pounds a year until the end of her life in 1800. Fulfilling the restrictions of the trustees that the land grants could pass only to a male heir, Horton's five-hundred-acre grant on Jekyll Island passed into the hands of his second son, Thomas, his older son, William, either having died or no longer living in the colony at the time.[96] Young Thomas Horton, already deeply involved in his own life, took no interest whatsoever in the land he had inherited on the north end of Jekyll. He had apparently accepted his father's word without question that the island was "totally unfit for cultivation." Focusing his full attention instead on his Ogeechee plantation, he abandoned Jekyll Island, leaving it to others to take his father's place.

CHAPTER THREE

From Royal Colony
to Revolution

If there is any man so base or so weak as to prefer a dependence
on Great Britain to the dignity and happiness of living a member of a
free and independent nation, let me tell him that necessity now demands
what the generous principle of patriotism should have dictated.

SAMUEL ADAMS

HE DEATH of William Horton and the indifference of his heir toward Jekyll left the island, once again, with an uncertain future. For the rest of the eighteenth century, Jekyll and its owners would be caught up in family disputes and the political upheavals of a colony in turmoil. Their sequential stories reflect the final days of the trustees' colony, the advent of the royal colony, the conflict of the American Revolution, and finally the beginning of the plantation era at Jekyll Island.

The arrival in Georgia in April 1749 of an English captain, George Dunbar, seemed at least briefly to clarify Jekyll's role. The captain stepped off the vessel *Francis and John* carrying orders to deactivate Oglethorpe's Forty-second Regiment at Fort Frederica. The troops held their final formation on the Frederica parade ground on May 29.[1] Soldiers were given a choice of remaining in the military by enlisting in one of the three Independent Companies of South Carolina that Dunbar had been authorized to form, or else they could remain in Georgia as settlers. Those who chose to stay in Georgia would receive a grant of fifty acres of "good land, five pounds sterling, and provisions for a year for themselves, their wives and their children."[2] For the most part, the soldiers scattered, some returning to England and others volunteering to stay and become settlers in the colony. Only a handful reenlisted in the newly organized Independent Companies. Among them were Paul and Raymond Demeré, into whose hands Jekyll Island would fall.

The disbanding of the regiment was the death knell of Frederica. With the departure of the soldiers and their families, so essential to the town's economic survival, the tradesmen and artisans also began to leave for greener fields. However, also contained within Dunbar's orders was a provision intended "to shew his Majesty's Care of his Subjects in Georgia."[3] That unremarkable clause would determine the immediate future of Jekyll Island. The army, the orders declared, would maintain at least a token presence of soldiers in the area. One sergeant, one corporal, and twelve men were to be stationed on Jekyll Island, which was still valuable both as an outpost against any invasion from the south and for the beef and barley it supplied.

Paul Demeré, whom Horton had recruited as a lieutenant into his company of grenadiers in 1740, was assigned to oversee the small unit of soldiers stationed on Jekyll, which for the first time became a true military outpost. Although plans for "a Battery and Redout [sic] with a Guard-House" on the island had been drawn up in 1740 by the engineer John Thomas, the fortifications had never been constructed.[4] Thomas had died even before the plans were completed, and evidently the limitations on funds prevented the building of the battery.

For little more than a year, beginning in June 1749, Lieutenant Paul Demeré commanded the small contingent of troops on the island, but in September 1750 his older brother, Captain Raymond Demeré, took over command of the island and would remain part of its history until his death in 1766.[5] With his brother, Raymond Demeré had also served with William Horton during his command in Frederica. Like the settlers led by Jean Ribault two hundred years earlier, the Demeré brothers were French Huguenots who had taken refuge in England during a period of persecution. They came from a French village called Nérac on the banks of the Baise River in the Gascon region of southwestern France. Nérac had once been a Huguenot stronghold and the capital of Henri IV, a French Protestant king who had converted to Catholicism in order to be crowned. Although during his rule he protected the Protestants and brought the wars of religion in France to an end, in 1685 Louis XIV revoked Henri IV's Edict of

Nantes, an important document that had guaranteed to Protestants freedom of worship. The Reformed Church was once again outlawed, and the door of Catholic persecution of Protestants was again opened wide.

As soon as they were old enough, Raymond and Paul Demeré left for England and purchased commissions in the British Army, with the encouragement and help of a half-uncle, Captain Francis Cayran, himself a British officer since 1719.[6] The English were no doubt pleased to have the Demeré brothers both in their army and in their drawing rooms, for the young men were sociable, well educated, and fluent in English as well as in French. Raymond soon added Spanish to his linguistic skills when he was sent to Gibraltar, where he served for ten years as an aide to Brigadier General William Stanhope, the first Lord Harrington.

Demeré's knowledge of Spanish, as well as his previous service in the hot climes of Gibraltar, made him a particularly desirable officer for service in the Georgia regiment that Oglethorpe recruited in England in 1737–38. Demeré received his commission as a lieutenant in Major William Cook's company, one of the six companies that would make up Oglethorpe's Forty-second Regiment of Foot, on August 25, 1737, the same day that Oglethorpe received permission to raise the regiment from King Gorge II.[7]

The new regiment, consisting of 684 officers and men, Raymond Demeré among them, reached the Georgia colony on May 8, 1738. He was soon chosen to serve as interpreter for an envoy to St. Augustine and to the governor of *La Florida*, Manuel de Montiano. Montiano described in detail his meeting with Demeré in a letter to the governor of Havana written on April 3, 1739:

> James Oglethorpe recommended to me Don Raymond Demere, a lieutenant in his regiment. . . . when I was informed of this by the Adjutant, Don Alvaro Lopez, . . . I asked him who was this Don Raymond and the others who came in the sloop, and he informed me that the envoys from St. George [Charles Towne] were two members of the Parliament House and a secretary, a boy of 16 years, more or less, . . . and a lieutenant of the troops that are in the chief towns to the north, who was coming both as interpreter . . . and at the same time also to pay his respects to me on the part of Don James Oglethorpe. . . . I agreed that they should lodge in my house in order to deprive them of the opportunity to treat with those who incautiously would tell them what was not proper or to see the Castillo or the line of fortifications.[8]

Demeré and Montiano discussed many things that day, among them some deserters from Frederica who, Oglethorpe thought, might have taken refuge with the Spanish, though the governor denied it. Demeré also confided to Montiano that Oglethorpe was not well liked by all, which might be seen as a ploy to gain his confidence. However, what Demeré said was true. Some of the newly arrived men were already "in a surly mood."[9] They found their surroundings primitive; they grumbled about the lack of rum; and they had not yet received the extra pay they had expected for the voyage to Georgia. Montiano commented in his account that Demeré "handled the [Spanish] language sufficiently well." The visitors stayed several days in St. Augustine and were treated in a cordial manner, even feeling at ease to ask before they left whether they could take with them some chocolate and candy, treats they rarely enjoyed in Frederica. As they set sail, they exchanged seven-gun salutes with the Spanish.

One year later Demeré and Montiano would not be on such friendly terms. The following October saw the beginning of the War of Jenkins' Ear, named for the ship's captain whose ear was severed by a Spanish search party on his vessel. Captain Jenkins brought the severed ear back to London and displayed it to members of the British Parliament, who were so horrified and indignant at the bloody sight that they declared war on Spain. King George II sent orders to General Oglethorpe to capture St. Augustine, a task that proved easier said than done. This second siege against St. Augustine, which lasted for many months, was no more successful than that of 1702. This time Demeré's language skills were less important than his military prowess. But he must have remembered, even as he besieged the fortress, the hospitality he had enjoyed at Montiano's house such a short time before.

The unsuccessful siege consisted primarily of useless land maneuvers and efforts to blockade the port and prevent the Spanish from receiving food and supplies. Although Demeré did not particularly distinguish himself at St. Augustine, it was a different story in the defense of Frederica at the battle of Bloody Marsh two years later.[10] This time the Spanish were the attackers, and Demeré, thanks to the intervention of Oglethorpe, became known that day as a hero. Recognizing that the British were greatly outnumbered at Bloody Marsh and dismayed by the relentless noise of the Spanish shouts and drummers whom they could not see through the smoke of musket fire and the constant drizzle, Demeré and three "fugitive platoons" thought it was a rout and quickly retreated. Oglethorpe, still hearing some of his men firing at the Spaniards, ordered Demeré and his troops back to the front. Whatever misgivings they might have had, to their credit, Demeré and his men returned to the battle and fired persistently at the Spanish grenadiers who were still stumbling through the marsh. Unaware that many of the British troops had fled, the Spaniards began to retreat.[11] Without the return of Demeré's men, the British might well have lost the day and ultimately the colony of Georgia. That skirmish was the last time Demeré would face Spanish guns.

No doubt both Paul and Raymond Demeré were loyal and vigorous soldiers. In fact, in a letter written later to the governor of South Carolina, William Lyttleton, Raymond Demeré spoke of his own military determination: "as long as I can craul [*sic*] about and shall have a Drop of warm Blood in my Veins, I shall fight. I flatter myself to have as much Courage as any Man . . . [and] I have done my Duty to the Utmost in every Shape, and let me die or live, I shall have Nothing to reproach myself with."[12]

Only a few years after Raymond assumed responsibility at Jekyll, the Georgia trustees, denied funding by Parliament and having no other fiscal recourse, decided to abandon entirely their idealistic experiment—the "charity colony" of Georgia. They found themselves with insufficient funds from the government and diminishing private support. Many of their original backers, weary of all the wrangling and gossip that reached them from the colony, had lost interest in the effort. Even Oglethorpe had stopped attending meetings of the trustees.[13] On June 23, 1752, they gave up the project and relinquished their charter rights to the Crown a year before they were scheduled to expire.

For the first time in its history, Georgia would become a royal colony, with a governor appointed by the king and a council composed of twelve royal appointees, all notable citizens of the colony. In 1754 Georgia governance began a process of reorganization, and by 1758 it had a fully developed structure with a governor and a two-house assembly, the Commons House elected by the voters, and the Upper House, made up of members of the council, meeting without the governor.[14] That same year the colony was divided into eight parishes north of the Altamaha River. They did not include Jekyll Island, which was technically still part of Spanish Florida. During the life of Raymond Demeré, however, it would come to be without question a part of English territory. But arriving at that point would not be easy or peaceable, and the Demeré brothers would both play significant roles in the process.

This drawing, *Peter Manigault and His Friends*, by George Roupell provides the
only known image of Captain Raymond Demeré, who is seated at the head of the table,
in front of the fireplace. (Courtesy, Winterthur Museum)

Thomas Spalding, a well-known Sapelo planter, described Raymond Demeré as "a French Huguenot of considerable fortune." The minutes of a
meeting of the president and assistants for the colony of Georgia depicted
him as "a very industrious and worthy Gentleman and particularly addicted
to the Cultivation of lands."[15] Not only did Demeré enjoy the use of the
500-acre plantation at Jekyll Island, but he also had a large plantation on
St. Simons—Harrington Hall. Initially the plantation consisted of only 50
acres, but in August 1760 he was granted an additional 150 acres on the
south side of the original 50.[16] Spalding seemed to admire the plantation,
which, he noted, Demeré had ornamented "in the French taste," no doubt
quite formal and elegant.[17] William Logan, who visited both Demeré and
Horton during his 1745 trip, left a somewhat less splendid picture. His first
glimpse of Harrington Hall came during an after-dinner walk he took "with
several Gent[s] . . . out to Captn Demmery's Plantation abt 1½ mile from

Town [Frederica]." It was, he said, in "a very poor flat, sandy spot, but stocked with young trees, peaches, apples, oranges, pomegranate etc."[18]

Given the fact that Demeré's main residence was on St. Simons, his interest in Jekyll was most likely for military reasons, for it guarded the entrance to the sound that led to Frederica. Jekyll had also served as the residence of the former military commander of Frederica, which no doubt gave it a particular prestige. And it was essential for providing the troops with meat and drink. Even though Demeré petitioned colonial officials for the provisioning of the troops stationed under his command at Jekyll, he also invested much of his own time and money in the property. Like Horton, he seems to have supplied provisions to the soldiers from his own private stocks there.[19] Since Demeré maintained the property, it is reasonable to assume that he used the Horton house from time to time, though not as his permanent residence. It (or the overseer's residence) also housed the soldiers stationed there. Certainly he treated the plantation as his own, renaming Jekyll Creek, Demeré Creek, and at his own expense repairing buildings and even adding new ones.

It may indeed by then have been a less mournful place than Frederica, which, since the disbanding of the regiment, had fallen into ruin. The wealthy planter Jonathan Bryan, who owned considerable property in both South Carolina and Georgia, including land on Cumberland Island, passed through Frederica in 1753 and bemoaned its condition. He had seen it years before in its better days. But now, he noted with sadness, it lay "all in a ruinous Condition, the Melancholy Prospect of Houses without Inhabitants, Barracks without Soldiers, Guns without Carriages and the Streets grown over with Weeds, appeared to me with a very horrible Aspect, and so very different from what I once knew it, that I could scarce refrain from Tears."[20]

Although Bryan was aware that "Capt Demere has a Company [with] about Fifty Men for this Place, . . . they were either out on Detachments or upon Furloughs." Only twelve or so soldiers were in the town upon the arrival of Bryan and his party, which included the well-known cartographer and military engineer William DeBrahm. Though they were well-entertained and fortified with fruit and punch, Bryan could not help but mourn the lost potential that was Frederica. Very early the following morning they went to the south end of the island, and where there had once been a "Battery of ten or twelve Pieces of cannon to secure the Inlet," they now found it "quite defenceless, and the cannon almost buried in the Sand."

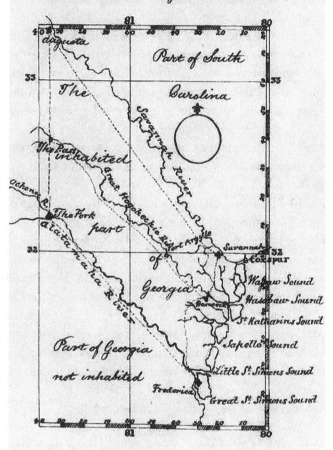

This map, drawn in 1756 by the famous cartographer
William DeBrahm, who had visited Jekyll Island three years earlier,
does not include Jekyll in the "inhabited part of Georgia," which
suggests the lingering dangers of such a southernmost outpost.
(Courtesy of Hargrett Rare Book and Manuscript Library/
University of Georgia Libraries)

Taking advantage of the flood tide, they rowed over to Jekyll Island to visit what they still referred to as "Major Horton's Plantations and Buildings at Jekyl." Here, to the contrary, Bryan was favorably impressed and found much more than he had expected:

> I was Surprizd at the extraordinary Expense this Gentleman must have been at in the Setling and improving of this Place. he has a handsome dwelling house of about forty foot long by twenty wide, neatly finish'd and Glazed, a good House for his Overseer about thirty by twenty, a Malt House of Eighty or one hundred foot long by thirty, all these of Tabby, also a large Brew-house of wood with all Conveniences for Brewing, a large Barn and Stables and other Conveniences too numerous to mention; he has a large Orange Garden, now loaded with Fruit, a good Stock of about three hundred Head of Cattle and one hundred Head of Horses. This place is about ten Miles from Frederica; the Island is about nine Miles long and two miles wide it is very fit for Stock and some good planting Land on it. there is now only a Soldier to take care of the Buildings.[21]

It had been more than four years since William Horton's death, and the island, abandoned by his son Thomas, was clearly being used and well maintained by Raymond Demeré.

Although the immediate danger from the Spanish in Florida seemed to be over, the claims among the English, French, and Spanish for territory in the New World had never been settled and continued to simmer. In July 1754 English officials received a warning from Havana that the Spanish and French had joined forces to build forts and commission Native Americans "in preparations for War against the English." Colonial records make it clear that the British did not take the warning lightly. Although they "hoped the Indian Report wou'd not prove as represented," they nevertheless thought it best "to be upon their Guard."[22]

The Demeré brothers would not have long to wait before their military service was needed again, for the French and Indian War erupted in 1756. Raymond Demeré took over command of Fort Loudon, North Carolina (now in Tennessee). However, he suffered from ill health, probably from a dangerous combination of malaria and asthma from the time he arrived in Cherokee country, and unable to fulfill his duties to his own satisfaction, he requested relief from his command, which was finally granted on August 14, 1757. He returned to his plantations on the Georgia coast to recuperate.

Raymond Demeré II (son of Paul Demeré) fought for the colonies during the American Revolution and was an aide to George Washington, while his cousin, Raymond Demeré Jr. (son of Captain Raymond Demeré) remained loyal to the crown. (Courtesy of the Margaret Davis Cate Collection, Fort Frederica National Monument, Georgia Historical Society)

It was his brother, Paul, who replaced him, only to lose his life in a brutal Cherokee attack in August 1760 following a long siege against Fort Loudon.

Less than three years later the Treaty of Paris brought a formal conclusion to the French and Indian War, or the Seven Years' War as it was known in Europe. In the treaty, signed on February 10, 1763, the Spanish crown officially ceded to the king of Great Britain "Florida, with Fort St. Augustin [*sic*], and the Bay of Pensacola, as well as all that Spain possesses on the continent of North America, to the East or to the South East of the river Mississippi." Furthermore, the French ceded to Great Britain not only Canada but also all the territory east of the Mississippi. The treaty, sweeping in its implications for America, quietly ended an important era in Georgia history and put Jekyll Island firmly and indisputably in English hands.[23] That same year the royal colony created four new parishes south of the Altamaha. Two years later, on March 15, 1765, a legislative enactment decreed that "the Island of Jekyl shall from henceforth be and forever continue a part of the parish of Saint James."[24]

Raymond Demeré, now in his sixties, and with all immediate dangers from foreign encroachment at an end, was finally able to focus his full attention on his own estates. With the leisure and resources to do so at last, he and his sisters began a lawsuit in 1763 to recover the substantial wealth of their grandmother in France. He also began to make petitions to seek additional land grants in the Georgia colony.[25]

One of these grants involved Jekyll Island. On July 1, 1765, he petitioned the council to give him full possession of Horton's five hundred acres "for the term of his Life." He was well aware that Thomas Horton was the rightful heir, but he also knew that young Horton had not set foot on the island for the past fifteen years. Acknowledging the younger man's rights, Demeré agreed that after his own death, the land should "descend to the heirs of the said Major Horton." Recognizing that the council would need some persuasion to make such an unusual grant, he pointed out that from the time of Horton's death until the present, he had had responsibility and possession of "that Part of Jekyl Island improved and built on by the late Major Horton." He informed council members that he had gone to great expense on the Horton property, that he "had kept up and repaired the Buildings thereon as well as made additional ones." He underscored as well that he already had "on the said Island a very large Stock of Cattle and Horses and had a Family Right for more Land than he petitioned for."[26] It was a long and earnest plea, unlike any Raymond Demeré had ever made.

Not only did Demeré request the Horton grant, but he also asked for an additional six hundred adjacent acres on Jekyll to use as a range for his cattle. The council was unsympathetic and reluctant to break with tradition. Although the members granted him the six hundred additional acres he requested, they denied him the acreage belonging to the Horton estate. However, their decision had little effect. Until his death the following year, Demeré continued to graze his cattle even on Thomas Horton's portion of the island, which, in fact, if not in deed, he already used as his own plantation.

Demeré's death did not escape the attention of a young man named Clement Martin, a member of the Royal Council, who was his next-door neighbor both in Savannah and in St. John's Parish, where the two men owned adjacent plots of land. In July 1766, only a month after the probation of Demeré's will, Martin requested that Demeré's "six hundred acres pass to . . . Clement Martin Esqr" and that "the Surveyor General do prepare and certify a Plan of the said land accordingly."[27] Evidently, as a member of the council that would decide the petition, he felt a sense of confidence in making the request despite Demeré's living heirs. He would not be disappointed.

The Clement Martin in question was Clement Jr., the son of a retired British sea captain, now a merchant, who still lived with other members of his family in St. Kitts (also known as St. Christopher) in the West Indies. Because only the younger Clement came into the colony of Georgia in the 1750s, colonial records and newspapers prior to, and sometimes even after, his father's arrival in 1767 record only the name of "Clement Martin" or "Clement Martin Esqr," making no effort to distinguish between the Junior and Senior Martins. Until both men had come to the colony, there had been little need to make such differentiations in public records. As a consequence, it has been sometimes difficult for historians to sort them out.

Clement Jr. had left St. Kitts, where he held a minor public service post as assistant registrar of deeds, to come to Georgia in 1754.[28] Not long after his arrival, on August 6 he petitioned the council for the usual five-hundred-acre land grant in the colony, indicating that he was "lately arrived from the Island of St Christophers" and that he was "desirous of setling [*sic*] and cultivating Lands in the Colony." He requested his acreage "on the South Side of the North Branch of Newport River near to Lands laid out for Elizabeth De St Julian," a young widow who, according to family genealogy records, would later become his wife, though the issue of marriage is by no means certain.[29] As luck would have it, Martin arrived in the colony only a short time before the first royal governor, John Reynolds, who reached Savannah on October 29. It would not take long for the forceful personalities of the two men to clash.

In mid-December the king received and approved a recommendation from the Board of Trade that Clement Martin Jr. be appointed to serve on the Royal Council in Georgia.[30] By virtue of this appointment, Martin also sat in the Upper House of the Assembly. Governor Reynolds later claimed that he was "extreamly [*sic*] concerned" to learn of Martin's appointment to the council, for he viewed him as "a young Man of a very Turbulent, Overbearing Spirit." According to the governor, "he came hither from St. Christophers (where his Father has been Master of a Vessel) and he arrived here a little before me, to Settle, with 12 or 14 very indifferent Negroes." The governor made abundantly clear his dislike for Martin, who, he alleged, "had no sort of Regard for His Majesty's Service."[31]

Nevertheless, the king approved Martin's appointment to the council at the Court of St. James on December 17, 1754. On April 28, 1755, he took his seat on the council, an honor enjoyed by only twelve men in the colony

at any given time.[32] He soon found himself embroiled in a major controversy. Georgia's first royal governor, evidently a man of poor judgment, had
bestowed on his private secretary and chief lieutenant, William Little, a
former naval surgeon, extraordinary powers and offices—including clerk of
the two-house assembly, clerk of the Crown and Peace, clerk of the General Court, secretary of Indian Affairs, and the governor's aide-de-camp.
Little did whatever it took to have his way, even falsifying minutes of the
Commons House of Assembly and failing to present to the governor for
his signature bills that the assembly had passed. The council was outraged
at his acts, with one member describing him as "a person . . . of the most
Despotic Principles."[33] As a group, council members decided to complain
of Little's actions to the governor, accusing him of slander, extortion, fraud,
falsification of minutes in his role as clerk, and forgery, and to demand his
dismissal. Unfortunately for Clement Martin Jr., it was he they selected to
deliver this message to the governor.[34]

The governor chose to punish the messenger and instead dismissed Martin from his seat on the council. Reynolds wrote to the Board of Trade, laying out his reasons and explaining that Martin "had the Impudence to tell
me in Council, that I had but half Cheated the Assembly, . . . and that same
Evening he made it the Subject of Conversation at a Tavern, in a mixed
Company." Martin, he fumed, had "always behaved with great Indecency
and Illmanners [*sic*] to me, in Council, ever since he has been a Member
thereof." He informed the board of his intent to dismiss Martin from office,
"without giving my reasons to the Council for so doing, in hopes that your
Lordships will Approve of them, and represent the matter accordingly to
his Majesty."[35] One week later, on September 30, 1755, he carried out his
intent. The council vigorously protested, to no avail.[36]

The governor's secretary denied the council's charges, calling them "false,
Malicious and Weak." Although he admitted to having withheld a bill "on
Account of its Insignificancy and Non-Importance" and also averred that
he might have committed "little Inaccuracies" here and there because of
overwork and his "not having been bred to the Law," he argued that these
matters were noticeable only when viewed "through the Magnifying Glass
of Prejudice and Malice."[37]

On top of the governor's squabble with the council came a similar argument with the Commons House the following year. Reynolds, increasingly impatient with those who did not bow to his authority, summarily

dissolved what one councilor called "the best Assembly he'l [*sic*] ever probably meet in Georgia."[38] This time, however, Reynolds had gone too far. Prominent Georgians began to write to officials in England, criticizing his dictatorial actions and his inability to govern. Reynolds and Little defended themselves vigorously, but ultimately to no avail. Despite Reynolds's efforts to create a new assembly that would favor his actions, the Crown soon sent another governor, initially given the title of lieutenant governor, to replace him.

Henry Ellis, the new appointee, arrived in Savannah on February 16, 1757, to the cheers of its residents. Still unhappy about the mistreatment of Clement Martin Jr. at the hands of Governor Reynolds, the council petitioned the new governor (as he soon became) for Martin's reinstatement on the council. But Ellis was much more cautious and circumspect than his predecessor, and he did not want to make sudden changes without careful consideration. He seemed nonplussed as to what he should do about Clement Martin. He wrote to the Board of Trade on February 10, 1759, asking their advice about two council members who had been previously suspended by Governor Reynolds. One of the former members had been renominated; but Ellis was reluctant to reappoint him without reappointing Martin, who still had support in the council. He wanted to avoid "censure at home" and giving "great offence" in Georgia. Thus, he decided to do nothing until he could learn the king's "pleasure."[39]

In fact, Martin would not be restored to his seat in the council until after Henry Ellis was replaced by the third (and last) royal governor, James Wright, who took office in 1760. When two vacancies occurred in the council in 1761, Governor Wright sent six names of possible replacements to the Board of Trade. One of those names was Clement Martin. Regarding him he wrote, "With respect to Mr Martyn my Lords I understand he was formerly in Council and Suspended by Mr. Reynolds. How that matter Stands & the Reasons for that Suspension your Lordships best know." But he included Martin among those he judged "to be Sensible, discreet, well bred Men, and their Characters Extremely good & fair."[40]

Wright subsequently reappointed Martin to his council seat. The record is absolutely clear that both appointments refer to Clement Martin Jr. While some scholars have contended that Clement Martin Sr. also served on the council, there is no evidence of it.[41] Although council records give the name most of the time simply as "Clement Martin Esqr.," whenever

Portrait of Governor James Wright, the
third and last governor of the Royal Colony
of Georgia. (Courtesy of the Georgia
Historical Society)

there is a specific designation to the council member in attendance, it is always to Clement Martin Jr., never to Clement Sr. As one final piece of evidence, Governor Reynolds, in explaining his dismissal from the council, referred to him as a "young man." He cannot possibly be referring to the father, who would have been over fifty-five years old at the time.

The first clear mention we have of Clement Martin Sr. is a grant he received on March 5, 1756, for five hundred acres of land near those of his son in the district of Newport.[42] On the same day Clement Martin Jr. was also granted an additional five hundred acres in that area. However, if Clement Sr. had come to the colony at that early date, he evidently did not remain, for there is no further public record of him in Georgia until 1767. It is possible that his son made the request on his behalf to increase his own holdings or in an effort to persuade his father to come to Georgia. Three other petitions were approved that same day for "Clement Martin, Esqr." It is impossible to tell whether these refer to father or son, though in all likelihood, they were for the son. Had the petition been from his father, it would surely have been clarified for the record. In one of these petitions on May 6, 1755, the new councilman (Clement Jr.) noted that he was "desirous of erecting a House in Savannah," where his council work would often require him to be. He requested one of the reserved lots in Heathcote Ward, known by the letter *O*.[43] Later that same year he requested another five hundred acres on the north side of the Little Ogeechee, five hundred acres in the district of Newport, half a lot in Savannah, and a lot in Hardwicke No. 63, next door to lot No. 65, which belonged to Raymond Demeré. The petitions were all granted on March 5, 1756.[44] Another son of Clement Sr., John Martin, requested one hundred acres of land at Midway on July 4, 1758, stating that he had been in the province for three years, which suggests that he came to Georgia the year after his brother.[45] One other family member, possibly a brother, came to Georgia with Clement Jr. in 1754, and when the latter applied for his first five-hundred-acre grant south of the north branch of the Newport River, he also petitioned for an equal amount of land to adjoin his own on behalf of William Martin.[46]

On March 28, 1763, Clement Martin Jr. applied to Governor Wright for a leave of absence, noting that he was "going on a voyage to the West Indies."[47] He requested a nine-month absence, but by September 6 he had already returned and was attending council meetings. During his absence from the colony, it is probable that he visited his family in St. Kitts, seeking to persuade them to come to Georgia, where land was abundant for planting and where he was a man of distinction. His trip was evidently successful, for on August 6, 1765, he noted that he now had "forty Persons in Family for whom he had obtained no Land" and was petitioning for a grant of two thousand acres on "the River St Mary in the Southward part of the Province lying at a Place called Butter Milk Bluff."[48] Even then, however, his father apparently still remained in St. Kitts.

Clement Sr. did not, in fact, come to the colony to live until two years later. The *Georgia Gazette* chronicled his arrival with his family from St. Kitts aboard the *Nassau*, captained by Christopher Prince, on July 3, 1767.[49] Clement Sr. had emigrated to the island of St. Kitts, the "mother-colony of the British West Indies," sometime before 1723, the year in which he married a young woman named Jane Edwards there.[50] The couple began a family, with children including Clement Jr., John, Elizabeth (called Betsy), Ann, Jane, and Susannah.[51] Clement Sr. was a ship's captain and merchant in St. Kitts, and given the number of slaves he brought to Georgia, he was very likely also a sugar planter.[52] Sugar cane had long ago begun to outstrip cotton there as the primary cash crop. In fact, the West Indies had

Portrait of Clement Martin Sr.
(Courtesy of the Margaret Davis Cate
Collection, Fort Frederica National
Monument, Georgia Historical Society)

come to be known in England as the "sugar colonies."[53] When Martin had first come to St. Kitts from England, the island was considered the garden spot of the West Indies. In the early days of that colony, St. Kitts served as the first settlement and the seat of the West Indian colonial government. For a time, the English and French had shared the island, and its capital city and best harbor, Basseterre, still bore a French name. In 1713, however, with the Treaty of Utrecht, France had given over the island of St. Kitts to the English, in whose hands, for the time being at least, it seemed secure. Nevertheless, it was in all probability a good time to be leaving St. Kitts.

Subject to storms and hurricanes, which repeatedly wreaked havoc on the crops, St. Kitts had also become a favorite haunt of pirates and privateers, and the sixty-eight-square-mile island was always vulnerable to attack, as is evident from the presence of three English forts there. Worst of all, the lands had begun to play out, requiring more and more labor to make them productive. In 1707 fewer than 3,000 Negro slaves were on St. Kitts. By 1756 that number had increased to 21,891, while the numbers of whites on the island decreased between 1724 and 1756 from 4,000 to 2,713.[54] Fearful of slave uprisings, the colonial government had begun to place increasing restrictions on the enslaved peoples and harsher penalties for any violations. As the slaves' resentment increased, so did the danger of the situation for those who would keep them in chains. In fact, in 1761, while many members of the Martin family were still in the West Indies, a conspiracy to massacre all the whites was uncovered on the adjacent island of Nevis.[55] As a consequence, wealthy planters were beginning to return to England or, like Clement Martin, move on to other colonies, leaving their lands in the hands of overseers. One English visitor to St. Kitts in 1774 reported that the island had been "almost abandoned to Overseers and managers."[56]

In addition, in the wake of the Treaty of Paris, Great Britain had taken possession of four islands, Dominica, Grenada, St. Vincent, and Tobago, all of which were underdeveloped by St. Kitts's standards and had fertile, veritably virgin soil. Unfortunately for those at St. Kitts, these four islands were ideal for sugar planting and soon began to attract a new generation of planters from England. By 1767 these so-called Ceded Islands were putting economic pressure on the other planters, lowering prices, and taking away markets.[57]

Given the deteriorating situation, Clement Sr., now in his sixties, finally decided to leave St. Kitts and settle nearer his sons in the colony of Georgia. It was clear to him that his eldest son had become a man of some consequence there. In fact, the year after Clement Sr.'s arrival, Clement Jr. was authorized, along with other Georgia notables Joseph Habersham, Noble Jones, and Archibald Bulloch, on April 11, 1768, "to correspond with . . . Benjamin Franklin [who had been appointed an agent for the Georgia colony in Great Britain] and give him such Orders and instructions from time to time as they shall judge to be for the service of this Province."[58]

The esteem in which his son was held must have benefited Clement Sr., at least at the outset, and the two appeared at first to be on good terms. Only seven days prior to his son's prestigious committee appointment, he submitted his first request to the council after arriving in Georgia. His petition noted that "he was lately come into the Province with his family in Order to settle and take up lands Therefore praying for an Island called Jekyl lying to the Southward of the Province he having one hundred Negroes." This petition was approved, but only on the condition that Martin "obtain five hundred acres of land to be laid out and granted unto Thomas Horton in lieu of a settlement long since made on the said Island by his father the late Major Horton deceased or the matter otherwise adjusted."[59] Evidently Martin was able to come up with a satisfactory arrangement with Horton, because on April 5, 1768, Clement Martin, designated as "The Elder," was

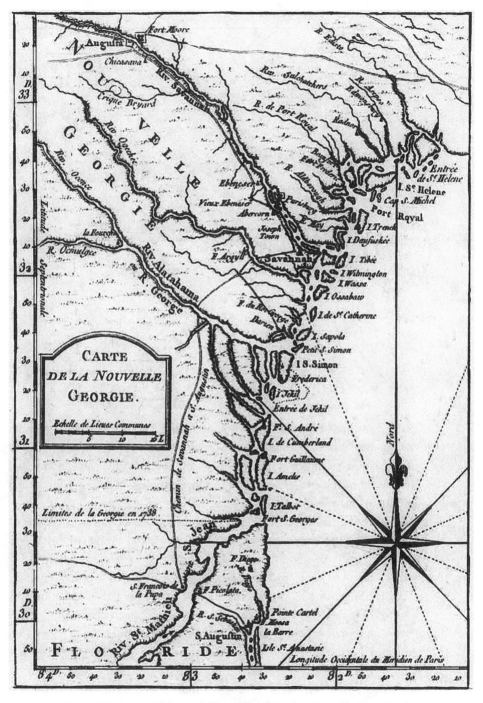

Map of "La Nouvelle Géorgie" (or pre-Revolutionary Georgia), drawn in 1764 by cartographer Jacques-Nicolas Bellin. (Courtesy of Hargrett Rare Books and Manuscript Library/University of Georgia Libraries)

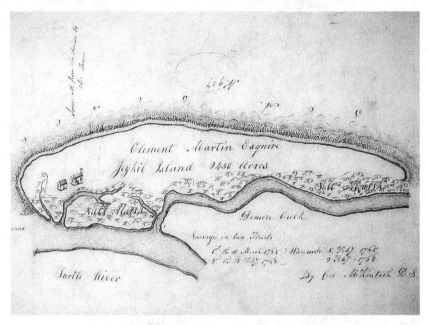

Jekyll Island was surveyed in two tracts for Clement Martin Sr. and his son
in 1765 and 1768. The Horton house is indicated at the island's north end.
(Courtesy of Georgia Department of Archives and History)

granted "all that Island or tract of land known by the name of Jekyl, containing two thousand four hundred and fifty acres, situated and being in
the Parish of St. James in our Province of Georgia."[60] He thus became the
first owner of the entirety of Jekyll Island, a privilege that had been denied
to both William Horton and Raymond Demeré.

Clement Jr. had applied for and received a grant for the Jekyll lands of
Raymond Demeré the year before his father arrived in the colony. It was
an opportunity too good to resist. It is likely that Clement Jr. knew of his
father's plans to come to Georgia and acted simply as a placeholder for
Clement Sr. until his arrival. One month before his father's petition was
granted, Clement Jr. resigned the eighteen hundred acres he held on Jekyll
(twelve hundred of which he had quietly acquired since the original 1766
petition) in exchange for other lands in the colony.[61] On the same day that
Clement Jr. applied for Raymond Demeré's six hundred acres on Jekyll,
his brother John reminded the council that he had earlier applied for five
hundred acres on "Buffelo [sic] Swamp" to adjoin land he already had, but
since it had not been surveyed within the limits of the grant, he was making

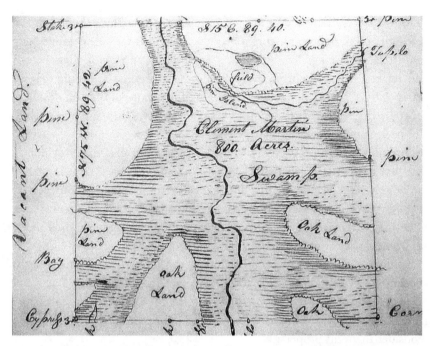

Various other coastal properties were surveyed for Clement Martin Sr.
over the years. Although much of this plot is swampland, there is nonetheless
both oak and pine timberland on the surrounding islands.
(Courtesy of Georgia Department of Archives and History)

a second request for the land.[62] The family was clearly planting deep roots
in the colony.

By Georgia standards, Clement Martin Sr. was a wealthy man when he
arrived. Few colonial petitions ever claimed ownership of as many as one
hundred slaves. It appears that he acquired still more slaves after his arrival
in the colony, for on March 5, 1771, he petitioned the council for additional
land, noting that he "was yet Possessed of ten Negroes for whom he had
never Obtained any Land." He was, therefore, "Praying for five hundred
Acres of Salt Marsh in St James's Parish between Carters Point and Egg
Island."[63]

Although slavery had not been permitted in Georgia at the beginning
of the trustees' colony, the trustees had finally capitulated in 1750 to the
incessant demands of the colonists who claimed they could not adequately
work their lands without slaves or compete with the Carolina colonists who

did own slaves. Thus, on January 1, 1751, slavery officially became legal in Georgia. Until that year Georgia had stood alone as the sole colony where only free people could live and work. Clement Martin Sr. took advantage of the relaxed policies to bring to the island the first enslaved people that we can positively identify on Jekyll, though we know none of their names. It is, of course, possible that Raymond Demeré had slaves on the island as well, for he certainly owned slaves at St. Simons and elsewhere, but we have no record of it.[64] In short, Clement Martin Sr. was, from all available evidence, the first slave owner on Jekyll Island.

Exactly what Martin planted on his Jekyll plantation and his other lands is uncertain. One thing seems clear: he intended to raise livestock there. The *Georgia Gazette* of October 12, 1768, during the organizational phase of his new plantation, carried a notice, signed by Clement Martin Sr., that "there are considerable numbers of cattle and hogs, as also some horses, now upon the Island of Jekyll." These had evidently belonged to Raymond Demeré, whose heirs had done nothing to remove them. Martin declared that unless the livestock were removed within the specified time, he would consider them his property.

In the beginning the Martin family seemed to thrive in their new home, the old Horton house. Clement Sr.'s daughters quickly became active in coastal social life, and he found influential friends, some of whom were also associates of his son—men of the status of James Habersham, who would serve as acting governor of Georgia, and George Baillie. Clement Sr. served with Baillie as a justice of the peace from Christ Church Parish and had the opportunity, through his son John, a justice of the peace from St. John's Parish, to meet Button Gwinnett, who would later be a signer of the Declaration of Independence.[65] It was also in Georgia that Clement Sr.'s daughters met their future husbands. The first to marry was Betsy, whose wedding was announced not long after the family arrived in the colony. On July 27, 1768, the *Georgia Gazette* carried this notice: "On Monday last John Simpson was married to Miss Betsy Martin, daughter of Clement Martin, Sen." Unfortunately, Betsy was dead within three years of her marriage, leaving behind a little boy, Clement Jacob Simpson, named for his grandfather.[66]

Ann was the next to wed, and on Wednesday, March 30, 1774, the *Georgia Gazette* published the following announcement: "Married James Phillips Esq. To the amiable Miss Ann Martin, daughter of Clement Martin, Sen.

Esq. And sister to the Hon. Clement Martin Esq." That same year a young Irishman named Richard Leake, who had come from Cork, Ireland, and settled first in New Jersey, then in North Carolina, arrived in Georgia. He was a surgeon with experience in both the East and West Indies, and evidently he and Jane Martin found that they had much in common. They too were married the following year.

No doubt Clement Sr. and his wife, Jane Edwards, if she still lived, enjoyed watching their children wed, settle into their new homes, and start their families, but they must also have observed with concern the growing discontent against England in the colony. Martin was fairly typical of older colonists who had been born in Britain and who tended "to form a conservative group that generally went along with British actions," unlike those Americans, born in the colonies, who gathered in Savannah taverns to discuss their more radical views.[67] Arriving in Georgia, Martin discovered the existence of a group of "malcontents" calling themselves the Sons of Liberty (though Governor Wright liked to refer to them as the "Sons of Licentiousness"). The "Liberty Boys," as the press dubbed them, had begun to meet in October 1765 at Machenry's Tavern in Savannah to talk about the unfair burdens they felt that officials in London had recently imposed on them, especially the Stamp Act, which was to go into effect in Georgia on November 1. They were determined to be free from such perceived injustices and, as their talks evolved, even from England itself if necessary.[68] In the eyes of the Martin family, they were no doubt dangerous radicals. Both Clement Sr. and Jr. clung tenaciously to their royalist loyalties, even as resentment among the colonists increased against the Crown for indignities such as the Boston Massacre and the so-called "Intolerable Acts." But the Martins were not, in this regard, very different from the majority of those who would gather in Philadelphia for the First Continental Congress in September 1774.

However, unlike those in Philadelphia, neither father nor son would have an opportunity to change his mind or choose sides in the oncoming revolution against the British. The *Georgia Gazette* of October 11, 1775, bore the announcement that "Early this morning died at Yamacraw, the Honourable Clement Martin, Esq., one of the Members of his Majesty's Council for this province." He had attended his last council meeting on August 15.[69] One month later, on November 22, 1775, the *Gazette* carried a terse notice of his father's death as well: "[Died.] At Sunbury, Clement Martin, Esq." He may well have gone there to visit his son John, who had by this time become a military officer stationed at Sunbury.

No reason is given for either death, but, in the case of Clement Sr., it was not very likely grief over his son's death, for by this time the two men had quarreled, and they died with deep bitterness between them. Clement Sr. had apparently come into the colony with significant wealth, but he clearly did not prosper there. His financial problems are suggested by a notice in the *Georgia Gazette* of November 16, 1774, announcing that he, among others, had not paid the necessary fees for 250 additional acres of land that had been granted him. In fact, he died considerably in debt, blaming his son, who, he claimed, had cheated him of six thousand pounds. In an effort to settle the dispute, the two men had appealed to their friends Button Gwinnett, Joseph Clay, George Baillie, and James Read to serve as arbiters.[70] Unfortunately, their arbitration did little or no good, and the father and son were never reconciled but went to their graves with the unforgiven grievance between them. Clement Jr., who died first, never heard a reading of his father's will (though he may have been aware of its contents), in which Clement Sr. left him only "six dunghill fowls for having cheated me of six thousand pounds, by my keeping no acc[ou]nt against him."[71]

In the will, which had been drawn on September 9, 1771, Clement Sr. had bequeathed Jekyll Island, his most valuable property, in equal shares to his younger son, John, and to his daughters Jane and Ann. He also left to another daughter, Susannah, the wife of Thomas Anderson, "one Negro woman named Debra, one boy her son named Tom Fountin and one boy named Punch." To his grandson Clement Jacob Simpson, "the son of John Simpson of Savannah & my late daughter Elizabeth Simpson," he left nine hundred acres of land "situated on Turtle River." Clement Martin Sr. willed that "my children [with the exception of Clement Jr.] . . . shall have the use of and occupy the said nine hundred acres of Land until my said grandson Clem't Jacob Simpson shall attain the age of twenty one and in the case of his death without issue then I will that the afore'd nine hundred acres of Land shall rever[t] to and be equally divided among each of my children as are hereafter mentioned." He named only John, Jane, and Ann. Under no circumstances, the will made clear, was any portion of his estate to go to his son Clement Jr. or any of his children.[72]

In his own will, Clement Martin Jr. appealed to his children "to live to-gether in the strictest Union as I am convinced their own good and happiness depends almost totally on their keeping together and assisting each other." If he had learned nothing else from his rift with his father, perhaps, he had come to understand the importance of family harmony, something he no longer enjoyed with either his father or his brother John. Should all five children be deceased or unable to inherit, the will declared, "then I do hereby in the most solemn manner debar [from inheriting my estate] my brother and all his Children, John Martin more especially or his Heirs or any person whatever that may claim under any pretence of blood relationship on the side of my Father." The property should instead "devolve in the nearest of kin from my mother's side."[73]

Clement Jr.'s five children were still minors at the time of his death, except for the eldest, Alexander, who was to be executor of his estate and guardian of the other four children—three daughters Ann, Dorothy, and Elizabeth, and their younger brother William—all of whom he acknowledged to be the children of Elizabeth Jackson and himself. Just who this Elizabeth Jackson was and the nature of their relationship remains a mystery. One Georgia historian has assumed that she and Clement Jr. had cohabited without the benefit of marriage in a "long and unsanctioned liaison," which must have begun almost immediately after his arrival in the colony.[74] Quite possibly she was already married but separated from her legal husband, which would explain why the couple never married. To have lived together long enough to have five children, and his ready acknowledgement of his paternity, certainly suggests a deep commitment. According to family tradition, as noted above, Clement Jr. was, in fact, married to a woman named Elizabeth de St. Julian, a widow who owned land adjacent to his own. Whether these women were one and the same remains to be clarified.

Alexander Martin, Clement Jr.'s son, perhaps sensing that he needed to close his father's estate quickly, advertised in the *Georgia Gazette* of November 1, 1775, that "All persons having demands against the Estate of the Hon. Clement Martin, Esq., deceased, are desired to send in their accounts properly attested, and such as are indebted to said Estate are desired to make immediate payment." In the same ad, he also noted that he was "in want of an Overseer who thoroughly understands the management of a Rice Plantation." Either he was himself too inexperienced to manage the lands he had inherited, or he was planning to leave the colony.

Clement Sr.'s executors were all important men who served in various official capacities in the royal colony—James Habersham, Anthony Stokes,

Lewis Johnston, George Baillie, and James Habersham, the younger. It was, however, Baillie and Johnston who assumed the real responsibilities. They too made an effort to settle his estate not long after Clement Sr.'s death, advertising on December 20 that anyone having demands against "the Estate of Capt. Clement Martin" should submit his accounts, while anyone indebted to it should "make immediate payment."[75] It did not take long to realize that any settlement of the estate would involve primarily trying to pay Martin's debts, for he had "died considerably indebted to the full amount (as it is said) of the estate which he left behind him."[76] But the coming revolution would impede their efforts.

Martin's son John, a loyalist who proved to be on the wrong side of the conflict, was desperate for money, and he sought, before the estate was settled, to sell his father's slaves. The administrators appealed to Archibald Bulloch, president and commander in chief of Georgia, and the Council of Safety, to put a stop to the sale. At the council's meeting on October 10, 1776, Bulloch ordered that "all persons whatsoever who have, hold, or detain the said negroes, under any pretence whatsoever (as they will answer the contrary at their peril) to deliver up the said negroes to Lewis Johnston and George Baillie, Executors of the estate of the said Clement Martin (or their agent) in order that due and proper administration of the said estate may be made and the creditors receive their demands, etc., given."[77]

Not surprisingly, the Council of Safety ruled against John Martin, who had already been adjudged on June 26 as one "dangerous to the liberties of America."[78] His Tory sympathies were well known. By 1779 the disputes involving the heirs and executors of Clement Martin Sr.'s estate had become so embroiled that, in an effort "to determine all Controversies[,] suits and demands" and resolve "all Disputes," the parties finally agreed to arbitration. The arbiters were James Spalding and John Wood. They ruled on July 14 that executor George Baillie owed to the heirs "One hundred & thirty two pounds two shillings & ten pence sterling," while John Martin, who was evidently living on Jekyll, owed to the estate the amount of "three hundred and sixty two pounds fifteen shillings sterling."[79]

Both Clement Sr. and Clement Jr. had lived long enough to learn of the battles at Lexington and Concord, news of which had reached Savannah on May 10, 1775. But they were never compelled to take sides in the conflict as their children would have to do, though it seems likely that they would have remained staunchly loyal to the Crown, as did John Martin. He agreed with Governor Wright that "It is the due course of law and support of [the British] Government which only can insure to you the enjoyment of your lives, your liberty, and your estates; and do not catch at the shadow and lose the substance."[80] In the wake of the news from Lexington and Concord, powder magazines and military storehouses were broken open and their contents stolen. On the night of June 2, cannons on Savannah's battery were thrown down a bluff in an attempt to prevent their being fired in celebration of the king's birthday, and the battle lines between those conservatives who would remain loyal to England (the Tories) and the patriots to the colony who favored revolution (the Whigs) were being drawn. Even so, Georgia was slow to enter the discussion at a national level and sent no representatives to the Continental Congress in May 1775. The three delegates who had been elected refused to go, contending that Georgians wavered between "a passion for liberty and a desire for economic convenience and security."[81]

John Martin was, thus, not very different from many other Georgians in believing that his best interests lay in siding with the British. But the tide quickly turned. On July 6, 1775, Georgia's provincial congress voted to approve the Declaration of Independence and to send delegates to the Second Continental Congress. On January 18, 1776, the Georgia Council of Safety arrested the royal governor. And on June 26, 1776, John Martin's name appeared on a list of men "whose going at large is dangerous to the liberties of America."[82] Many loyalist Georgians fled to east Florida, only to return to Georgia in 1778, when the British Army recaptured Savannah and restored Governor Wright to his former position.

British supremacy, however, did not last. In the spring of 1781 General Nathanael Greene began an offensive against the British, recapturing Augusta on June 5. But Savannah was still held by the British. Finally, under continued pressure from General Anthony Wayne, continental commander in Georgia, the British surrendered Savannah in July 1782 in order to make a stand against the colonists in South Carolina. By this time some who had earlier sworn allegiance to the king had capitulated and joined the colonists, who now held all of Georgia. Not so with John Martin. When the British evacuated Savannah in July, they took a thousand loyalists with them for their protection. It may have been on that occasion, if not earlier, that Martin left Georgia.[83] But it is probable that he had already departed the state, for his name had appeared on the attainder of May 4, 1782, as "John Martin [of] Jakill, his heirs devisees or Assigns" (along with Raymond Demeré

Jr.) as one of those accused of high treason "to be banished from the State forever," and whose lands were confiscated and his civil rights abolished for being on the wrong side of the conflict.[84] Royalists, even those previously condemned by the Whigs, were given a new opportunity after the capture of Savannah to join with the patriot forces of General Wayne and receive "full pardon and protection." But those who refused were condemned as traitors.[85] Among them was John Martin of Jekyll Island.

When the American Revolution finally ended, the colonists, now full-fledged Americans, were victorious. Those, like John Martin, who had sided with the British found themselves unable for a time to return home and claim their property in Georgia. Such sanctions against loyalists, now considered "traitors," were enforced primarily against those who had considerable property or who had been particularly vehement in their support of the Crown. Under the royal colony, Martin had held only minor posts as tax collector of St. James's Parish and Frederica, a post to which he had been appointed in 1768, and as justice of the peace for St. John's Parish, hardly high offices.[86] But he must have been vigorous in his opposition to American independence. Whatever the case, he took refuge with other Tories in east Florida. He was among a group of loyalist refugees who surrendered to Colonel Johnson in Effingham County and who were restored to "the Rights of Citizenship" on July 31, 1782.[87]

The executors of Clement Sr.'s estate who had originally accepted the responsibility for the task, Baillie and Johnston, had both been loyalists, and Baillie had died before the Revolution ended in 1783. A new administrator would need to be appointed. Most of the Martin family had sided with the British and left the colony during the Revolution. Ann Martin and her husband, James Phillips, had moved to the West Indies. John Martin eventually also left the area to take up residence in the Caribbean, probably in the Bahamas.

Perhaps the only member of the family who maintained relative goodwill with the new government was John Martin's brother-in-law and Jane Martin's husband, Richard Leake. Family tradition contends that he too was a loyalist, though, if so, his name never appeared on any attainder list. And he clearly thought himself in favor with the new government, for even as John Martin was still under the shadow of banishment, Leake was applying for a position with the new House of Assembly on July 20, 1782, as "a Clerk of the Court." By October he was buying confiscated lands of those who had been banished.[88] In November 1782 he also applied for and was granted a "Commission of a letter of Mark" for his vessel.[89] Thus, Leake was the logical person to try finally to settle Clement Martin Sr.'s estate.

As soon as possible, Leake had himself appointed administrator and, on January 21, 1784, posted the following notice in the *Georgia Gazette*: "all persons having demands against the estate of Clement Martin the elder deceased will deliver them in, duly attested, on or before the first day of March next, after which day none will be received or the estate be liable for payment. Savannah, Dec. 8." It was signed Richard Leake, Administrator. Before all matters could be resolved, the sheriff of Liberty County seized Jekyll Island to sell at auction the confiscated lands of John Martin. Leake protested the sale, arguing that the land did not yet belong to John Martin but was still in the estate of Clement Martin Sr., which had not yet been settled. When he had no luck in convincing the sheriff, Leake bid the land in himself at twelve shillings per acre or five hundred pounds. However, according to his own testimony, he refused to pay, and the land was resold the following day at ten pence an acre. Once again he bid it in at thirty-four pounds and eleven shillings, which apparently included a small auction fee.[90] The county then sued him for the difference. Even so, it was a less cumbersome way to acquire a clear title to the island than to have to deal with all the heirs and creditors. And Leake was eager to have the island for agricultural purposes, for, in addition to being a physician, he was a planter with ambitions to expand his plantation holdings.[91]

He was particularly interested in experimenting with various types of cotton and was an innovator in introducing Sea Island cotton to the Georgia coast. Leake was not the first to grow the long-staple cotton; that credit would go to James Spalding, the father of Leake's future son-in-law; to Josiah Tattnall; and to Nicholas Turnbull of Savannah, who had grown it on an experimental basis in 1785 and 1786. But Leake does claim to have been the first to grow cotton for profit. He wrote to Thomas Proctor of Philadelphia in 1788, claiming to be "an adventurer (and the first that has attempted it on a large scale,) in introducing a new staple for the planting of this State—the article of cotton." He planned to raise about five thousand pounds the following year from only eight acres of land, and the year after that "to plant fifty or one hundred acres, if suitable encouragement is given." His son-in-law, Thomas Spalding, who made the claim that he "saw this [first] field of cotton growing," speculated that Leake had received his seed from "his brother-in-law, then resident in the Bahamas," probably John Martin, who left the state after the Revolution. Thus, in 1788 on Jekyll Island, Richard Leake raised the first crop of Sea Island cotton grown in Georgia for commercial purposes. [92]

In March 1788 he noted in his "Plantation Book" that he "carry'd ten Negroes to Jekyl" and "hired Mr. Dudley this year as an Overseer on Jekyl Island." In November he recorded that he "brought back some of the negroes from the Island" and paid them, so they were evidently not his slaves. The following season on April 20, 1789, he "set of[f] for Jekyl," where he "left 38 bush[els] of corn in the corn house" and "observed severall [*sic*] of the cotton plants cut by the worms." [93] Despite such minor setbacks, by 1792 he had concluded that cotton was "likely to become one of the most valuable productions of this country." [94]

Leake was also cutting oak timbers for the shipping industry and keeping cattle on the island. [95] In 1788 he hired "Mr. Bess and his wife to take charge of my stock on Jekyl." At the time Leake and his family were not living on Jekyll, and it may have been either Mr. Dudley, the overseer, or Mr. Bess and his wife who were living in the Horton house. Leake's agricultural use of Jekyll was evidently strictly seasonal, and he seems to have limited his trips to the island to brief visits to oversee his cotton crop and livestock, which consisted of horses, cattle, goats, sheep, and hogs. If he and his wife ever lived there, it was for only a brief time, for in June 1785 they moved to his "Little Ogeechia" plantation. Despite Leake's clear preference for living at the "Little Ogeechia," he continued to farm Jekyll for at least the next five or six years.

In 1791 Leake set his sights anew on land in McIntosh County, where he moved the following year. He leased the Belleville plantation on the Sapelo River for several years before finally buying it in 1795. On November 12 that same year at Belleville plantation, his daughter, Sarah (called Sally), the granddaughter of Clement Martin Sr., married Thomas Spalding, the son of their neighbor on St. Simons Island. [96] Spalding would become an agriculturist well known for his intellect and writings. He and his wife would later purchase Sapelo Island and make it their home. Leake and Spalding no doubt had much in common, particularly their interest in experimenting with Sea Island cotton, and both men are associated with its introduction into Georgia.

Although he lived until March 11, 1802, Richard Leake kept his Jekyll property for less than a decade.[97] In preparation for his move to Belleville, in April 1791 he sold his Little Ogeechee plantation to a Captain Wadlington for £850 sterling. Six weeks earlier, on February 15, he had sold Jekyll Island to a Frenchman by the name of François Marie Loys Dumoussay de la Vauve for a recorded price of £2,000. He also hired "ten Negroes to the first of January 1792" on behalf of Dumoussay, who evidently intended to begin planting right away.[98] This agreement between Leake and Dumoussay ended more than half a century of British domination of Jekyll and would lead to nearly a century of ownership by the French du Bignon family.

CHAPTER FOUR

The Land of Liberty

The only freedom which deserves the name is that of pursuing
our own good in our own way, so long as we do not attempt to
deprive others of theirs, or impede their efforts to obtain it.

JOHN STUART MILL

ITH THE END of the American Revolution, Georgia severed all colonial ties with England and the true plantation
era began at Jekyll Island. The new state of Georgia adopted
its first constitution in 1777, with article 4 providing that the
three parishes of St. John, St. Andrew, and St. James (where Jekyll Island
was located) "shall be another county, and known by the name of Liberty."
In 1789, however, a legislative enactment approved on December 20 annexed
"all the islands [including Jekyll] on the south side of the Altamaha to the
river Little Satilla and St. Andrews Sound" to Glynn County.[1]

That same year a new revolution erupted, this time in France, which
would have an impact on the history of Jekyll Island for nearly a century.
How the French du Bignon family came to own Jekyll in the 1790s is an
extraordinary tale of seafaring, adventure, and the need for refuge. It began
in 1739 with the birth of Christophe Anne Poulain du Bignon, the oldest
surviving son of a poor nobleman from Brittany named Ange-Paul Poulain
and his wife, Jeanne Louise Le Franc.[2] As a young man Christophe had
never even heard of Jekyll Island, much less set foot on its shores. It was a
circuitous route that brought him to the coast of Georgia.

He went to sea at the age of ten as a cabin boy aboard the *Hercule*, a vessel
of the French India Company *(Compagnie des Indes)*.[3] Three years later he
received an appointment as a student pilot aboard the *Lys* and worked his
way up to second ensign. When Louis XV abolished the company in 1769,

thirty-year-old Christophe was pensioned at one hundred livres a year.[4] He then entered the merchant marine, passing the examination to become a captain in 1775. During the next ten years he served as his own master, sailing to Portugal, India, South America, and the Isle de France (present-day Mauritius). His voyages were often dangerous, but they brought handsome profits to the adventurous young man. He became a privateer during the Seven Years' War, and when France signed an alliance with the United States in 1778 and officially entered the American Revolutionary War, du Bignon once again became a privateer, this time in the service of Louis XVI.

During a layover on the Isle de France, he met Marguerite Anne Lossieux Du Jong de Boisquenay, a twenty-eight-year-old widow with three children. As both the daughter and the widow of sea captains, she knew full well what life would be like with her husband often away for long stretches of time.[5] Nonetheless, she accepted du Bignon's proposal, and Christophe and Marguerite were married in France on August 29, 1778. After only four months together, he set off for another voyage. His life at sea was both exciting and arduous, involving lengthy trips to the coasts of India, Africa, and the Americas, his adventures nearly costing him his life when ships twice sank beneath him. But now that he was married, and perhaps at the persuasion of Marguerite, he was more eager to put his seafaring career behind him. Having accumulated a substantial sum during his many voyages, he renounced the sea in 1784 at the age of forty-five, six years after his marriage. Nine months after his return to France, his first son, Joseph, was born.

A member of the merchant nobility with high economic aspirations, Christophe settled his family in his native Lamballe, France, purchasing an abandoned domain known as la Grande Ville-Hervé, and began to consider ways he might invest the profits of his thirty years at sea. He tried a variety of economic ventures, among them a china factory in Nantes, but his timing could not have been worse. Rising inflation in France began to eat away at the profits he had worked so hard and taken so many risks to acquire. The economic situation, the result in large measure of massive government debt brought on by a century of wars and exacerbated by excesses among the nobility, was growing worse. A persistent drought in the summer of 1788 and a bitter cold the following winter brought severe famine to the country. Scarcity doubled the price of bread, and discontent grew dramatically throughout the country. The king, isolated in the grandiose world of Versailles, was out of touch and unable to deal with the impending crisis.

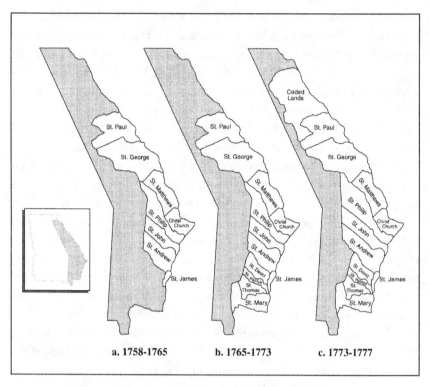

a. 1758-1765   b. 1765-1773   c. 1773-1777

This map shows the parishes of colonial Georgia from 1758 to 1777.
Jekyll Island was added to the parish of St. James in 1765. (Courtesy of the
Carl Vinson Institute of Government, University of Georgia)

Finally, in 1789, the storming of the Bastille in Paris marked the onset of the
French Revolution. France was hardly a safe environment for a man who
wanted to preserve his fortune and protect his family.

As luck would have it, that same year a Frenchman by the name of
François Marie Loys Dumoussay de la Vauve made an agreement in America with John McQueen, better known to Georgians as Don Juan Mc-
Queen, to purchase the islands of Sapelo, Blackbeard, Cabretta, and Little
Sapelo off the coast of Georgia. Dumoussay quickly recruited as a partner to his venture his friend Julien Joseph Hyacinthe de Chappedelaine,
who was also eager to invest in American land and who saw the island
of Sapelo, where the two hoped to found a little colony, as a veritable
"Eden."[6] Chappedelaine, excited about the possibilities, returned to France
and, armed with a letter from Dumoussay that laid forth the possible profits
that Sapelo could produce, met with a group of potential investors, among

them du Bignon. Chappedelaine spoke in glowing terms of Sapelo's beauty and possible productivity as a plantation site. Du Bignon was particularly taken with the description of the massive live oaks that would be good for building ships, and on November 8, 1790, in St.-Brieuc, he signed an agreement to purchase one-fifth of the island.[7]

Du Bignon wasted little time in planning a voyage to Georgia to look over the property and make certain it would be a suitable home for his wife and children, who now included a second son, Henri Charles, born at la Grande Ville-Hervé on August 3, 1787. He departed before the month's end, taking with him his elder son, five-year-old Joseph, on the *Silvain* but leaving behind his pregnant wife and younger son. His intentions to emigrate were clear and showed keen foresight, for not only was France's rising inflation a threat to his fortune, but the increasingly volatile and violent political situation was also beginning to pose a serious danger. Châteaux of noblemen in the area had already been burned, and the violence was intensifying in Paris and beginning to spread to other parts of France. Upon his departure, du Bignon, perhaps in recognition of his status as a property owner in Georgia or perhaps for protection from the revolutionary government, signed himself on the ship's passenger list as a "citoyen des états-unis" (citizen of the United States). Dumoussay and Chappedelaine, who accompanied him on the voyage, also listed themselves on the *Silvain*'s roster as American citizens.[8]

Chappedelaine, du Bignon's shipmate, held the prospect of life in America in high hopes, for this was not his first visit to the colonies. During an earlier trip in 1788, thanks to his noble title and the French government's support of the recent American Revolution, he had moved easily among the landed gentry of his new country and had even been hosted by George Washington during an overnight visit to Mount Vernon. Upon the *Silvain*'s arrival in Savannah, Chappedelaine wrote to Washington, recalling his "friendship and kindness" during the earlier visit and announcing his arrival once again in Georgia "with the heads of these noble families of Bretagne [Brittany], who have come over with me to establish themselves on the Isle of Sapelo." He proclaimed himself to be "their intercessor with you, to engage you to look with a favourable eye upon the new Colony which we are about to found," a boon they would view as "a happy presage."[9] Chappedelaine's letter to Washington is dated January 9, 1791. Although there is no record of a reply, Washington visited Savannah that May, where, presumably, he had an opportunity to give his blessing first-hand to the newly formed "Sapelo Company." But all would not go well. Within just over three years, Chappedelaine would lie dead on Sapelo, struck down by a kinsman's bullet, and the little colony would be in chaos.[10]

The enterprising, but not always trustworthy, Dumoussay seemed intent on increasing his holdings in the Georgia Sea Islands. It was during this particular trip to America that he signed the agreement with Richard Leake to purchase Jekyll Island.[11] But Dumoussay, who had purchased five islands in less than three years, had evidently overextended his economic resources and failed to pay the taxes levied against the property. As a consequence, the tax collector seized Jekyll once again and sold it at public auction for one hundred pounds sterling on April 17, 1792.[12] The buyer was another one of the investors in the Sapelo Island deal—Nicholas François Magon de la Villehuchet. The French émigrés were a close-knit community, and Villehuchet, by apparent prearrangement, conveyed portions of Jekyll Island to three other Sapelo investors, including one-fourth to du Bignon, one-fourth back to Dumoussay, and one-fourth to Chappedelaine.

Well before the Jekyll sale, however, du Bignon, still planning to bring his little family to Sapelo and set up a new homestead, booked passage to return to France, leaving his son Joseph in the care of Chappedelaine.[13] Back in his native Lamballe, not only was he reunited with Marguerite and his son Henri, but he also for the first time met his third son, evidently a frail child who would not long survive the family's move to America, and whose name has not been preserved. Upon his return, du Bignon discovered a France in the midst of a revolution growing ever more violent, and he was anxious to take his family out of harm's way to a safer haven in Georgia.

In preparation for his return to the Sea Islands, he attended a ship auction in the port city of St.-Malo, where he bought a small seagoing vessel, which he rechristened *Le Sappello*. On March 5, 1792, with Marguerite and their children, he set sail for Georgia. With them on the ship were Thomas Dechenaux and his wife, Sophie. Dechenaux would become one of du Bignon's most reliable friends and often his agent in America.[14] Before leaving Georgia and in anticipation of his family's arrival, du Bignon had begun to build a house called "Bel Air" on Sapelo.[15] His property was later described as being "on the Hermitage Plantation upon Kettle [Teakettle] Creek."[16] After his arrival back in Georgia, du Bignon seized the opportunity to buy the one-fourth interest in Jekyll Island.

It would prove to be a fortuitous purchase, for, upon his return to Sapelo, du Bignon found his house unfinished and the little French colony in complete disarray. High hopes had turned to cynicism among the émigrés as they were forced to recognize that life in such harsh circumstances and without their accustomed luxuries could be difficult. Not only had conflicts begun to develop between the older and younger members of the group, but also Dumoussay, and evidently to some extent Chappedelaine as well, had played rather fast and loose with their finances. The French colony had begun jointly to farm and raise livestock, and plans were under way to build a sawmill to take advantage of the abundant timber on the island, primarily for shipbuilding. But the situation at Sapelo had quickly deteriorated, and one of the French consuls in Charleston noted of the group, "They are all at daggers drawn and this establishment cannot maintain itself."[17] Du Bignon was the first of the group to decide that he had had enough, though by 1794 the entire Sapelo colony would be dissolved. Abandoning Sapelo altogether, du Bignon settled his family instead on his newly acquired Jekyll property, which was infinitely more tranquil, though he still held no legal title to either of his properties in Georgia.[18]

The deeds to Jekyll had been lost at sea when Villehuchet had sent them back to France "for the purpose of obtaining a renunciation of dower" from his wife. En route the vessel was "chased by an enemy," not an uncommon circumstance, and the deeds and other papers were "thrown overboard and entirely lost."[19] The lost deeds did not seem a problem, however, when, on June 14, 1794, du Bignon signed an agreement to exchange his portion of Sapelo Island for the two-fourths of Jekyll belonging to Dumoussay and Chappedelaine.[20] It proved to be a wise decision. As it turned out, three of the investors in the Sapelo Company died in 1794. Villehuchet made the unfortunate mistake of returning to France, where he was guillotined on June 20.[21] Dumoussay succumbed to fever on September 10, and five days later Picot de Boisfeuillet, yet another of the investors in the Sapelo Company, shot and killed his nephew, Chappedelaine, following a quarrel provoked most likely by property disputes and long-standing resentments between the two men.[22]

Du Bignon put up the bond for Boisfeuillet, and thanks to the eloquence of his attorney, Joseph Clay, he was either acquitted or never brought to trial. Jeanne Marie Melanie, Boisfeuillet's daughter, eventually married Ralph

Clay, the son of her father's lawyer. As for Boisfeuillet himself, he lived but a short time longer, dying of a virulent fever in 1800.[23]

Du Bignon was, thus, one of the few survivors of the Sapelo Company, and he no doubt felt himself lucky to be already settled on Jekyll before the demise of so many of his partners. However, in 1796 the heirs of the deceased Dumoussay and Chappedelaine apparently demanded that the issue of Jekyll ownership be clarified, and du Bignon began his efforts to legally restore the deeds that had been lost at sea, so that he might gain a clear title to his three-quarters of the island. He was able to wrangle a legislative enactment on February 19, 1796, to enable the Glynn County Superior Court to hear testimony and take depositions attesting to the sale of the island property and the transfer of the lost deeds.[24] Du Bignon's friend Thomas Dechenaux appeared before the court to give depositions to the validity of the deed.[25] Dechenaux and Charles Harris, who had also witnessed the exchange of the Sapelo lands for the Jekyll lands in 1794, testified on November 4, and, finally, the conveyance was legally recorded with the Glynn County Court.[26]

Du Bignon purchased the remaining one-fourth of Jekyll on October 14, 1800, for $2,142.85 from Pierre Grandclos Meslé, still another of the original Sapelo Company, who had barely survived the French Revolution by escaping from house arrest at his home in St.-Malo and seeking exile in England.[27] Thus, by the end of 1800, Christophe Poulain du Bignon claimed sole ownership of the entire island. For him, it was truly a refuge from the turmoil that had shattered his world. He expressed his satisfaction to a friend in France when he wrote, "I am alone on an island. . . . I quarrel with no one; I do what I please; here, it is truly the land of liberty."[28] At one time these French émigrés had owned or occupied much of the Georgia coastline, including all or part of the islands of Sapelo, Little Sapelo, Blackbeard, Jekyll, St. Catherines, and Cabretta.[29] Now only du Bignon still owned what he termed in that same letter an "important property."

During his first years on Jekyll, du Bignon, though plantation life was clearly an adjustment for him, apparently did reasonably well with his first crops of Sea Island cotton, for prices of this prized long-staple cotton were on the rise in the late 1790s. Du Bignon also raised livestock and cultivated potatoes and other vegetables in order to remain as self-sufficient on the island as possible. The family seemed happy and prosperous, and Christophe expressed his satisfaction to his business agent in France, René Peltier, in 1801, boasting of his "large estate" and his income.[30]

In 1798 he decided to sell at least some of his remaining French properties and to sink his roots even more deeply in Georgia soil. He oversaw his own plantation and invested heavily in slaves, many to tend the land and others to take on additional tasks essential to plantation life. It was no doubt a relief to be freed from the squabbles and tensions of the Sapelo Company, and with Marguerite he set out to make the long-neglected and by now run-down Horton house livable once again, moving his small family and his two serving girls, Françoise and Marie, into it.[31] Although family memoirs speak of the house being used by both Christophe Poulain du Bignon and his son Henri du Bignon, at some point before 1861 the family also built another house farther south and near the location of the present-day Jekyll Island Club. A Glynn County map dated 1869 and drawn by B. W. Frobel shows the du Bignon house at this later site, as do several subsequent maps. In addition, an article in the *New York Times* dated April 9, 1892, speaks of a Jekyll "manor house" that "was burned in civil war times." There is no archaeological evidence that the tabby house constructed by William Horton, after his earlier home was destroyed by the Spanish in 1742, was ever burned.

Only a few months before the du Bignons came to Jekyll, in March 1794 the well-known naturalist William Bartram passed through the area, paus-ing briefly on St. Simons, where he recorded nature and the lifestyle he witnessed there. As he departed St. Simons en route to Florida, he made some observations that pertain to Jekyll:

Next morning early, we again got under way, running by Jekyl and Cum-berland Islands, large, beautiful, and fertile, yet thinly inhabited, and con-sequently excellent haunts for deer, bears, and other game. . . . It may be a subject worthy of some inquiry, why those fine islands, on the coast of Georgia, are so thinly inhabited. . . . If I should give my opinion, the following seem to be the most probable reasons: the greatest part of these are as yet the property of a few wealthy planters, who having their residence on the continent, where lands on the large rivers, as Savanna, Ogeeche, Alatamaha, St. Ille, and others, are of a nature and quality adapted to the growth of rice, which the planters chiefly rely upon for obtaining ready cash, and purchasing family articles; they settle a few poor families on their insular estates, who rear stocks of horned cattle, horses, swine, and poultry, and protect the game for their proprietors. The inhabitants of these islands also lie open to the invasion and ravages of pirates, and, in case of a war, to incursions from their enemies [*sic*] armed vessels; in which case they must either remove with their families and effects to the main, or be stripped of all their moveables, and their houses laid in ruins.[32]

Bartram's observations were astute. Certainly while Richard Leake still owned the island, and before the du Bignons arrived there, the owner did live primarily on the mainland and settled others on his "insular estate" to care for his stock and crops. And the du Bignon family would eventually discover, as Bartram had predicted, their vulnerability to invasion, which would force them either to "remove" from the island or "be stripped" of their possessions on more than one occasion. But for now the island was about to begin a new era, with a resident owner who was making plans to develop a great plantation there. The *New York Times* article mentioned above, written almost a hundred years later, described what happened in the interim: "The island was a big plantation for many years, and many slaves were kept upon it, and there were, it is said, occasional merrymakings and jubilations in the old manor house in which the Du Bignons lived."

At first Joseph and Henri (called Henry by the Americans, though I shall continue to use his French name in an effort to distinguish him from his son Henry) grew up on the island and, no doubt, had as their playmates children from the slave quarters. But the du Bignons would not remain long on the island without other planter families for company. Several families, including those of Jean-Baptiste Goupy, Pierre Bernardey, and Alexander Campbell Wylly, either rented land at various times from du Bignon or worked for him and made their homes on the island. While most of the settlers along the Georgia coast from Darien south were of English or Scottish descent, Jekyll Island was unique as a predominantly French enclave. Even the slaves spoke French.

The hospitable and charming du Bignons soon had a wide circle of prominent friends, playing host to the Coupers and Spaldings from nearby St. Simons, as well as their French friends from as far north as Savannah. In May 1799 they provided unexpected hospitality to John McQueen. Before his arrival on Jekyll, as he wrote to his daughter Eliza Anne, he had been "drinking Port and Madeira Wine with Mr. Couper and Mr. Spalding, a liquor I have not been accustomed to make use of for many years." As he set sail for his home in east Florida, he was seized "with a severe fit of the Gout" and put in at Jekyll Island for help. Madame du Bignon (Marguerite), he reported, "was exceedingly attentive to me for four days that I was confined under her hospitable roof to my bed." As soon as he could be moved, he had himself lifted into his boat and continued on his way.[33]

Life on the Georgia coast was, for most of those who ventured beyond their own island plantations, by necessity a nautical life. The typical mode of transportation from Jekyll Island to Brunswick, Darien, Savannah, or even New York was by boat. In fact, Georgia's island planters in particular were exceedingly proud of their seagoing vessels, and the du Bignons' sloop *Anubis,* which engaged in coastal trade and ran regularly between Savannah and Brunswick, was well known in the area.

Du Bignon also owned a house and lot in Savannah, where the family may have stayed during certain social seasons and events, as well as a house in Frederica and additional land in Brunswick.[34] But their primary residence was without question Jekyll Island, and Christophe was overall deeply contented with his lot.

There is no question that the du Bignons missed their native France, and they took every opportunity to surround themselves with French-speaking people. When the possibility of a French bride for one of their sons arose unexpectedly, they did not hesitate to take advantage of it. Marriageable young women of the Catholic faith and of French descent were relatively scarce outside of Savannah since the collapse of the Sapelo colony. Therefore, when such a young woman, Anne Amelia Nicolau, just Henri's age, appeared as the houseguest of John Couper on St. Simons in 1804, it seemed a match sent from heaven.

Originally from Bordeaux, France, Amelia Nicolau came to St. Simons, separated from Jekyll by only a short boat ride across St. Simons Sound, at the behest of her brothers Joseph and Bernard, the latter of whom was her guardian. Joseph had been shipwrecked off the Georgia coast and, once rescued, had liked the area so much that he sent for his brothers, Bernard and Pascal, and eventually for their sister, Amelia. Not long before her arrival in the early summer, however, Joseph was caught offshore in a small boat by the howling winds of another storm. This time he was not so lucky and lost his life in the raging sea.

Another of Amelia's brothers, Bernard, had fallen sick shortly thereafter with the malarial fevers that routinely ravaged the coastal lands in the summer. He was still very ill when his sister arrived. She was accorded the

Miniature of
Anne Amelia Nicolau du Bignon.
(Courtesy of Henry Howell)

gracious hospitality of John Couper's Cannon's Point Plantation and had no knowledge of her brother's illness. During Amelia's visit, Aaron Burr, who had taken refuge on the Georgia coast after fatally shooting Alexander Hamilton in a duel on July 11, had settled for a time on the plantation of Major Pierce Butler, just across Jones Creek from the Couper plantation. We learn of the poignant situation of Amelia Nicolau from the letter that Burr wrote on August 31, 1804, to his daughter Theodosia:

> At Mr. [John] Couper's, besides his family, there are three young ladies, visitors. One of them arrived about three months ago from France to join a brother who had been shipwrecked on this coast, liked the country so much that he resolved to settle here, and sent for his sister and a young brother. About the time of their arrival the elder brother was accidentally drowned, the younger went . . . to make an establishment some miles inland, where he now lies dangerously ill. Both circumstances are concealed from Mademoiselle Nicolau. In any event, she will find refuge and protection in the benevolent house of Mr. Couper.[35]

The distressing news about her brothers was being kept from Amelia until Bernard was out of danger from his illness. In fact, Amelia had three brothers, as we have noted, not two, but, aside from this minor slip, which he later corrected, Burr's assessment of the situation was generally correct.

One of Anne Amelia Nicolau du Bignon's
brothers. (Courtesy of Henry Howell)

In the end Bernard recovered and would continue in the years to come to
oversee his sister's welfare.

It was doubtless John Couper, a jovial and florid Scotsman, who introduced Amelia to the du Bignon family, and Henri du Bignon would return the favor by eventually naming one of his sons for him. According
to one source, Henri's father, Christophe, met Amelia when he called at
the Couper plantation to express his condolences to her, as a fellow coun-
tryman, on her brother's death. As the story goes, he was "so struck by
her beauty and charm that he promptly offered her either of his two sons
in marriage."[36] One may certainly question whether such a proposal would
have been made on so inappropriate an occasion. However, a young woman
whose prospects looked a bit gloomy may well have found it welcome even
then. Even though Christophe was likely captivated by her fairness and
grace upon first meeting her, he probably waited until a later occasion to
propose the match, for the marriage did not take place until more than
three years later and only after "much gossiping" had begun about Amelia
and Henri du Bignon.[37]

When the prenuptial agreement was drawn up on April 30, 1807, between Henri Charles du Bignon, who was not quite twenty at the time,
and Amelia Nicolau, her brother-guardian, Bernard, and John Couper were

among the witnesses, along with Christophe and his older son, Joseph. The agreement gave the couple ten slaves and forty acres of cotton land on Jekyll for their use. They were married on Monday, January 18, 1808, by the rector of the Catholic church in Savannah only a few months before the birth of their first child. Henri's father, Amelia's brother and guardian Bernard Nicolau, and Thomas Dechenaux, among others, witnessed the ceremony. Their marriage document states that they had been "heretofore married by the civil authorities, agreably [*sic*] to the laws of the state."[38] The religious marriage placed the Church's sanction on their already consummated union.

Amelia's brother Pascal also came to live on Jekyll for many years, as the census records show, though he seems to have had a separate household. No doubt he was a welcome resident who assisted with the work of the plantation. The du Bignons took every opportunity to host French-speaking guests or to persuade French-speaking individuals to settle on Jekyll Island. One of these was a young man named Louis Grand Dutreuilh, who had gone to Santo Domingo in the summer of 1802 to check on his family's holdings there. The island had just gone through a major slave uprising that cost the lives of many plantation owners, one of whom, he learned during his visit, was his father. He wrote to his mother about the terrible incident: "On February 18, between 11 p.m. and midnight our poor father was taken to the river bank with the other 5 deputies, their arms tied behind their backs. Once there they were beaten to death with bayonets. Ah, how dreadful it has been for me to tell you all that."[39] Returning to the United States in 1809, the young Dutreuilh stopped over on the Georgia coast, penning another letter to his mother from the little town of Frederica on St. Simons, where he paused only briefly. "I have the pleasure of writing you to report to you that we are all well and that we hope to arrive at Mr. DuBignon's in about two hours."[40] Evidently du Bignon had come to meet him in Frederica, for he sent his regards to the young man's mother. During his lengthy stay with the du Bignons, Christophe invited him to live on the island, an incident that Grand Dutreuilh related to his mother on January 12, 1809:

> The Messrs Dubignon are urging me to settle on Jekyl. They are offering me a conveniently located house on their wharf to keep a store and they would put up half of the necessary capital to set it up. They are offering me besides as much land as I could cultivate. I cannot tell you, my dear Mother, all the expressions of friendship I have received from this worthy and excellent family

and how much interest they take in my unfortunate situation. I have not yet accepted their kind offers, wanting to know first how much I can expect from my speculation in Martinique, for with what means could I start a store if I receive nothing.[41]

Grand Dutreuilh eventually declined du Bignon's offer and returned to Trenton, New Jersey, where his mother lived. But three of his sisters did settle on the Georgia coast, where the Grand Dutreuilh, Nicolau, and du Bignon families would intermarry. One of the sisters, Marie Elizabeth Félicité Grand Dutreuilh (called "Treyette" by her family) had already wed Bernard Nicolau on December 6, 1808, while Louis's niece, Félicité Riffault, the daughter of another sister, Marie Anne Félicité ("Mimi") Grand Dutreuilh, would marry Joseph du Bignon, the son of Henri and Amelia. In fact, Marie Anne Félicité Grand Dutreuilh Riffault is buried beside her son-in-law in the little du Bignon cemetery at the north end of Jekyll Island.

Another French family who lived on Jekyll for an indeterminate number of years was Jean-Baptiste Goupy and his wife, Marguerite Vidal. Their daughter, Anne Georgienne Goupy, was born on Jekyll on October 22, 1800, and baptized there on July 16, 1801, by the rector of St. John's Church. Only three years earlier the Goupy family had been living in Savannah, where Jean-Baptiste had sold to du Bignon two slaves, thirty-five-year-old Pauline and her twelve-year-old son John Louis, on January 19, 1798, and yet another, a boy named Joel, on April 12. Goupy was listed as a planter on Jekyll Island when du Bignon purchased from him another three slaves on January 3, 1804.[42] Since Goupy clearly had slaves of his own and was not merely an overseer for du Bignon, it is probable that he leased land from du Bignon in order to grow his own crops.

Yet a third known French resident of Jekyll during the plantation era was Pierre Bernardey. One source identifies him as the son of a ship's physician "who had once served under the command of Captain Christopher Poulain Dubignon." The Bernardeys and their son, Pierre, had evidently lived on Sapelo Island, "where the father may have been plantation physician" for the Sapelo Company. When the du Bignons moved to Jekyll Island in 1793, the Bernardeys apparently accompanied them there, for Louis Grand Dutreuilh refers to "our good doctor," most likely Bernardey, in a letter written during his stay on Jekyll on January 12, 1809.[43] By 1820, however, it is his son, Pierre Bernardey, who is listed in the 1820 census as a head of household on Jekyll Island. Living with him was a middle-aged white woman, presumably his mother, and one female slave, most probably Marie-Jeanne, who became the mother of Bernardey's mulatto daughter, Elizabeth (called "Zabette"). Although, like his father, Pierre may have served as a plantation doctor, he also did some planting himself, for he had his own group of fourteen slaves. Only two years before Christophe du Bignon's death in 1825, Bernardey purchased property on Cumberland, a five-hundred-acre tract near Plum Orchard Landing and an additional five hundred acres called the Table of Pines. Now a landowner himself, he left Jekyll for his own Cumberland lands.

One of the few non-French residents on Jekyll during these years was Alexander Campbell Wylly (born in 1759).[44] Even today the island bears a trace of his residence there in the name of Captain Wylly Road—one of the oldest roads on Jekyll, second only to Major Horton Road at the extreme north end of the island. At the time the American Revolution began, Wylly was in England, where his father had sent him to continue his education. As a loyal subject of the Crown, he returned to Georgia to serve in the British Army, where he had risen to the rank of captain in a well-known unit called the King's Rangers. After the war Wylly, finding himself banished from the colony and his lands confiscated, went into exile in the Bahamas. There he met and married his wife, Margaret Armstrong, and their first seven children were born before they returned to America. But finally, about 1803, the family returned to test the political waters of the Georgia coast. Du Bignon, who had no vested interest in American Revolutionary politics, welcomed him to Jekyll and evidently leased him land and a homesite. In many respects, the two men had much in common: both had become exiles during a dangerous revolution, and du Bignon was no doubt "sympathetic to the plight of an aging refugee returning to a home forever changed."[45] The du Bignon family formed close bonds with the Wyllys, who remained on Jekyll Island until about 1809, with Margaret giving birth to three more children there.[46] Although the Wylly family lived on the island for more than half a decade, they, too, eventually left to set up a homestead on St. Simons at St. Clair, moving to an area on the eastern shore called The Village.

Even after they departed from Jekyll, however, the Wyllys maintained close contact with the du Bignons. Susan Wylly, the family's oldest daughter, who had been born in Nassau in 1788, was fifteen years old when the

Portrait of Susan Wylly, as she appeared at
the time her family lived on Jekyll Island.
(19th century. Oil on canvas, 26½ x 22½ in.
Telfair Museum of Art, Savannah,
Georgia. Gift of Harriet Huston from the
estate of Margaret Screven Duke)

family first came to Jekyll and a young woman of about twenty-one when
they moved away. Friends described her as vivacious, noting that she added
"life and spirit to all who meet her."[47] Her one surviving portrait has captured her beauty, and her charm is evident in a letter she wrote on June
16, 1824, to sixteen-year-old Louisa du Bignon, the first child of Henri and
Amelia, to thank her for "the beautiful cap" she had made for her mother,
Margaret Armstrong Wylly. "Everyone who sees it admires it & agrees in
thinking it the prettiest work they ever saw." Her mother had assured her,
she wrote, that "it will long be her favorite cap—and sported whenever she
wishes to look particularly smart."[48]

Du Bignon's granddaughter Louisa was also well known and admired in
the area for her talents and sweet disposition. But within a year of receiving
Susan's letter, Louisa was dead. As Christophe's first granddaughter, she
had been his favorite, and he never ceased mourning her until his own death
the following year.

The untimely death of Louisa was but the culmination of a series of problems that plagued Christophe and his family during his last two decades on
Jekyll. The good fortune, of which he had boasted to Peltier in 1801, and
which he enjoyed for more than ten years, was seriously fractured for the
first time in 1804, when he began truly to understand the various environ-
mental problems that beset the coastal planter in Georgia. While his early
plantings had apparently gone reasonably well, the summer of 1804 brought

Sea Island cotton was the primary crop grown on Jekyll during the plantation years, and slave labor was used throughout the process of growing, picking, and preparing it for market. (Courtesy of the Georgia Historical Society)

excessive heat, drought, and a plague of caterpillars that ravaged his cotton crop. Then, on September 8, one of the worst hurricanes ever to hit the Georgia coast pounded the island, flooded the cotton fields and the du Bignon home, and left only devastation in its wake. Though Christophe's tabby house, built by Horton, remained standing, his crops were ruined, virtually eliminating the income he had hoped for that year. For the first time since his arrival there, he openly expressed his discouragement to Peltier. In a letter written on September 20, he listed his losses and confided that he found himself financially in "a very precarious situation."[49] In the wake of the storm, cotton prices began to fall and fell precipitously for the rest of the decade, exacerbated by trade restrictions by the French and British and an embargo imposed by President Thomas Jefferson.

It seemed as though du Bignon's luck could get no worse when another severe storm hit the island in 1813. Though in terms of overall damage it was not as severe as the 1804 hurricane, it nonetheless ruined his cotton crop and undermined his annual income. But the worst was still to come. Perhaps

Ships like these could be seen off the coast of Jekyll Island during the War of 1812.
(Courtesy of the Library of Congress)

the most distressing of all the calamities that befell him in these last twenty years of his life on the island took place not long after the 1813 storm, when his family's tranquil island existence was shattered by an invasion that once again disrupted his financial stability and helped to break his spirit. It came in the waning days of the War of 1812. As most of the war raged, it had not disrupted their harmonious existence on Jekyll. Nonetheless, coastal Georgians, who had seen British ships along their shores as early as 1807, had tried to prepare for a possible invasion, appealing to President James Madison for help. On October 14, 1814, the plantation owner Pierce Butler received a letter from his overseer, Roswell King, complaining that still no help had come. "[W]e have no one to defend our coast," he wrote, and "a boat . . . can land from Warsaw [Wassaw] Island to Cumberland and take what they please."[50]

Six weeks later, after British forces under the command of Rear Admiral Sir George Cockburn sacked Washington, D.C., they headed south. On November 26 a frigate in Cockburn's fleet, the H.M.S. *Lacedemonian*, landed at Jekyll Island allegedly to investigate gunfire heard coming from the island.[51] Following the road that led from the beach to the Horton house, the sailors made their way to the du Bignon home, where they pillaged and plundered, carrying away large quantities of cash, silver, and

Admiral Sir George Cockburn's troops
twice invaded Jekyll Island during and just
after the War of 1812. (Courtesy of the
National Maritime Museum, London)

jewelry, as well as two gold-framed miniature portraits of Christophe and
Marguerite, and vandalized the property, destroying documents, clothing,
crops, and livestock.[52] When they left the island, they also took away
twenty-eight of the du Bignon slaves, including sixteen "prime field hands."
As du Bignon described them in the list he swore to on July 16, 1821, in hope
of compensation from the British government, they included a blacksmith,
carpenter, shoemaker, sailmaker, fisherman, packer, carter, seamstress, and
cook—all essential to the independent life of the plantation. Worst of all
was the loss of Big Peter, the plantation driver, who served as overseer to
other slaves and on whom du Bignon placed the highest value of $750.
All had apparently gone willingly when they heard the British promises of
freedom. Those who fled were, for the most part, young and at their peak
work capacity, in their teens, twenties, or thirties. Only two were over fifty,
while two were children of nine and ten.

A few weeks later, on December 24, the warring nations signed the Treaty
of Ghent, ending the war, but that did not prevent the British from returning once more in late February. By now the du Bignon family had taken

refuge in Brunswick, and British troops freely occupied the Horton house during their second raid. This time they finished the job of destroying the du Bignon plantation, burning the cotton house and gin, destroying five hundred pounds of ginned cotton and three thousand pounds of unginned cotton, shooting most of the cattle, and stealing the rice and a thousand pounds of salted meat intended to sustain the family and workers through the winter months. To add insult to injury, they pilfered from the house the few personal items they had left behind before, even taking Christophe's ivory and tortoise backgammon set, as well as his spyglass and quadrant, which had been his most essential tools during his career as a sea captain.[53] In the interim, on January 25, 1815, Admiral Cockburn had raised the British flag on Cumberland Island, setting up his headquarters at Dungeness, the mansion that had been built in 1802 by Phineas and Catherine Miller (the widow of General Nathanael Greene). It was now the home of Catherine's daughter, Louisa Greene Shaw. Although at first Cockburn did not know of the treaty ending the war, when he did learn the news on February 10, he chose to ignore it. There is no question that he knew the war had ended when his men invaded Jekyll Island for the second time.

One of the terms of the Treaty of Ghent allowed for compensation to Americans who had incurred losses during the war. Thus, before his death, Christophe filed a claim against the British government. Various people attested to the losses of the du Bignons' property. Du Bignon himself filed a deposition, as did his son and daughter-in-law. Among the others was Jane E. Johnson, who had been a visitor of Louisa Greene Shaw on Cumberland. She claimed to have recognized among the contraband slaves Madame du Bignon's waiting maid. Another who attested to du Bignon's losses was John Couper, who had befriended Anne Amelia Nicolau during her earlier hardship. He had even set out after the British ships (for they had taken sixty of his slaves as well), followed them as far as Bermuda, and received permission to board one of the ships, the H.M.S. *Brune.* There he saw Frederick, one of du Bignon's escaped slaves. Others, he learned, had already been sent to Melville Island and still others to Halifax, Nova Scotia.[54]

Another witness for du Bignon's claims was unexpectedly a British officer, Lieutenant John Fraser. During the stopover on Cumberland, Fraser had met Ann Couper, the daughter of John Couper, and the two had fallen in love. They eventually married, and when du Bignon filed his claims nine years later, Fraser attested to their veracity. For the loss of his goods and slaves, his labor, crops, profits, and interest, he asked $79,418.50. In the end, and only after his death, the British government compensated his losses at only a fraction of their value—$2,047.50.[55]

It is little wonder that many of du Bignon's slaves fled at the first opportunity, for the life of the enslaved on a coastal plantation was not an easy one. Slavery, forbidden in the early Georgia colony, had become legal on the first day of January 1751 and since that time had become a fundamental component of cotton and rice plantations on the coast. Although Georgia had been the last of the colonies to legalize slavery, the state of Georgia would also be one of the last to give it up. The incident of 1814 gives us a great deal of valuable insight into plantation life at Jekyll. The twenty-eight escaped slaves were valued at $15,450, an average valuation of just over $550 each. Twelve men and four women were listed as "prime field hands." The other occupations (carpenter, sailmaker, packer, fisherman, shoemaker, cook, and seamstress) reveal the ingredients of a thriving and relatively self-sufficient southern plantation. Du Bignon relied as little as possible on the outside world, growing his own food, maintaining his property, and producing even the homespun clothes and shoes, no doubt made from the hides of butchered livestock, he provided for his slaves. The workers who fled were thus among his most valuable "possessions." Their loss virtually crippled his plantation. Without such essential skilled labor, not only the du Bignon family but also the slaves who remained behind would suffer until others could be trained to take up these necessary tasks.

The fact that the enslaved workers apparently went so willingly with their British liberators tells us that many were dissatisfied with life on Jekyll Island. Du Bignon was apparently a hard taskmaster, expecting more from his slaves than did most of the slave owners at neighboring plantations. In 1821 he claimed that his best field hands picked "900 pounds of ginned cotton per season," compared to that of a nearby plantation, run by an overseer known by reputation to be demanding, where hands picked only 750 pounds.[56] Those who had escaped their life of slavery on Jekyll apparently had no regrets. In one account of the incident, as John Couper was climbing aboard the *Brune*, one of the slaves called out, "That is Mr. Couper. I wish my master was in his place. I should like to shove him down into the sea." The seaman who overheard the remark asked to whom the man belonged and was told, "He's one of the Frenchman's Negroes."[57]

Their desire to escape slavery should have come as no surprise to du Bignon, but like many slave owners, he viewed himself as a benevolent

Tilling the sandy soil on Jekyll Island required difficult
and constant manual labor. (Photo by Pierre Havens.
48162, Collection of the New-York Historical Society)

master and declared in his will "that my old Negroes be treated with all the
humanity & kindness accessory to the[ir] Comfort." His self-proclaimed
kindness did not prevent their thirsting for liberty, and it was certainly not
the first time some of them had tried to escape their bondage. As early
as 1794 du Bignon's friend and agent in Savannah, Thomas Dechenaux,
offered a five-dollar reward for the return of Philip, a runaway du Bignon
slave. "He has a spot on his face covered with hairs, and a crooked leg;
he absented himself about the 14th of July carrying a canoe from Sapelo
Island."[58] By 1808 the reward for a runaway slave had risen to ten dollars,
when du Bignon sought the return of Alexis, "a short, stout fellow, pock
pitted and about 45 years old—speaks French and English." He had escaped from du Bignon's sloop *Anubis* and was said to be "lurking about
the marshes, creeks, or islands on the river."[59] Then again, on September
5, 1810, Dechenaux, once again acting as du Bignon's agent, posted an ad

in the *Savannah Evening Ledger* offering another ten-dollar reward for a
runaway slave named Tom:

> Ran away about three weeks ago, from Jekyl Island, a NEGRO MAN, named
> Tom; about 36 years old; five feet, four or five inches high; has large whiskers,
> and is very artful. He took with him a small fishing canoe boat. The fellow is
> well known, and particularly remarkable from his being lame and disabled of
> the right arm, on account of a shot in the shoulder, which he received (being
> on the same errand) some time after his legal death and burial, about the year
> 1804; but notwithstanding, was found again, whereby the coroner was dis-
> appointed, having to return the fees. He was afterwards drowned; appeared
> again, and is again vanished. In the hope that he may once more re-appear,
> the above reward is offered and will be paid for him, on his being apprehended,
> dug or fished up, and delivered on the above island to Captain DuBignon, his
> owner; or lodged in Savannah gaol.

Tom's story, his wounds and infirmities, suggest his desperation for freedom, just as Dechenaux's sad attempt at humor indicates the callous lack of
understanding on the part of slave masters. Certainly the story of Tom helps
us to understand why, when the opportunity came during the War of 1812
for du Bignon's slaves to escape with the help of the British, many did not
hesitate to take advantage of it. Of the twenty men, six women, and two
children who boarded the British frigate *Lacedemonian* during its raid on
Jekyll Island, there was one Tom among them. One can certainly hope that
the Tom listed among the rescued slaves was the freedom-hungry Tom for
whom Dechenaux had advertised, if indeed he was ever caught. However,
we should also note that a Tom, valued at $450, was still listed among the
slave inventory at the time of du Bignon's death in 1825.[60]

What is perhaps even more interesting is that all the slaves from the
du Bignon plantation did *not* elect to accompany the British, which suggests that they may have foreseen the possibility of an even harder life elsewhere. One who stayed behind was Maria Theresa, to whom Christophe
would leave in his will an annuity of eighty dollars and that priceless possession, freedom—both for her and her daughter, Margueretta—insofar "as
the Laws of the Country will allow." He also left Maria Theresa a slave of
her own, "my Negro woman Nelly," and he put the two freed women under the care and protection of his executors, "who should allow them to
leave the State if necessary for their comfort."[61] He was evidently aware

that there might be difficulties if they remained in Georgia, where it was still illegal to free a slave as a bequest in a will. He had purchased Maria Theresa on June 13, 1806, when she was twenty-one years old, paying for her the highest price recorded for any slave purchase made between 1795 and 1807—five hundred dollars. She was described as West Indian born, "fair and clear complexion," and of short stature. It is probable, considering the description and his bequest to Maria Theresa in his will that her daughter, Margueretta, was also his daughter. At the time of the bequest, however, du Bignon noted that Maria Theresa was "in a helpless state of infirmity," though she would have been only forty years old. To his credit, whatever their relationship had been, he did not completely abandon her in her "helpless state."

In addition to du Bignon's humiliation by the British, the other matter that disrupted and distressed the last years of his life on Jekyll was the arrival on the island about 1810 of the grandchildren of Marguerite from her first marriage. In the days before they were wed, Christophe had taken Marguerite's son, Louis Jerome, under his seafaring wing, signing him onto his crew as a student pilot at the age of twelve. The boy had grown up to be, like his father and stepfather, a naval officer. But when the government reorganized the navy in 1796, Louis Jerome found himself laid off with only a meager pension and unable to support his family.[62] Although he had struggled on for a time, he finally sent three of his children, Marie Melanie, Clémence, and Louis Alexandre, to Jekyll to be cared for by his mother. The boy, Louis, died in 1817 at the age of eighteen, but the girls seemed to thrive. Over the years du Bignon took on an ardent dislike for his wife's granddaughters, believing them to be greedy and always after his money, and, indeed, they were costly to his household. To give them a good education and perhaps to minimize the conflict between the girls and her husband, Madame du Bignon put Clémence and Marie Melanie into boarding school first in Charleston and then in Savannah.

If things were not already sufficiently tense, Christophe's son Joseph fell in love with one of his mother's granddaughters. The one he had chosen was his half-niece, Clémence, the second daughter of Marguerite's son, Louis Jerome. It was, especially for a Catholic family, an uncomfortably close blood connection, one that in the eyes of the Church would have been viewed as consanguineous.[63] But that was not the only objection, and perhaps not even the most important one, that Christophe had to

Clémence. He detested the girl and believed that her intentions to snare his son were entirely mercenary. Despite the objections of his father, the determined Joseph married Clémence on October 27, 1819. It was the last straw. Christophe would never forgive his son and virtually disinherited him.[64]

Du Bignon was furious, disheartened, and fed up at the turn his life on Jekyll had taken. To make matters worse, the country was in the midst of a national economic panic, and the price of cotton in 1819 took another precipitous drop. Less than a month after Joseph's marriage, on November 16, and for several weeks thereafter, Christophe, at the end of his rope, ran an ad in the Savannah *Daily Georgian* offering the island for sale. It was "indisputedly the finest property on the sea coast of the Carolinas or Georgia," the ad boasted, "for the cultivation of Cotton or the enjoyment or preservation of health." It extolled as well the abundance of game and timber, and the "excellent water."[65] But apparently he had no takers.

Ironically, as he ran the ad proclaiming the salubrious environment of Jekyll, Christophe's own health was failing as was his eyesight. Like his health, his fortunes were ebbing. When cotton prices began to rise again in 1820, his yield proved lower than usual, and thus, his financial straits did not improve. He revealed his discouragement in a letter to his friend Peltier in January 1824, when he described both himself and his wife as "old and broken down."[66] His greatest consolation, other than his work as a planter, had been the pleasure of watching his younger son, Henri, and his bride, Amelia, begin their family. The death of their first child, Louisa, was the hardest blow of all for Christophe.

That same year, when yet another hurricane struck Jekyll Island on September 14 and 15, this one even worse than the one in 1804, it was the final calamity for Christophe. The heavy winds and rain tormented the island throughout the night, and the six-foot storm surge that followed once again destroyed a promising cotton crop and drowned some of du Bignon's cattle. The misfortunes of 1824 would prove to be too much for Christophe and Marguerite. Still mourning his beloved granddaughter, Christophe died one year to the day after this last, dreadful hurricane, on September 15, 1825. His family buried him beneath a live oak tree, no doubt in the area of the du Bignon cemetery that still stands on Jekyll Island today. Marguerite would follow him in death three months later on December 29.

From the grave, du Bignon meted out the final punishment to his son Joseph for what he had considered his outrageous behavior and unforgivable marriage, leaving him only an eighty-dollar annuity in his will and pointedly mentioning him only after "my mulatto woman named Maria Theresa," to whom he left an equal amount. It was to his younger son, Henri, whose growing family had helped ease the burden of his final years, that he left Jekyll Island and all his other properties. His will contained no provision, of course, for his wife's Boisquenay offspring, but his death did not end their expectations. He had long been plagued by demands on their behalf by their Savannah teacher, Luce de Cottineau, who had taken up their cause, believing that he treated them unfairly. At one point during a visit to France, she had even "talked Peltier out of six hundred francs of Du Bignon's money for Melanie and Clémence," without revealing its true purpose to him.[67] After du Bignon's death, Madame de Cottineau continued in her rancor toward his heir, Henri, on behalf of Joseph and Clémence. Again she complained to Peltier, alleging that Madame du Bignon had made some kind of contract in order to provide equally for her son Joseph. When Peltier contacted Henri du Bignon about her allegations, he replied:

> I was not at all surprised by what you told me concerning Mme Cottinau [*sic*]. It is yet a new machination from this conniving woman. I have known her for a long time; and my father knew her well also. . . . I, no more than you, have ever heard of this contract that she mentioned, and what she is trying to insinuate about my brother is pure spitefulness. It is true that my father left him only a very small pension, undoubtedly he had his reason for that—it is also true that he married his niece Clémence De Boisquenay (which was one of the principal causes for the displeasure of my father) but since I had no reasons to complain of my brother, I had intended to share as equally as possible with him the property that my father left at his death—a circumstance of which Mme de Cottinau was not unaware. I would not have gone into all these details, my dear Monsieur Peltier, if I did not fear that she wanted to give you a bad opinion of me.[68]

Despite his protestations, there is no indication that Henri ever shared any portion of his estate with Joseph. Without question, he was now the sole new master at Jekyll Island, which would enter a new era with his father's passing.

CHAPTER FIVE

Bitter Harvest

If you sow it in the rain

You got to reap it jus' the same.

You got to reap in the harvest what you sow.

HILE Christophe du Bignon had viewed the marriage of his firstborn, Joseph, as a curse, he considered the nuptials of his second son, Henri, which he had personally arranged, one of the great blessings of his life. Perhaps it is well for his own peace of mind that he did not live long enough to see how it turned out in the end.

Henri du Bignon and Anne Amelia Nicolau were both twenty years old at the time of their marriage in 1808. When Henri's father and Amelia's brother-guardian Bernard drew up their marriage contract, Christophe granted to the couple "forty acres of land planted in cotton (or more if necessary) on the island of Jekyl" and ten slaves, whose names were listed as Hanna, Sally, John, Rose, Category, Fanny, a second Rose, Rosetta, James, and Couper. Even at the beginning of their marriage, the couple were reasonably well provided for, and at Christophe's death in 1825, Henri inherited the bulk of his father's estate, valued at $30,500, no mean sum at the time, yet not enough to make him one of the area's wealthiest planters. The estate consisted of fifteen hundred acres on Jekyll Island, valued at $20,000; thirty-nine slaves, with an appraised value of $8,300; twelve hundred acres on the mainland listed at $1,200; and a house and lot in Savannah worth $1,000.[1] In addition, Christophe left his younger son considerable assets in France. Though the inheritance did not place Henri du Bignon at the very top of the economic scale in coastal Georgia, particularly compared to planters like James Hamilton Couper on St. Simons and Robert Stafford on Cumberland, it nonetheless placed him at a social and economic level that allowed him to mingle with the wealthier planters in the Brunswick area.[2]

Henri du Bignon had many advantages from the outset that his father had not had. As a second-generation American who had come to Jekyll as a small boy, he had lived almost his entire life in Georgia. Though he spoke and wrote French with ease, he was completely bilingual and equally comfortable with English. Therefore, he did not, as Christophe and Marguerite had done, seek out predominately French-speaking friends or try to create a French enclave at Jekyll. As a consequence, he moved more easily within coastal society than had his parents. No doubt he had known many members of the coastal community from his childhood, and he was conscious of the status his position gave him among them.

He also had the advantage of being a second-generation cotton planter, already familiar with the difficulties and advantages of growing the long-staple Sea Island cotton. He had learned from his boyhood, both from his father and his father's workers, many of the practical aspects of the cotton-growing process: the need for a careful selection of the black seeds that would produce the best crop; the constant demand for soil renourishment; the "ridge method" or mounding of the soil into oval beds or ridges on which the cotton seeds were planted; the frequent hoeing the fields required; and the problems that could arise from drought, insects, and storms that seemed always to come just as the cotton was ready for picking. He knew that frequent fluctuations in the price of cotton were inevitable and that he needed to be always prepared for them. Like his father, Henri did his own ginning on the plantation. It was a skill that Christophe had been forced to learn the hard way, but for Henri, who had spent his life observing and participating in cotton production, it was a familiar process. He knew how to clean the cotton by "assorting" the white from the yellow or stained cotton, how to brighten it by whipping it to remove trash before ginning, and finally the actual process of ginning, moting, and baling the cotton.[3]

He had, however, inherited a cotton plantation that had perhaps already seen its best days. Though cotton prices spiked in 1825 to fifty-four cents a pound, by 1827 they had dropped again to only twenty-one cents. The sandy soil was playing out, was perpetually in need of renewal, and had long since failed to provide the abundant yields of the du Bignon ownership's earlier years. More and more slaves were required to haul the fertile marsh mud or manure to the cotton fields every year in a desperate effort to provide a better crop. It was hard and dirty work, at best. The loss of twenty-eight slaves during the British raid on the island a decade before had taken its toll, and Henri's father had been able to replace only one of them before his death. The escaped slaves had represented the best of his workforce, and those who remained were, for the most part, aging and less productive.[4]

Nevertheless, Henri and Amelia, who had begun their marriage with only forty acres of cotton land and ten slaves, must have felt suddenly rich upon the inheritance; Henri slid into the role of plantation master with a natural ease. He had worked beside his father long enough to know how to profit from his predecessor's mistakes as well as his successes. He knew which fields yielded the best crop, which workers were best at given tasks, and how to supervise with relative fairness the task system, which assigned a specific amount of daily work to each slave. Above all, he had learned not to invest all his resources in a cotton crop that was unreliable. Over the years he would begin to make judicious investments in the enterprises of the developing town of Brunswick and the state of Georgia, with special attention to things such as bank and eventually railroad stock. What's more, by the time of his father's death, he already had three sons old enough to ride with him to the fields and begin to learn, as he had, at their father's side. Charles was sixteen, John Couper was thirteen, and Joseph was eleven—never too young to begin. And when they were old enough and had sufficient experience, the knowledge they would gain from their apprenticeship would free du Bignon from some of the personal supervision of the plantation and for other pleasures.

In the early years of Henri and Amelia's marriage, Jekyll Island was filled with the laughter of children. Not only their sons and daughters but also the children of the Wyllys and the Goupys enlivened the island during the first decades of the nineteenth century. Once the danger of British invasion no longer hung over the islands, the state had begun to grow at a steady pace. Although by 1807 the capital of Georgia had moved from Savannah to Augusta to Louisville and, finally, to Milledgeville, the coastal area still remained, for a time at least, the most populated and lively part of the state. For Henri and his young family, times were increasingly good, and his resources seemed adequate to weather downturns such as the drought in 1830. His confidence grew in his role of a respected planter with diverse interests, and he began to develop as well the reputation of a man who had significant responsibility and respect within the community. The sporting men of the area also knew him well, for he loved to pit his boats against theirs in various local and regional regattas.

His marriage was fruitful, and during its first eighteen years Amelia was pregnant most of the time. On May 31, 1827, not long after his father's death, Henri du Bignon wrote to the family's business manager in France, René Peltier, to describe his family: "My father had written to you of my marriage to a demoiselle Nicolau of Bordeaux; I have had eleven children, eight of which survive. I had the misfortune in 1824 of losing my eldest daughter Louisa, aged sixteen—a charming and favorite child for her sweet amiable character, and for her superior talents. It was a terrible blow for my parents, as well as for her mother and myself. I have also lost a little boy of seven and a girl of six."[5] The surviving children—Charles Joseph (born in 1809), Eliza (1810), John Couper (1812), Joseph (1814), Sarah (1819), Catherine (1823), Eugenia (1825), and Henry Charles (1826)—were no doubt a comfort to their parents. Henri and Amelia must have felt a deep sense of satisfaction as they watched their children grow up, marry, and begin to have children of their own, and they had good reason to be proud of them. Three of their sons would serve in the Georgia legislature, and one in particular, their oldest son, Charles, would leave a considerable mark in the state of Georgia.

Charles showed an early interest in law and politics. Born on Jekyll on January 4, 1809, he left the island as a young man and went north to continue his education. When he returned to Brunswick, he read law with an eminent Glynn County attorney, R. R. Cuyler, who was also the president of Central Rail Road and Banking Company, one of the companies in which Henri invested heavily. Elected in 1841 to represent Glynn County in the state general assembly, Charles moved to Milledgeville, by then the seat of Georgia government. He cut a dashing figure in the capital and was evidently held in high regard. While in Milledgeville he met and married in 1844 Ann Virginia Grantland, the daughter of a newspaperman and a senator, Seaton Grantland, who had come with his brother Fleming from Richmond, Virginia, where they had worked in the printing business. Once in Georgia, they established the *Georgia Journal*, which would evolve into the *Southern Recorder*. Grantland was also reputed to be one of the wealthiest men in Georgia. It seemed an ideal marriage for both Charles and Ann, even though he was fourteen years older than his bride. (He was thirty-five and she was twenty-one when they wed.) Such a marriage was no doubt a boost to du Bignon's status, for Grantland was an influential man. In all probability, Charles was considered quite a catch as well, and one source describes him as "a magnificent specimen of southern manhood and chivalry."[6] The couple chose to make their home permanently near Milledgeville, where Charles became a captain in the governor's Horse Guards.[7] He was therefore not involved in some of the later activities on Jekyll Island that would cause his two surviving brothers difficulties in future years. Instead, he kept busy elsewhere, serving in the Indian Wars and during the Civil War as a captain in Cobb's Legion, where he was dubbed "Our French Field Marshall."[8] Eventually he gave up both politics and law to manage Woodville Plantation (about five miles from Milledgeville), which his wife inherited from her father.

In naming his sons, Henri du Bignon had seemed intent on honoring his brother, Joseph, who at the time was still in favor with his father. Not only was his firstborn son, Charles Joseph, named for his brother, but so also was his third son, who was called simply Joseph. Born in 1814, he was five years younger than his brother Charles, whom he evidently much admired. Joseph seemed to model his life after that of his older brother, and judging from his later career, he, too, apparently read law, perhaps also with Cuyler. For a time after his marriage, however, Joseph returned to Jekyll Island with his young family. On January 22, 1839, he had married Félicité Riffault, the niece of the Louis Grand Dutreuilh to whom Joseph's grandfather had offered such generous hospitality in 1809, and the young couple began their domestic life on Jekyll. On March 20, just two months after his wedding, Joseph wrote to his cousin Joseph Nicolau, "Well, Joe, here I am, settled on Jekyl, an old *married man*, & as happy as I can wish to be—loving my dear little wife more & more every day." His happiness bubbled over in the letter as he advised his cousin, "Joe, get married as soon as you can. I never knew what it was to be happy until I was married—The further I go, the more I am convinced of that fact.—Were I a single man now on Jekyl I would die, whereas with my wife with me I am perfectly happy & contented." Their life on the island seemed idyllic. Joseph helped his father with the planting each year, but when his duties were done, he was free to follow his own pastimes, and he and his brothers apparently enjoyed "playing gentlemen." He expressed his delight with the life he was leading. "All my old pursuits have returned to me very naturally—& I find a great deal of pleasure in them, such as hunting, fishing, shooting, swimming, etc.

Charles Joseph du Bignon, the oldest and most successful of the sons of Henri du Bignon, served in the Georgia legislature and as captain in the Governor's Horse Guards. (Courtesy of Henry Howell)

Ann Virginia Grantland, daughter of senator and newspaperman Seaton Grantland, married Charles Joseph du Bignon in 1844. (Courtesy of Henry Howell)

etc. I have Emmet & Cracker [his horses] in fine order & enjoy my rides on the beach much more than I used to in consequence of the company of *ma chere petite femme* [my dear little wife]."[9] The couple built a house about a mile south of his parents' home and lived there for the next fifteen years, and it seemed for a time as though they would spend the rest of their lives there. At least the first four of the six children of Joseph and "Cité," as he called Félicité—Mary (1839), Josephine (1841), Henry Riffault (1843), and Louise (1845)—were born on Jekyll.

Their decision to leave the island did not come about until 1845 after Joseph's brother Charles married and decided to make his home in Milledgeville. As a Baldwin County resident, he could no longer represent Glynn County in the legislature. Thus, Joseph was elected to replace his brother as the county representative in the Georgia House of Representatives, where he served for two terms from 1845 to 1847 and again from 1849 until his death. He also served during this period as a justice of the Inferior Court in Glynn County, from January 13, 1846, until January 6, 1849.

Joseph was an attractive young man who had been chosen at the age of twenty-four as lieutenant of the Glynn Hussars, a military unit considered "an honor to our county and the State."[10] To make his legislative and legal duties easier, the couple decided to move from Jekyll into Brunswick. He seemed to have a good career in politics and the law ahead of him, and his little family continued to grow. The couple had two children after their move into Brunswick—Félicité (1846) and John Eugene (1849). John Eugene, the youngest, liked to claim that he, too, was born on Jekyll, and it is, of course, possible that Joseph brought his wife to the island to be cared for by his mother during her deliveries. But once they moved into Brunswick, Joseph's mother, Amelia, visited them more often there. Joseph was, no doubt, away much of the time, and Félicité needed help with the children, particularly little Josephine, who was, according to her grandmother, "puny, very thin," and subject to frequent nosebleeds. "She sleeps with me but will not quit her mother," Amelia wrote in a letter.[11] Little Josephine clung to her mother tenaciously, as though fearing to lose her. However, it was not her mother but her father whom she lost at an early age.

Joseph was struck down in the prime of his life, at only thirty-six years old, when he came down with what was diagnosed as pneumonia but was more likely some type of contagious viral infection. He died on April 27, 1850, leaving behind his young widow and six children. Joseph du Bignon was buried in the family plot at Jekyll, only to be joined in death a week later by his mother, who died in Brunswick on May 4 from a combination of grief and the same illness that had taken Joseph's life.

Neither of Henri and Amelia's other two sons, John Couper and Henry Charles, ever married. John Couper, second of the four brothers, was named as the administrator of his brother Joseph's estate and upheld the family tradition by being elected to serve one term (1853–55), after the death of his brother Joseph, to represent Glynn County in the Georgia House of Representatives.[12] It was a life not to his liking or abilities, and he soon returned home to Jekyll Island, the only place he ever felt truly content. John evidently had at least one romance in his life that caused a good deal of gossip. On August 24 (no year) his sister (Sarah?) wrote to her mother, "tell John that I begin to think that there is some truth to the report about him. There is nothing that would please me more than to see him well married and I know he would not intentionally trifle with the feelings of any lady but tell him to be prudent & think as well as he acts."[13] It is possible

This charming sketch of Joseph du Bignon's wife, Félicité Riffault, was made in 1829 by Charles R. Floyd. (Courtesy of Doris Finney Liebrecht)

that the lady in question was his cousin Fanny Nicolau, who on one occasion wrote to John's sister Eliza to assure her that neither she nor her mother was "vexed with him" and that "my friendship for John is that of a kind sister." Whatever indiscretion he may have committed seems to have created a brief rift in the family, though Fanny wrote that she and her mother wanted to forget the incident and were prepared "to let this forever rest in oblivion."[14]

Of the girls, only Eliza, the eldest surviving daughter, would remain single throughout her life. In 1839 her sister Sarah, at age twenty, married Captain Tom Bourke, who was active in the same social circles as her father and older brother. Henri must have wondered if his other two daughters would ever marry, for both were still single when their mother died. Catherine was already thirty-three when she wed Dr. Robert Hazelhurst Jr. in 1856. And Eugenia, the youngest of the daughters, married Archibald T. Burke in 1853 when she was twenty-eight.

The incessant strain of bearing eleven children in eighteen years and losing three of them, who had survived infancy, had no doubt helped to fade the delicate beauty of Amelia over the years. By contrast, Henri du Bignon, only thirty-nine when their last child was born, considered himself still in the prime of his life. He was no doubt more comfortable in his role of southern plantation owner than his father had been, and he had learned to

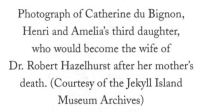

Photograph of Catherine du Bignon,
Henri and Amelia's third daughter,
who would become the wife of
Dr. Robert Hazelhurst after her mother's
death. (Courtesy of the Jekyll Island
Museum Archives)

accept the vicissitudes of plantation economics, always setting enough by
to get through the hard times when the crops did not produce as he would
have liked. He also made prudent investments and was actively involved in
the Brunswick community, which helped him to be less dependent on the
plantation economy.

Shortly after he had come into his full inheritance, he was elected captain
of the local militia, the Twenty-fifth District Company of the Seventh Battalion of Georgia's Third Regiment. Three years later he rose to the rank of
colonel, a title he would bear with pride and honor for the rest of his life.[15]
Even as early as 1809, when he was still a lieutenant, he was a man of style
and a certain élan who had occasionally been singled out for special honors.
Once, when chosen to receive the colors from the militia's commander, Major Page, he responded with self-conscious eloquence, "Accept, sir, through
me, on this occasion, the thanks of my brother officers and soldiers; and
we pledge ourselves never to part with this standard but with our *lives* and
liberties." His little speech, which also complimented Major Page's patriotism and hailed "our happy constitution" and its "well regulated militia,"
no doubt met with loud huzzahs from the troops. An elegant officer in
his uniform, du Bignon paraded for the next three hours with his battalion,
which then took "an excellent dinner" at the invitation of Major Page. They
"retired at sunset in the utmost harmony."[16] His career and reputation had
only improved since then, and life was good.

If Henri had economic worries, they involved the continued low price of cotton coupled with the depletion of the soil after so many years of production. Hauling marsh mud and compost and spreading dung to coax yet another yield from the depleted cotton fields were never-ending and time-consuming tasks for his slaves, yet as an overseer from a nearby plantation had concluded, nothing "in the way of cotton could be grown on the sea island lands without the application of compost and manure."[17] Nonetheless, on the surface Henri seemed to live a rich social life without serious care. He visited frequently back and forth among the various plantations, as did his children. The diary of Charles Rinaldo Floyd records many visits from members of the du Bignon family to his own plantation, Fairfield, as well as to others in the area, notably Belleville, now the plantation of Floyd's father, General John Floyd; and Dungeness on Cumberland Island. Du Bignon was often accompanied by his three oldest sons, Charles, John, and Joseph, and sometimes by his daughters, especially the two eldest, Eliza and Sarah.[18] Other planters, yachtsmen, and hunters in the area also visited Jekyll, where they were hospitably received, occasionally staying for overnight visits.[19] But nowhere was du Bignon better known than in the boating community. When the Aquatic Club of Georgia was organized on January 12, 1836, Henri du Bignon was elected recording secretary, one of the club's four officers.[20]

As a sportsman, du Bignon clearly was at his peak. Like his father, he was drawn to the sea, and he was a stylish and much-touted figure in regattas and boat races along the Georgia coast with his vessels, especially the *Goddess of Liberty*, well known in the racing community, and the *Sarah and Catherine*, named for two of his daughters. Du Bignon had no doubt learned many of his nautical skills from his father and was consequently a sailor proud of not only his seafaring prowess but also his boats. The *Goddess of Liberty* was a sleek, white vessel "with a blue band bearing twenty-four stars."[21] She was a familiar sight in the coastal towns of Georgia, like Brunswick and St. Marys, which often hosted the boat races. On June 8, 1837, the *Brunswick Advocate* noted that, following a sale of thirty-seven city lots on May 25, "a large company sat down to the first dinner furnished at the 'Oglethorpe House.'" Following the dinner came speeches and a boat race between two of the "Island Lords," one of whom was Colonel Henri du Bignon of Jekyll Island, whose boat, the *Goddess of Liberty*, built by his friend and master boat builder Charles Rinaldo Floyd of Camden County, had once again taken first place in the day's races. The newspaper article described the boat as one that "is dug out of a Cypress log, and is the most perfect model of symmetry we have ever seen. She has been victorious at several of the races of the St. Simons' Club and deserves for her beauty alone to win the prize."[22]

On June 15, 1837, following his victory in the Brunswick races, du Bignon, along with fellow sportsman Charles R. Floyd, posted a notice in the *Brunswick Advocate* on behalf of the Aquatic Club of Georgia challenging any of the boat clubs in the city of New York to a race. He noted that the Georgia club members had "frequently heard of the fleetness of your Boats and skill of your Oarsmen" and "are desirous of comparing the speed of one of their Boats, with the speed of one of yours." They proposed a wager of ten thousand dollars to pit the four-oared canoe boat the *Lizard* in a mile-long race "opposite the city of Savannah in fair and calm weather" against "any four Oared Plank Boat built in the City of New York, not over 27 feet 3 inches on the keel (which is the length of the Lizard's)." Apparently there were no takers.

Thus, the Aquatic Club yachtsmen had to content themselves for that season at least to race against each other. The *Brunswick Advocate* reported on September 7, 1837, a race the preceding Monday between Colonel du Bignon's *Goddess of Liberty* and "Mr. [Francis M.] Scarlett's boat." The article also noted that the "Whitehallers," as locals called the New Yorkers, had not taken up the wager of the Brunswick club and must therefore be contented "to wear the 'white feather,'" which in polite circles was a symbol of cowardice. Stung by the rebuke, the "Whitehallers" indicated that the reason for their refusal was that they would "not consent to row against black servants," whereupon the Aquatic Club of Georgia responded obligingly that the *Lizard* would be "manned by gentlemen, who we warrant, shall be the equals of the Knickerbockers in bone and muscle, blood and breeding."[23]

Finally, unable to avoid the challenge any longer, the New Yorkers arranged for certain parties in Savannah to represent their interest. The race, or "trial for superiority between the Georgia dug-outs and the Whitehall wherries," was arranged for January 15, 1838, the day of the second annual Regatta of the Aquatic Club of Georgia. As the *Brunswick Advocate* gloated on December 28, 1837, the trial had long "been avoided by the New York gentry, under an affectation of refinement." But, despite the excellent weather, the race did not take place. Members of the Aquatic Club

again had a fine regatta only among themselves, with repeated races between du Bignon's *Goddess of Liberty*, described in the newspaper account
as "the reigning belle of our waters," and the *Devil's Darning Needle*, owned
by Captain Richard F. Floyd, with the latter victorious. Undaunted, the
Goddess of Liberty raced again, against the *Leopard*, this time winning by
four lengths. And so the races went on for the full afternoon, with vessels like the *Emma Sarah*, the *Thomas F. Bryan*, the *Caroline King*, and the
Lizard vying repeatedly for victory.

In May 1838, however, though the New Yorkers still refused to accept
the challenge directly, a Savannah group, which had organized themselves
into the Lower Creek Boat Club, took up the gauntlet in a northern-made
vessel, the *Star*, to compete against the Aquatic Club of Georgia's *Lizard*.[24]
It was a breathtaking race, as the *Savannah Georgian* described it, with the
vessels, "one having been formed and fashioned in the icy bound regions
of the Hudson—the other hewn from a log, from the banks of the warm
Satilla," neck and neck for much of the race. A huge crowd, black and white
alike, lined the Savannah River to cheer on their rowing teams, the rowers of
the *Lizard* sporting red turbans while their opponents in the *Star* wore blue.
The *Lizard* was the victor by 105 feet, but the local newspaper nonetheless,
in a spirit of noblesse oblige, lauded the "strength and spirit" of the oarsmen
of the defeated northern vessel. And the victors, represented by Henri du
Bignon and Charles R. Floyd, in a gesture of magnanimity, presented the
losers with the boat that had defeated them.[25] The race, which had been so
long promoted by du Bignon and Floyd, was to become an annual event,
with the Lower Creeks winning victory the following year in their gift from
the Aquatic Club's officers, the *Lizard*, and another vessel that they had
built in honor of the *Lizard*'s generous owner, the *Floyd*. The friendly spirit
of competition between the northern and southern vessels could not presage
the bitter and bloody struggle in which these regions would be engaged only
a few decades later.

The regatta held on January 15, 1838, ended with another elegant dinner
at the Oglethorpe House, "in due observance of the rites of conviviality and
good fellowship." The reporter noted the importance of such days for the
coastal planters, who led, in many ways, lives of relative isolation. "Living
as they do at a great distance from each other, some such association is
needed to bring them together occasionally, and revive the feelings which
otherwise imperceptibly grow dull."[26] Thus, such challenges between boat

owners on the Georgia coast were not unusual. It was part of plantation life, particularly among the sea islanders during boat racing's heyday from 1830 until the Civil War. Wagers were not always of the magnitude of that against the New Yorkers. They could be anywhere from "a cigar, a glass of toddy, a beaver hat, a pair of Durfee's best made boots, to $500 or $100."[27] Du Bignon did not always win, though he continued to participate in the "manly recreation" of boat racing as long as he could. In the 1840 regatta he raced with the *Sarah and Catherine,* this time going down in defeat. But the *Weekly Georgian* newspaper noted, by way of consolation, that "Little Jekyl showed herself game every inch. She exhibited the Sea Island pluck which, we venture to say, will not stay *beat.*"[28]

Slaves were especially valued for their ability to row, and some of them made up the finest crews on the coast. They were highly sought after for their prowess in the races and for their ability to hollow out the logs to create the smaller boats like the *Lizard,* which were famed for sleekness and speed. The rhythmic rowing songs of the slaves were familiar sounds in the marsh streams and inland waterways, and their owners bragged of the strength and quickness they displayed in their rowing. If accounts of their white masters can be given credence, even the enslaved men enjoyed these outings: "The negroes too, as full of the excitement as their masters, hailing their acquaintances, gibing each other about their boats, made the banks ring with their shrill laughter."[29]

Henri du Bignon was one of a convivial group of sportsmen who regularly enjoyed each other's company. A journal kept by a Darien physician, James Holmes, popularly known as Dr. Bullie, recounts an incident that took place at this opening event of the Oglethorpe House, in which he himself was the butt of the joke, and du Bignon was one of the jokesters. Dr. Bullie was a notorious mimic who enjoyed imitating his friends, one of whom was Charles R. Floyd. On the occasion of the boat race and the opening of the Oglethorpe House, du Bignon approached him "with his peculiar, polite address that belongs to all the family." Tapping his snuff box, du Bignon informed him, "Dr. Bullie, I am called upon by General Floyd to demand satisfaction from you for 'taking him off' [doing a take-off of him] at your table for the amusement of your guests. I beg your reference to some friend with whom I may correspond on the subject." It suddenly dawned on the genial doctor that he was about to be challenged to a duel. It seemed quite plausible, particularly since the gentlemen in question, General Floyd and

Colonel du Bignon, were both dueling men, and because such duels were an acceptable southern way of settling arguments. Dr. Holmes was no doubt aware that five years earlier in October 1833, du Bignon had fought a well-known duel with rifles against another doctor, H. D. Holland. It had been du Bignon's son Charles who had originally challenged Dr. Holland to a duel, and Henri had carried his son's challenge to Dr. Holland in June 1833, but Dr. Holland had declined. However, on September 27, Dr. Holland delivered a challenge himself, this time to the father. As "the challenged party," Henri had at first selected "the small sword" as his weapon of choice, but after learning that Dr. Holland was "unacquainted with the use of such a weapon," he agreed instead to the rifle duel.[30] He used the *"famous dueling rifle"* of his friend Charles R. Floyd, at whose home he practiced before the event. His efforts paid off. From the duel, which took place shortly after noon on October 3, 1833, on the beach at the north end of Amelia Island, a popular dueling spot just across the border in Florida, du Bignon emerged victorious, having wounded the doctor "through the upper part of both thighs." According to Floyd, who witnessed the event, both men "behaved well on the field of combat," though in his opinion du Bignon had "the advantage in *training* and weapon."[31]

Dr. Holmes, who now found himself in the uncomfortable position of the "challenged," had no inclination for such doings, but as a man of honor, he could not very well refuse.[32] When the gentleman designated to be Dr. Holmes's "second," Tom Forman, walked away with du Bignon and then returned, Holmes asked with resignation, "Well, Tom, . . . pistol, rifle, or double barrel guns? In short, let me hear the terms." Forman handed him a piece of paper. The note stated that Dr. Holmes was to repeat his performance in the presence of General Floyd's friends "at a champagne party at the hotel this evening at eight o'clock, and the satisfaction he demands is that you grant his request." The relieved doctor, who had noticed the sly smiles of the conspirators, did his "level best" to comply, and they no doubt all enjoyed a convivial evening.[33] Although du Bignon, like the others, was a drinking man, he usually kept it under control. Once, however, he showed up at Fairfield Plantation, seeking to act as a go-between in another quarrel, but according to his host, he was so "*'used up*' with brandy" that he was unable to carry out his task.[34]

Despite such occasional incidents, Henri du Bignon prided himself on being a sportsman and something of a sophisticated bon vivant among his

Southern gentlemen often used the north end of Amelia Island,
Florida, for their duels, as did Henri du Bignon and his adversary,
H. D. Holland, in 1833. (Courtesy of the Library of Congress)

friends. But he did not entirely neglect his plantation. Though his crops
suffered the usual problems brought about by drought, excessive rain, and
the fluctuation of prices, an example of which he experienced in their precipitous tumble during the Cotton Crash of 1839, his cotton production was
generally good. That, along with his other investments, yielded enough to
support his family in relative comfort and not only provided ample seed for
his own planting but also from time to time allowed him to share as much
as ten bushels of his "fine cotton seed" with his friends.[35] His plantation
was well-ordered, and, despite the fact that his father's enslaved driver had
deserted Jekyll when the British liberated him in 1814, du Bignon still clung
to the belief that a black driver was preferable to a white overseer.

We are fortunate to have an extensive description of slave life on the du
Bignon plantation under Henri's supervision. An enslaved woman named
Julia Rush (her married name) left an account of her life there with her

mother and three sisters, all of whom lived together in a log cabin in the slave quarters behind the du Bignon house. Born in 1826, the year following Christophe's death, Julia would live much of her life under the supervision of Henri du Bignon. Although both her parents had worked on the Jekyll plantation, Colonel du Bignon, as she referred to him throughout her account, had sold her father away when she was only a baby, and she never knew him. She did, however, recall being the playmate of Henri's youngest daughter, Eugenia, who had been born in 1825. Her earliest memories were happy ones, when "all she had to do was play from morning till night." When she was old enough to help, she was put to work in the kitchen of her master's house, a position that afforded a certain privilege. Later, however, for reasons she does not mention, she was sent to the fields to work alongside her mother and sisters. Even so, she contended with a certain pride that she could "outplow" any man. According to Julia's account, Colonel du Bignon's black driver would awaken the field hands before dawn and set them to work. The slaves toiled under the task system. Each worker was assigned a certain amount of labor to complete and could expect a whipping if it was not finished. Breakfast was sent to them in the fields, but at lunchtime they were permitted to go home to eat and, no doubt, to escape for a while the worst heat of the day. Julia and her family also prepared their own evening meals in their individual cabins. All able-bodied slaves worked, she pointed out, even women with young babies, who carried their infants to the fields in a basket on their head.

Living conditions for the slaves were sparse but not unbearable. The houses that du Bignon provided Julia's family and his other slaves had wooden floors, beds, benches, and a fireplace where they did their cooking. Chinks in the wall were filled with mud. The colonel issued them clothing twice a year, once in summer and once in winter. Summer issues for men consisted of two shirts, two pairs of pants, and two pairs of undergarments, all of cotton and all made on the plantation. Women received two dresses, two underskirts, and two pairs of underwear. The slaves went barefoot in the summer, but in winter du Bignon issued shoes along with their clothing. Julia particularly recalled a pair of "heavy red leather brogans" that she received in the winter issue. Du Bignon also provided them some food, though not enough to sustain without their own effort. Corn was issued on a daily basis from the "corn house." The slaves dug their own potatoes from the colonel's garden. "It was up to the slaves to catch fish,

This slave cabin fits Julia's description of her home on Jekyll Island.
(50473, Collection of the New-York Historical Society)

oysters and other sea food for their meat supply," Julia indicated. Such an arrangement was not unusual on the Sea Islands, where fish, oysters, and small game were abundant. Du Bignon also permitted them to raise chickens, vegetables, and watermelons, "which they could either eat themselves or sell to others."[36]

Julia's description is particularly valuable because she was on Jekyll from the time Henri received his inheritance until he left the island, dividing his slaves among his children and leaving his two unmarried sons, John Couper and Henry, to manage the plantation. At that time Julia was given to her old playmate, Eugenia, and went to live in Carrollton, Georgia. After she left Jekyll, her life changed considerably. According to her account, she was frequently abused by her mistress, who in a rage once cut Julia's "long and straight" hair and sometimes made her sleep under the house, because she was jealous of the attentions Julia received from her new master, Eugenia's husband, Archibald Burke. It was apparently not an uncommon problem between mistress and female slave.[37]

From Julia's recollections, we can surmise that Henri du Bignon followed many of the typical practices on the Sea Island plantations. He demanded much from his slaves and did not spare the whip if they did not perform satisfactorily, but Julia did not complain in her account of the work assigned to her, nor did she seem to find it excessive by the standards of the day. The wooden floors she mentions in individual slave cabins suggest some degree of concern for the workers' comfort, for many Georgia slave cabins at the time had only dirt floors. But the only furniture that was provided was a bed and several benches. No doubt the Jekyll workers' freedom to raise their own poultry and have their own small gardens, allowing them to sell produce and eggs, was valued by the slaves and provided them with a small degree of independence and a sense of ownership.

Perhaps because he was less exacting and somewhat more indulgent than his father, Henri does not seem to have had the same problems with runaway slaves that Christophe had. It is possible that they had merely become resigned to their situation. More likely, they found life somewhat better under the son, who had grown up on the plantation and probably understood his workers and their needs better than his father had. When Christophe died, he left in his will the provision that his elderly slaves should be treated with "humanity and kindness," and, he added, "I rely upon the honour of my son Henry Charles DuBignon for the Execution of this clause in my will."[38] There is no reason to believe that Henri did not carry out his father's request to the best of his ability. He may well have learned the costliness of being an overdemanding master from his father, and by and large, his more lenient attitudes toward the slaves merely mirrored the practices among other nearby coastal planters of his day.[39]

Duties on his plantation, which grew to include fifty-seven slaves, did not prevent du Bignon from taking part in community activities. Although it was his property and the relative success of his plantation that gave him an elite status in the Brunswick area, he seemed to spend less and less time as a planter. By the mid-1830s he was not engaging in such close personal supervision of the plantation as had his father, and he may little by little have turned over more responsibility to his sons. Well aware of the dangers of relying solely on the cotton crop for his income and knowing of the many things that could go wrong—a late frost, heavy rains at the wrong time, unexpected infestations of insects—not unlike many other Sea Island planters of the time, he began to invest energies and money in diversifying his interests.[40] He had been chosen about 1814 as a commissioner of the public school system of Glynn County and was serving by 1818 as treasurer of Glynn Academy (which had been founded in 1788, the oldest public school in the state), just in time to oversee the funding of the academy's first building, erected in 1819. Twenty years later, in 1839, the year before the second Glynn Academy building was constructed, he was again elected treasurer of the Board of Trustees, alongside James Hamilton Couper (son of John Couper and a man of distinction in his own right), who was elected president.

He served, as well, as a commissioner for the town of Brunswick and lobbied to establish the Brunswick Canal and Rail Road Company to bring more business to the area. At one point he served as tax collector and on another occasion as justice of the Inferior Court.[41] When delegates were selected to the state convention in Milledgeville in 1838, he was elected to chair the delegation, which included other well-known plantation owners in the area, among them Thomas Butler King, Urbanus Dart, Francis M. Scarlett, and William A. Howard. He clearly enjoyed acceptance in the highest social and political circles of the area. In the mid-1830s, as Brunswick experienced a short-lived "boom," du Bignon was deeply engrossed in efforts to promote the economic strength of the city.

When the newly organized Bank of Brunswick was established in 1838, he was elected to serve as its first president. Announcing his election, the *Brunswick Advocate* noted that "Col. Dubignon is extensively known and highly esteemed, and is every way qualified to discharge the duties of the office."[42] Ultimately, neither the bank nor the city of Brunswick thrived from his efforts, but du Bignon continued to be well regarded. He was selected, along with Robert Stafford of Cumberland Island and Lewis Bachlott of St. Marys, to serve as arbitrator in a property dispute between Marguerite Bernardey and her daughter-in-law, Catherine, the widow of Pierre Bernardey, who had once lived on Jekyll Island.[43] In short, du Bignon was a man much respected in the community, a man of means valued for his public spirit and his efforts on behalf of Glynn County.

What could have caused such a civic-minded and successful man to flaunt community values and conventions in the following decade one can only speculate. Certainly, the irregularity of his behavior put a rather abrupt end to his political and social prominence. In any case, in the late 1830s, when

William Turner du Bignon, one of the sons
of Henri du Bignon and Sarah Aust,
changed his name to William Turner in
1875. (Courtesy of E. Lynn McLarty and
Charlotte Granberry Gillespie)

his reputation in and around Brunswick and the islands was at its zenith, a woman in her midthirties named Sarah Ann Maccaw Aust, the widow of an Englishman, George Butler Aust, came with her young daughters, Mary and Margaret, to live on Jekyll Island and serve as a tutor to the du Bignon children.[44] Sarah Maccaw had married George Aust on January 26, 1830, and her first daughter, Mary, was born that same year, aboard a ship en route to America.[45] A second daughter, Margaret, was born not long thereafter. But Sarah's husband, George, died unexpectedly on January 22, 1838, and the need to support herself and her two little girls was suddenly thrust upon her.[46] She had little choice but to accept an offer from Henri du Bignon to become a tutor to his children. Between 1839 and 1848, she was also his mistress. During those years she bore him three children— Leonidas (born 1840), William (1843), and Rosalia Elizabeth (1848). Du Bignon had not been completely scrupulous in his fidelity to Amelia even before. He had fathered at least one child named Charlotte, by Margaret, a free woman of color in the mid-1830s. The record of the child's baptism in 1836 acknowledged Charlotte to be "a free colored person and illegitimate child of Henry Du Bignon."[47]

It may be that Amelia du Bignon, after eleven pregnancies, had had enough and did not really object to Henri's turning his attentions elsewhere. Nonetheless, in the ten years before her death, she was confronted constantly with the situation and seems, after 1845, when her son Joseph and his family moved into Brunswick, to have spent more and more of her

Leonidas Turner (formerly du Bignon),
son of Henri du Bignon and Sarah
Aust. (Courtesy of Rose D. Glaiber)

time away from the island. Amelia divided her time between the mainland, where she could enjoy her grandchildren, and Jekyll, where she could not completely ignore her husband's illegitimate children. But she does not seem to have been devastated by the situation. On July 14, 1845, she wrote to her daughter Eliza from Brunswick, commenting on her life there and her concerns for the children: "Poor F[élicité] keeps going like a clock. Her health is good. I hope she will be lucky, her children stick to her and she is not willing to shake them off." She described her life in Brunswick as "a lazy life," and noted that she was "anxious to get home having nothing to do here and many little concerns on the island."[48] Nevertheless, her "many little concerns," which no doubt included her husband's unfaithfulness, may also have driven her inland on many occasions.

Despite Henri du Bignon's flagrant infidelities, at Amelia's death on May 4, 1850, at age sixty-three, only a week after the death of their son Joseph, he paid her all the honor that a grieving (or perhaps guilt-ridden) husband may have felt he owed his wife. The occurrence of her death in Brunswick, where she often visited, may imply a separation between the spouses, but no record indicates such estrangement. In fact, it is quite possible, as suggested above, that she was content with the arrangement as it was. Whatever the case, her funeral cortege back to the island was heart rending. As one account described it:

> The funeral procession; the coffin in the first boat, the crew dressed in mourning garments, followed by a long line of boats filled with relatives and friends, the rowers chanting "Spirituals" in low tones was an impressive sight, as it came down the river from Brunswick, crossed the sound, and slowly wound its way through the tortuous channel of the little creek to the old landing. . . . From there the cortege following the coffin, walked to the little burying ground and mid the last impressive rites, Amelie Nicholai [*sic*] was laid by the side of the old chevalier and of her brother, who had met so tragic a death years before.[49]

Though the two graves mentioned in this account are unmarked, that of Amelia, laid to rest next to her son Joseph, was commemorated by a fine tombstone. It is still visible today, along with those of Joseph and his mother-in-law, in the little du Bignon cemetery on Jekyll Island. There, intricately carved are the words her husband chose to describe her: "Highly educated in France . . . amiable and courteous." With the death of Anne Amelia, a gracious way of life ended on Jekyll. "She bid adieu," as her tombstone proclaims, "to a devoted family / And a large circle of friends / Who prized her highly for her many / Sociable virtues, and respected her / As an ornament of society." Her children had grown up and some of them had gone their separate ways, but during her lifetime, the du Bignons visited back and forth with their neighbors from plantations on St. Simons and Cumberland. Their children attended balls, learned the waltz, and enjoyed a lively social life. She taught her daughters needlework and the domestic arts she thought they would need to make good wives. Now the children who still remained at home, listed in the 1850 census as Eliza, John, Catherine, Eugenia, and Henry, had only their father to turn to, and his attentions were clearly directed elsewhere.

To the astonishment of his sons and daughters, after their mother's death in 1850, Henri du Bignon did not focus his affections more fully on his

To this little cemetery near the Horton house on Jekyll Island, Henri du Bignon brought both his wife and his son Joseph to be buried following their deaths only one week apart in 1850.

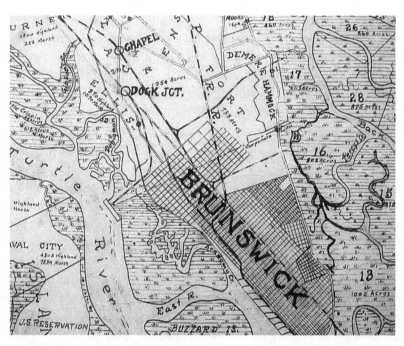

Just northwest of Brunswick is Ellis Point, where Henri du Bignon took his young bride and daughter. The little creek adjacent to their property was renamed Dubignon Creek. (Courtesy of the Public Records Office, Brunswick)

mistress, Sarah Aust, as one might have expected. Instead, at age sixty-three, he sought solace with her twenty-year-old daughter Mary. He had his first child by her, a baby girl named Virginia Elizabeth, in 1851, only one year after Amelia's death. On November 23, 1852, Henri and Mary were married, and in the next twelve years she bore him four more daughters: Emily Amanda (born ca. 1854), Agnes Sarah (ca. 1859), Valeria Marie (ca. 1862), and Gertrude Louisa (September 16, 1864).[50] Following his marriage to Mary Aust, Henri du Bignon left Jekyll Island and established a new home at Ellis Point just north of Brunswick on Yellow Bluff Creek, where he lived out the rest of his life with his young wife, forty-three years his junior, and their five daughters and the two sons, Leonidas and William, born to him by the woman who was now his mother-in-law. Whether Henri left Jekyll by choice is uncertain. He had spent sixty years of his life there, and it must have been a difficult move for him. But his young wife and Amelia's children may have agreed that it was best for all concerned that he and his children by Sarah and Mary Aust leave the island.

Before his move, Henri du Bignon divided his slaves among his children and left Jekyll Island forever, entrusting the plantation to the care of his two unmarried sons, John and Henry. Their associations and activities in the years to come would for the first time imprint the name of Jekyll Island indelibly on the national consciousness.

CHAPTER SIX

From the Wanderer *to War*

O God! How large a portion of the ills

Of human kind derives itself from man!

JAMES GRAHAME, "Africa Delivered"

N NOVEMBER 23, 1858, a curious notice appeared in the *Savannah Daily Morning News*, warning "All Persons . . . against landing on the Island of Jekyl . . . or in any way trespassing on said island." It was signed by John du Bignon and Henry du Bignon Jr.—the second and youngest sons of Henri du Bignon, who had left Jekyll Island in their care after his move to the mainland six years earlier.

At approximately the same time the notice appeared, the brothers also discharged the white overseer they had employed after their father's departure.[1] Five days later, at sunset, two men rowed a small boat across St. Andrews Sound to a lighthouse on Cumberland Island. Using false names, they introduced themselves to the assistant lighthouse keeper and indicated that they were seeking a pilot to take their vessel, anchored offshore, to Jekyll Island in order to deliver some gentlemen who planned to visit the island. The lighthouse keeper, James Clubb, whom they finally located on the south end of Jekyll, was suspicious of their intentions from the outset. But he agreed to pilot them to the island for five hundred dollars, an exorbitant fee for a service that typically cost less than twenty dollars. They had no choice but to pay it. Thus, under cover of darkness and just before dawn on the morning of November 29, Clubb guided the *Wanderer* past the sandbar, through St. Andrews Sound, and into Jekyll Creek, where it would anchor surreptitiously to debark its human cargo.

From the decks and hold of the vessel stumbled forth an estimated 409 miserable souls, enslaved Africans, many of them sick and hardly able to

Painting of the *Wanderer*. (Courtesy of the Jekyll Island Museum Archives)

stand.[2] Six weeks earlier these people, who came from various regions and tribes, had all been herded together onto the yacht near the mouth of the Congo River. According to a notebook in the captain's handwriting found on the vessel (but not its official log), the ship had set out with 487 passengers in addition to the twelve-man crew.[3] The survivors of the so-called Middle Passage, that ocean of horror and grief that lay between Africa and America, had been transported on the *Wanderer,* from the sands of their native continent to the shores of Jekyll Island. In the stinking hull of the roiling vessel, reconfigured and outfitted as a slave ship, they had been stacked like spoons, each occupying an area of not more than five or six square feet, to live or die in excruciating circumstances.[4] Some of them had not survived, but had succumbed to the fetid air and sickness trapped in the bowels of the ship. Those who had died in passage, an estimated seventy-nine among them (there had been at least one birth during the voyage), had been unceremoniously tossed overboard. Perhaps some of them had been still alive when they were thrown into the sea, for it was not uncommon for slavers to discard some of their human cargo, dead or alive, if they needed to lighten the load or if food or water was running in short supply.

The landing of the *Wanderer* was undoubtedly the most significant and best-known event that occurred on Jekyll Island during the late plantation era, and surely the most shameful. It represented the last known successful and major shipload of slaves imported into the United States from Africa.[5] It is an event that should be remembered not only for its historical significance but also to commemorate those who, against their will, endured its horrors.

The du Bignon brothers lent their yawl and personally assisted in the effort to unload the survivors, who stumbled awkwardly from the vessel, blinking against the bright morning light. Among them were women and men with names like Manchuella and Tahro. The majority were adolescent boys between twelve and eighteen, among them Zow Uncola, Mabiala, Cilucangy, and Pucka Geata, names they would not get to keep for long. Even small children, too young to later remember their African names, emerged timidly from the vessel.[6] At the time of their arrival, the Africans were suffering from scurvy, intestinal infections, and skin diseases. John and Henry du Bignon contacted their brother-in-law, Dr. Robert Hazelhurst, husband to their sister Catherine, to see to the sick among the newly enslaved.[7]

Word of the arrival was quickly sent to Charlie Lamar, the backer of the expedition, in Savannah, who hurried to the island on the iron steamer *Lamar,* pausing only briefly in Brunswick on December 2 to pick up Captain Thomas Bourke, another brother-in-law of the du Bignons. As they approached Jekyll from the Turtle River, Henry du Bignon rowed out from the north end of the island to show them where to anchor. Time was critical, for news of the landing had quickly leaked out, and Lamar knew that his human cargo would be confiscated if he could not dispose of it with dispatch. The group quickly loaded as many Africans as the *Lamar* would hold, an estimated two hundred. Still sick and stiff from their earlier confinement on the *Wanderer,* the Africans must have been horrified at the thought of another sea voyage. Under cover of darkness, the vessel crept by Savannah, taking them about sixteen miles farther north to the South Carolina plantation of John Montmollin. One of the Africans, already sick, died en route.[8] Five days later, about December 12, another vessel, the *Augusta,* picked up some of the newly enslaved and took them up the Savannah

Zow Uncola (given the slave name of Tom Johnson), survivor of the slave ship *Wanderer*. (*American Anthropologist*, 1908)

Manchuella (Katie Noble), survivor of the slave ship *Wanderer*. (*American Anthropologist*, 1908)

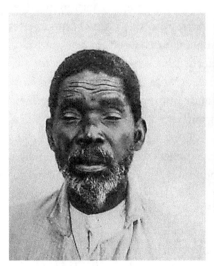

Mabiala (Uster Williams), survivor of the slave ship *Wanderer*. (*American Anthropologist*, 1908)

Lucy Lanham, survivor of the slave ship *Wanderer*, who was too young upon arrival to remember her African name. (*American Anthropologist*, 1908)

Sophia Tillman of Edgefield, South
Carolina, bought thirty slaves from those
brought to America aboard the *Wanderer.*
She was the mother of "Pitchfork"
Ben Tillman, later U.S. senator from
South Carolina.

River to a wood yard about two miles below Augusta. From there they were delivered to various other spots, including the Tillman plantation in Edge-field, South Carolina, where the widowed mother of a future United States senator, known as "Pitchfork" Ben Tillman, purchased thirty of the slaves. The steamer *Lamar* had long since headed back to Jekyll, where for two weeks after the landing the other Africans were "quietly distributed from the Jekyll Island area" to various rice and cotton plantations of prominent coastal planters in Georgia, South Carolina, and Florida.[9]

For their part in the ugly business of slave trading, the du Bignon brothers allegedly received $15,000. In today's dollars, conservatively estimated, that is the equivalent of about $326,000, and it might have purchased for them as many as twenty-five to thirty new slaves to work the plantation. Nonetheless, one might wonder why John Couper and Henry would have involved themselves in such an unsavory trade. They no doubt saw it as a lucky windfall, an unexpected opportunity to try to get the Jekyll plantation back on its feet. When their father had left the island and divided his slaves among all his children, he left fewer than half of them at Jekyll to tend the land, not enough for the du Bignon brothers to bring in a large crop successfully. To make matters worse, only two years after John and Henry took over the island, they suffered in 1854 the devastation of another major hurricane, which flooded their fields and wreaked havoc on their crops and livestock. Since then, cotton prices had remained relatively high, dropping below an average of thirty cents a pound only in 1858, and the exportation of Sea Island cotton was on the rise. Nevertheless, producing a decent cotton crop on Jekyll was much harder now than it had been during their father's time on the island. Their diminished labor force combined with the increasing exhaustion of the soil was making it more and more difficult to survive financially by farming. Thus, $15,000 could have represented to them a much-needed financial boost. To be paid merely for the *Wanderer* to land and unload its illicit captives on their island took relatively little effort or risk on their part (or so they thought). They probably perceived the opportunity as a boon and did not ask too many questions.

What's more, the expedition's primary backer was an acquaintance from a prominent and wealthy Savannah family—Charles Augustus Lafayette Lamar. To say that Charlie Lamar was a colorful figure is to put it mildly. Every aspect of his life seemed to be an adventure. His first moment of distinction came at his baptism in Christ Church, Savannah, in the arms of his godfather, the Marquis de Lafayette, who had come to Georgia in March 1825 to be honored for his support in the American Revolution. From that moment on, one might have guessed that young Lamar's life was going to be unusual, to say the least.

At fourteen he had his first encounter with danger and death, two things he would never run away from. He was the son of Gazaway Bugg Lamar, a Savannah businessman who was one of the wealthiest and most prominent men in the South. His business interests included various plantations, a cotton press, an insurance company, a commission house, several banks, railroads, and finally steamships. And in his son's fourteenth year, he launched a much-touted new vessel called the *Pulaski*. Lamar was very proud of his vessel, and on its maiden voyage from Savannah to New York in June 1838, he had brought his entire family, his wife and six children, aboard for the run. Unfortunately, the vessel exploded at sea in the middle of the night on June 14. Despite his youth, Charlie Lamar did what he could to rescue his younger siblings, but he could not save his mother and his five brothers and sisters, all of whom died in the accident. One younger brother was saved from drowning but later died of exposure and dehydration as they floated on the debris of the wreckage for days, praying for rescue. The only members of the family to survive the disaster were Charlie, his father, and his aunt

Charles Alexander Lafayette Lamar. (From *Roll of Officers
and Members of the Georgia Hussars*, Savannah, 1906.
Courtesy of the Georgia Historical Society)

Rebecca, who left a heart-rending account of the ordeal.[10] In spite of, or
perhaps because of, this early brush with death, Charlie tended to be reck-
less, sometimes even foolhardy, as though he thought himself invulnerable.

Perhaps to a certain degree he was—for he was certainly protected by
wealth, family name, and important connections. The family was well
known from Savannah to New York. The Lamars could claim family connections by marriage to Secretary of the Treasury and one-time presidential
candidate Howell Cobb; to Mirabeau Bonaparte Lamar, a former president
of the Republic of Texas; and to U.S. Senator, Secretary of the Interior, and
later Supreme Court Justice Lucius Quintus Cincinnatus Lamar.

The wealth and distinction of Charlie Lamar's family gave him a social
prominence that made him a good match for his bride, Caroline Nicoll,
daughter of a well-respected United States district judge and former mayor
of Savannah, John C. Nicoll. But Nicoll could not have been more different

in personality and conviction from his new son-in-law. He was devoted to the law and to the Union and was a man of sober convictions, while his son-in-law, an ardent secessionist, has been described by one as "fiery, articulate, and opinionated," by another as "Sanguine, impetuous, choleric . . . loud-spoken" and "quick to quarrel," while still another depicted him as "a brazen-faced and vociferous soldier of fortune." In short, Charlie Lamar seemed to create controversy wherever he went.[11]

There is no question that he is best known in southern history for his involvement in the expedition of the slave ship *Wanderer,* which catapulted him to national notoriety. He knew quite well that the importation of slaves from Africa was against the law of the United States (as it would also be against the law of the Confederacy). But he openly opposed the law, which had been passed by the United States Congress fifty years earlier. In fact, in 1858, prior to the *Wanderer* episode, Lamar engaged in a public debate over the issue with the U.S. secretary of the treasury, his kinsman Howell Cobb.

The debate had broken out over another of Lamar's efforts to import slaves on a vessel called the *Richard Cobden.* That time he had openly stated its purpose of "taking on board African emigrants in accordance with the passenger laws and returning with the same to a port in the United States." But the ship was refused clearance at the port of Charleston.[12] Lamar protested and penned a lengthy pamphlet on the issue, clearly setting forth his views, and published it for all to read. He had noted that the French were engaging in the slave trade by calling their African captives "apprentices." It seemed to Lamar merely an issue of semantics, but he was willing to play the game. However, openly proclaiming his intent had not worked for him and, to Lamar's annoyance and vociferous protests, had nipped in the bud the expedition of the *Richard Cobden.* Lamar became widely known as "the gentleman who made himself famous throughout the country by his able controversy with the Secretary of the Treasury on the subject of the importation of apprentices, and the foreign apprentice trade."[13]

In his opinion, it was no worse to import slaves from Africa than from Virginia. "Did not the negroes all come originally from the coast of Africa?" he wanted to know. Southern politicians and even ministers from the pulpit preached that slavery was a positive good, for, they said, it took Africans from their heathen land and brought them to a Christian nation where they could be saved. Why then was it not a benefit to bring more Africans into such a "blessed state"?[14] As strange as it seems today, many considered that to be a valid argument.

As a consequence of his open advocacy of slave importation, Lamar's vessels inevitably fell under intense scrutiny from officials and were often searched prior to landing. Such incidents made it clear to Lamar that he would have to be surreptitious about his slave importations and take care in the future to dissociate himself publicly, as much as possible, from any planned slaving expeditions. Thus, when he and a group of seven other associates decided to purchase the 243-ton, ninety-five-foot yacht the *Wanderer* as a slaver, he was careful to have the ownership registered in a name other than his own.

Lamar had first spotted the yacht in January 1858, when it was brand new, having been completed only the previous year in Port Jefferson, Long Island, where it was viewed as a nautical masterpiece. The *Wanderer*'s original owner, Colonel John D. Johnson, a Louisiana sugar planter who summered on Long Island, New York, had enjoyed a summer cruise to New Bedford before turning south toward New Orleans. En route he paused for several days in Charleston and then at Savannah to show off his new yacht. "Among the persons who saw the *Wanderer* at Savannah, and met her owner socially, was Charles A. L. Lamar."[15] Johnson next stopped over in Brunswick to participate in the first annual regatta, where the *Wanderer* defeated all the other local vessels by her dazzling speed of up to twenty knots.[16] The yacht was not only fast but also splendid, sleek, and luxurious. Lamar's close friend and the mayor of Brunswick, Carey Wentworth Styles, presented the victory cup to Johnson, and it is possible that once again Lamar, and even the du Bignon brothers, were in attendance. In any case, Lamar made up his mind that he must have her, for she would provide excellent cover for his slaving operations.

It is amazing that Lamar and the du Bignons ever became coconspirators in such an undertaking, for in the same month he first laid eyes on the *Wanderer,* on January 9, Lamar had almost killed Henry du Bignon. It happened on a misty Saturday afternoon after the last race at the Ten Broeck racetrack in Savannah. On the day following the event, Lamar wrote to his wife, Caro, to describe an "unfortunate occurrence," which had taken place following the final heat. After "the races were over and all the ladies had left," he wrote, "I was forced to shoot Henry Dubignon."

This startling pronouncement was followed by Lamar's self-justification. "He made at me with a knife in his hand, when he was arrested by the bystanders, and taken away out of the house." But du Bignon returned about fifteen minutes later, still brandishing his knife and once again menacing Lamar, who was by now "at the dinner table in the Ladies stand." When Lamar's elderly uncle [Phinizy] "took hold of him & begged him to stop," he grabbed a champagne bottle and menaced the old man. Lamar warned him, "That old grey headed man is my uncle, & if you strike him I will kill you." Despite the threat, du Bignon struck the old man with the bottle, seemingly out of control in his anger, then "jerked up a large glass inkstand" and hurled it at Lamar. In response, Lamar took out his pistol and shot du Bignon in the face. The gun's ball penetrated "just beneath the right eye."

Amazingly, the two men were reconciled the next day, by which time they both regarded the incident as little more than a minor squabble between southern gentlemen. In fact, Lamar did not even see fit to record the nature of the disagreement. At first it seemed that no permanent harm had been done. Du Bignon had received medical attention, and doctors thought at first that he would not lose his eye. Lamar pronounced that he was "doing remarkably well & is quite cheerful & suffers but little pain—the ball is still in him."[17] Although Lamar does not clarify which "Henry Dubignon," father or son, he was "forced to shoot," it is almost certain that it was the younger man. The elder Henri, who was almost always referred to as "Col. du Bignon," was over seventy-one at this point, and it seems highly unlikely that a man of his age would seek to take on the much younger and very robust Lamar in a knife fight, even though he had been a dueling man in his earlier days.[18] The younger Henry, however, was thirty-two and a contemporary and friend of Charlie Lamar. According to a letter from W. D. Duncan, another witness to the event, writing two weeks later, du Bignon "is recovering slowly but will lose the sight of one eye." The reconciliation between du Bignon and Lamar, which relieved the tensions following the incident, may have brought the men even closer together and helped to seal the pact that led to the landing of the enslaved Africans on Jekyll Island. In any case, they became conspirators in an act that would gain notoriety up and down the eastern seaboard and as far away as New York City, where newspapers followed the unfolding of the incident with as much relish, if not more, as they did in Savannah.

It is probable that Lamar had Jekyll Island in mind as a landing place for the *Wanderer* well before the incident at the Ten Broeck racetrack. On December 26, 1857, he had written to a possible investor in one of his slaving expeditions: "I can show you, when we meet, the place or places I propose to land them,—where you can go in and out by one tide—the bar straight and deep, and no persons about—and the men, both in reference to standing in the community and reliability in case of difficulty—who own the place."[19] He was most likely speaking of John and Henry du Bignon, though, in fact, the island still belonged to their father.

In spite of all efforts at secrecy, news of the landing of the *Wanderer* spread quickly, and a deputy soon arrived at Jekyll Island and tried unsuccessfully to serve a subpoena on John Couper du Bignon, who could not be found, for complicity in the affair. In order to make a case against Lamar and the du Bignon brothers, as well as their fellow conspirators, the government had to prove that the *Wanderer* had indeed brought illegal slaves into the county. One of the essential components of such proof was to produce Africans who had been a part of the *Wanderer* "cargo." It was, thus, the job of Lamar and his cohorts to conceal any Africans who may have served as evidence. For the most part, they were successful. Perhaps the closest authorities ever came to seizing evidence was their capture on Jekyll Island of a boy about thirteen or fourteen years of age, who appeared to fit the bill. The child had been injured during the voyage and was unable to run and melt into the undergrowth of the island as others did.

Once in Savannah, where the boy was detained first in a police barracks and then, because of his weakened condition, in a slave hostel/hospital, five hundred visitors allegedly came to see the "wild African boy." The *Savannah Daily Morning News* reported him to be a youth "of rather pleasing and intelligent countenance" who "seemed to 'bear his honors' with commendable modesty and good humor."[20] But federal authorities soon lost their prize. On Christmas night two white men and one black man showed up and whisked away the boy, never to be found again.

Another thirty-six of the Africans, accompanied by three "native negroes" and an elderly African who had been in the country for many years, were taken into custody by a deputy United States marshal in Telfair County, Georgia, in early March 1859. The deputy marshal contacted his superior in Savannah to find out what he should do with his captives. The officer in Savannah telegraphed Washington for instructions, received no reply, and subsequently recommended their release.[21] Thus, once again, the necessary "evidence" had slipped through the hands of federal officials. Charlie Lamar, delighted by the apparent incompetence of his adversaries and seeming to relish the consternation of the authorities, swore out a warrant for the arrest of the deputy marshal and his men, who were forced to come to court and defend themselves against the charge of "stealing certain negroes, to wit: Reuben, Charles and Cyrus," who belonged to Lamar.[22]

Later that month Lamar, growing ever more sure of himself and bolder in his arrogance toward federal authorities, took for a drive in his carriage through the streets of Savannah a "distinguished stranger, a bright intelligent looking boy," whom he introduced to all he saw as "Corrie," a sly and not-so-subtle allusion to the *Wanderer*'s captain, William Corrie. Lamar explained to all who would listen, including one federal official who tried to look the other way, that the boy, who seemed polite and respectful, was "a *bona fide* live African" from the *Wanderer*.[23]

In spite of repeated sightings of the Africans throughout the region and the boasting of planters that they now owned a *Wanderer* slave, none from the voyage were ever recovered long enough for presentation in court. Lamar had little compunction now about openly avowing "that he was the owner of the Wanderer,—that she sailed under his directions; that by his orders she brought a cargo of slaves to this country." Although it seemed obvious to one reporter that there should be no difficulty proving Lamar's guilt, since he confessed it openly, "it is evident that Mr. Lamar expects a different verdict. He clearly looks for an acquittal,—not because he even pretends to be innocent of the acts alleged, but because he holds these laws to be unconstitutional." The reporter conceded that Lamar's "acknowledged personal influence in Savannah and [his] high-handed manner" suggested that his expectations were well-founded.[24] And indeed they were. Lamar was so sure of himself that he wrote, at one point in 1855, of his own invulnerability should he engage in the slave trade: "Gen'l Pierce and his whole Cabinet, were they here, could not convict me or my friends. That is the advantage of a small place. A man of influence can do as he pleases."[25]

Despite Lamar's posturing, the government did intend to prosecute the case. On April 22, 1859, both John and Henry du Bignon of Jekyll Island were finally indicted, and their cases were put on the docket for April 1860, to be heard by the circuit court. After a brief trial, John Couper du Bignon was found not guilty on May 18, 1860. The case against his brother Henry, who claimed not to have been living on Jekyll at the time (though he was clearly present when the *Wanderer* landed), was not prosecuted.[26]

Others involved in the incident were also indicted, among them Charlie Lamar. But one of the two federal judges who heard the case against Lamar was none other than his father-in-law, John C. Nicoll. After a distinguished career as mayor of Savannah and judge of Chatham County Superior Court, Nicoll had been appointed as a United States district judge in 1839 and given jurisdiction over the case. Despite the appearance of favoritism that his serving as judge may have, Nicoll seems to have conducted the hearing without prejudice, and it was he who ordered in the Admiralty Court that the yacht be confiscated and sold at auction. When the time came for the auction, Lamar showed up to buy it back. He opened the bidding with one dollar, anticipating that no one would have the audacity to bid against him. He was wrong. A jailer named Charles Van Horn, who allegedly had a grudge against Lamar, bid the price of the yacht higher and higher. Lamar grew increasingly angry as the price of his vessel rose. When he finally bid four thousand dollars, the auctioneer, evidently sensing trouble, quickly banged down his gavel in favor of Lamar. As soon as the bidding ended, an infuriated Lamar knocked Van Horn down, only to give him "a sort of apology—such an apology as he generally makes," according to Van Horn, the following day.[27]

At one point on the evening of May 1, 1860, Lamar and a band of followers, among them his friend Carey W. Styles (who, following his political career as mayor of Brunswick, became a journalist and helped to found the *Atlanta Constitution*), appeared at the Chatham County jail and demanded at gunpoint the release of Egbert Farnum, another of those involved in the *Wanderer* incident. They were later obliged to return him to his jailer, and Lamar and three of his accomplices, including Styles, were arrested and indicted by a federal grand jury for "the rescue of Farnum." This time they pled guilty and were fined $250 and sentenced to thirty days in jail, serving their time, according to Styles's daughter, "in Mr. Lamar's sumptuous business rooms where citizens of Savannah plied them with flowers, champagne, pate [*sic*] de foie gras, and every known extravagant indulgence."[28] While she may have exaggerated the splendor in which they lived, there is no question that their confinement was something of a farce. They had picnics, made political speeches, and generally enjoyed themselves throughout the incident. It was the only crime associated with the *Wanderer* and its crew for which Lamar would ever be found guilty.

After so much to-do, the prosecution of all the cases from the *Wanderer* episode amounted to nothing. Many Savannah residents were relieved; others, indignant. One editorial may best have captured the reaction: "If Africans are to be imported, we hope in Heaven that no more will be landed on the shores of Georgia."[29]

One might wonder why the *Wanderer* received so much national attention when the South already had so many slaves. No doubt the timing of the incident played a major role in the debate. The controversial *Dred Scott* decision of the U.S. Supreme Court, which ruled that a slave who had been living in a free state was still a slave, had been rendered only a year earlier in March 1857 and focused attention sharply on regional differences concerning slavery. The northern press depicted the *Wanderer* incident as an attempt to revive the slave trade in the South as a challenge to national sovereignty. Lamar was viewed, even in the North, as a powerful man, and the *New York Herald* commented on March 29, 1859, that "Mr. Lamar has a formidable organization at his back, of speculators and politicians, resolved at all hazards to revive this contraband African traffic within the Southern States, as a speculative enterprise and as a political movement." The writers of the article described the *Wanderer* episode as part of a "disunion programme" aimed at provoking a "sectional contest upon slavery."

Already the Union was on shaky ground over the issues of slavery and the right of the southern states to chart their own course. The United States was not yet thought of, at least in the South, as a single nation, but rather as a confederation of states that should determine their own economic base. The chasm between the two regions had grown wide and deep in the wake of the 1857 *Dred Scott* decision, recent slave rebellions, and the publication of *Uncle Tom's Cabin* in 1852. Southerners were already talking of secession from the Union. While the *Wanderer* came to represent the southern perspective in the popular northern press, another incident that occurred less than eleven months after the landing of the *Wanderer* came to represent the northern perspective in the popular mind of the South: the abolitionist John Brown, hoping to spark a slave rebellion, led a raid against the federal arsenal at Harpers Ferry in October 1859. Distrust between the two regions was gaining momentum, and these two cases—John Brown and Charlie Lamar—became causes célèbres among extremists in the two regions.

Throughout its coverage of the affair, the northern press treated Charlie Lamar with utter contempt and virtually made him the whipping boy of southern slavery. He was, proclaimed the *New York Times* on March 21, 1859, "a kidnapper of Negroes" and "a felon" who engaged in "cowardly pilfering and spiritless piracy" and who chose "to snap his fingers in the face of the law." Southern newspapers treated John Brown little better. But the fates of the two men were markedly different. John Brown was hanged and became a martyr to the abolitionist cause, while Charlie Lamar was never even brought to trial for his slave importation.

The involvement of Lamar and the du Bignon brothers in the *Wanderer* affair exemplifies two of the issues most critical to the South in the 1860 election—slavery and states' rights. Southerners continued by and large to defend their way of life on moral grounds, and the *Wanderer* episode gave them ample opportunity to remind the nation of their position.[30] As one newspaper put it, "If a cargo of Africans have been safely landed on our shores, they are much better off to-day than if they were in their native Africa, or in New England, and we hope they will be put to useful employment, and that they will be well taken care of and not sent back to African barbarism."[31] The northern press saw the incident from a vastly different perspective—as representative of the cruelties and injustice inherent in slavery and even, in certain newspapers, as evidence of the need for its abolition. The controversial presidential election of 1860 and the views of the candidates would soon loom large in discussions of these issues, displacing the *Wanderer* episode from the headlines in the nation's newspapers. But the incident would not be soon forgotten.

Tensions continued to escalate throughout the 1860 presidential election. Charlie Lamar's kinsman Howell Cobb sought the Democratic nomination for president as a favorite son from Georgia. But, thanks in part to efforts by Lamar and his followers to block his nomination, Cobb was easily defeated in the June Democratic convention in Baltimore by Stephen Douglas, following a walkout by various southern delegations.[32] One historian wrote, "Lamar did not start the Civil War, but he helped remove one more of the possibilities of its being averted."[33] When the Republican Abraham Lincoln triumphed in the general election over Stephen Douglas by winning a mere 39 percent of the vote, it was virtually inevitable that southern states would move to secede from the Union. While Lincoln was not an abolitionist and did not propose to end slavery in the southern states, he was nonetheless a "free soiler" who believed slavery to be a moral, social, and political wrong that "ought not be extended" into new states being formed.[34] Douglas, by contrast, relegated slavery to a mere legal issue, arguing for "the right of every community to judge and decide for itself, whether a thing is right or wrong, whether it would be good or evil." This freedom, he argued, was "dearer to every true American than any other under a free government."[35] He, thus, avoided the question of morality altogether.

Even so, southern states supported neither party nominee. Following a walkout from the national Democratic convention, they nominated their own candidate, John C. Breckenridge, who ran on a platform that *supported* the institution of slavery. His nomination was little more than a gesture of defiance on the part of the southern delegations, and they must have known that he had little chance of victory. Lincoln, however, demonized in southern newspapers, was from their perspective the worst possible choice.

Though some still longed for a peaceful solution to the sectional problem, others were starving for battle. Among them were members of the du Bignon family and Charlie Lamar, who wrote to his father twenty days after Lincoln's election: "We have for ten years been calling upon the abolition states, to repeal their laws & I am opposed to any farther calls—it would involve too much time & force us to live for a time, at least, under Lincoln's rule, which I shant do. If Georgia don't act promptly we, the military of Savh, will throw her into Revolution, & we will be backed by the Minute Men all through the state—We do not care for what the world may approve of—We know we are right & we'll act regardless of consequences."[36] The "Revolution" Lamar had in mind was secession from the Union and war, if need be, to free the South from what he viewed as the federal yoke.

On December 20 South Carolina became the first state to secede from the Union. Others followed shortly thereafter. Georgia was the fifth state to secede, which it did on January 19, 1861. That night guns were fired in Savannah "in honor of the glorious event, and the cheers of the delighted people," one of whom no doubt was Charlie Lamar, were heard throughout the city.[37] Southern nationalism was a rolling snowball, gathering increasing support along the way, and members of the du Bignon family, like Lamar, were its strong supporters.

On February 4, delegates met in Montgomery, Alabama, to draw up a Confederate Constitution. Although several of its clauses recognized and protected slavery, article 1, clause 1, section 9 prohibited "the importation of negroes of the African race from any foreign country." Thus, even under Confederate law, the *Wanderer* episode would have been illegal. The clause merely represented a continuation of the status quo, and southern planters, in an effort to curry favor with the French and English, by far the most important importers of southern cotton and whose aid they hoped to enlist in the war effort, were willing to concede that no additional slave importation would be accepted. It was not a major concession on their part, for such slave importation was, in fact, no longer truly needed. Enslaved Africans had been brought legally and illegally from their homelands into Georgia for more than a century, and their African American offspring, now being born into slavery, were adequate to meet the labor needs of plantation owners.

On February 9 Jefferson Davis was elected provisional president of the Confederacy, and Alexander H. Stephens was elected his vice president. Lincoln, however, did not accept the secession of southern states and sought instead to conciliate them by proclaiming in his inaugural address on March 4, "I have no purpose directly or indirectly to interfere with the institution of slavery in the States where it exists." But it was not enough for southerners eager to press the issue of states' rights.

The firing of Confederate troops on Fort Sumter, a federal fort located within Confederate territory in Charleston, South Carolina, on April 12, 1861, marked the outbreak of the seemingly inevitable war. One week later, on April 19, Lincoln ordered a naval blockade of the Confederate coast, seeking to prevent trade among the southern states and with European countries, thereby crippling their economy. His call for troops was a major turning point that compelled the upper southern states to follow those of the Deep South and secede from the Union.

The coastal area was poised to become a battlefield between Union and Confederate forces. As one Georgia resident wrote, "Many of our planters along the coast are removing their negroes to places of safety: the negroes generally are very unwilling to go, but this seems attributable to fear, local attachment, and an unwillingness to lose their pigs, poultry, &c."[38] John and Henry du Bignon were no exceptions. They abandoned the Jekyll Island plantation and took their slaves into the Georgia interior to keep them out of Union hands.[39] It is not known for certain where they spent the war years, but they may, like many planters from St. Simons, have gone inland to Waynesville or joined a refugee colony called Tebeauville, near Waycross.[40]

By July all 3,550 miles of Confederate coastline were under blockade, and little by little, the South Atlantic Blockading Squadron moved down the coast of North Carolina and South Carolina, seizing military installations along the way. The Union blockade alarmed local residents and threatened the security of Georgia's coast. Confederate leaders particularly feared the possibility that Union troops would try to seize Georgia's two primary deep-water ports—Savannah and Brunswick. The islands that flanked the entrance to Brunswick Harbor—Jekyll and St. Simons—were considered key factors in Brunswick's defense. By December the city of Brunswick had become for the most part "a deserted village." Women and children had been ordered to evacuate, and the men had been instructed to burn the town "if the Yankees passed the Batteries."[41] The batteries in question were those on the islands of Jekyll and St. Simons, which were under construction to protect Brunswick Harbor from attack. The military fortification of Jekyll Island began in October 1861, and twenty-three officers, 359 men, and six pieces of heavy artillery were settling into place. They were evidently reinforced by December, when their commander reported to Adjutant General Henry C. Wayne that he had "Six Guns—& 558 men." In all, Confederate records report 563 people present on the island.[42]

The commander of the seven companies of the Twenty-sixth Regiment of Georgia Volunteers that constituted the Jekyll forces was none other than Lieutenant Colonel Charles Augustus Lafayette Lamar, who had played such a major role in the notorious *Wanderer* episode. This was the war he had longed for and helped to bring about. He had written to his father on November 5, 1860, "I hope Lincoln may be elected. I want dissolution, & have I think contributed more than any man South for it." In preparation for the coming conflict, he notified his father in that same letter that he had received approval to organize a military company and a promise of reimbursement for his expenses from Georgia's governor, Joseph Brown. Toward that end, "I have ordered 100 pistols & 100 sabers this day of Saml Colt Hartford."[43]

When the war came, Lamar volunteered, entering the Confederate Army on May 24, 1861, having organized at his own expense a cavalry company to which he provided eight of his own horses.[44] His company was needed and accepted, and Lamar, along with his friend Carey Styles, with whom he had once been "jailed" during the *Wanderer* episode, was soon sent south to help build Georgia's coastal defense. In order to guard St. Simons Sound,

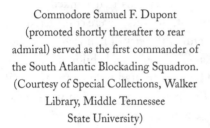

Commodore Samuel F. Dupont (promoted shortly thereafter to rear admiral) served as the first commander of the South Atlantic Blockading Squadron. (Courtesy of Special Collections, Walker Library, Middle Tennessee State University)

the gateway to Brunswick, Lamar accepted the responsibility of building fortifications on Jekyll Island, while Styles commanded the forces on St. Simons. Though Lamar would no doubt have preferred a more glorious role in the war's early years, he accepted his duty and determined to do the best job he could to build the staunchest possible fortifications on Jekyll. His time on the island, where he encountered "the most pleasant climate I ever was in," is captured in a series of letters that he wrote to his father; to his wife, Caro; and to various military leaders.[45]

Things did not go well at the outset. A measles epidemic among the men slowed the work, and some of them, as well as the engineers sent by his commanding officer, were not to Lamar's liking. When the first engineers came to Jekyll in the waning months of 1861 to design and construct the batteries at the island's north end, overlooking the sound that stood between Jekyll and St. Simons, Lamar believed they completely botched the job. He wrote a long letter to his commander, Brigadier General Hugh W. Mercer, in early December complaining of their work and so offended the chief engineer that he refused to return to the island.

The consequence was that Lamar was compelled to undertake the construction work himself. He decided that if he had to perform the task, his batteries would be the best ones that could be built. On December 18 he wrote his father, "I should not be surprised if the enemy were upon us, as you say, before my Battery is completed, if so, it will not be my fault. I

General Hugh Mercer was the superior
officer of Col. C. A. L.
Lamar while he was
in charge of the troops on Jekyll Island.
(Courtesy of the Library of Congress)

have all the heavy framing done, & have sent to Brunswick a detachment of 30 men to load the Boat with the lumber for the Bracing every day, since last Thursday, yet it has not yet been rec'd. It only reached B[runswick] yesterday, though it has been ready at the Mill for delivery for a Week!!!" Even then there were delays. Once again he sent his detachment of men to Brunswick and they came home empty handed because General Mercer had informed him that they could not unload the train cars and load the boat that particular day. In all that time, Lamar lamented, they had "accomplished nothing—save the killing of a man." Since the soldiers had nothing to do in Brunswick, they "stole off, got drunk on mean whiskey, & one killed the other." Lamar expressed his lack of confidence in General Mercer: "I am disgusted with such management—The Genl. gives an order, & no more attention is paid to it, than if it had been issued by a Private."[46]

On December 22 he complained again, this time about General Mercer's unresponsiveness to his demands, commenting that he was of no more use in Brunswick than if he had been in Savannah, "indeed, not as much so, for if he were away, Styles & myself would arrange matters to suit ourselves, & at the same time, to further the cause of the Gov'mt." It was his opinion that the general should have his headquarters on the islands rather than in his comfortable quarters in Brunswick. "If he were on the Islands, he would feel too the necessity of having them properly fortified, & with as little delay as possible. I am getting more and more disgusted every day," Lamar wrote. He was determined to finish his task, but no more than that. By late December he was truly fed up. "I will not hold on much longer," he wrote his father on December 26, "but resign & go home."[47]

His fortitude was no doubt bolstered on January 11, 1862, when an important contingent of officers arrived at Jekyll to inspect the fortifications. Among them were General Robert E. Lee and General Mercer with members of their staffs. General Lee was pleased with what he saw and seemed to think the fortifications "would effectually resist shot." They found the batteries "sunken nearly to the water level, the parapet is the earth in its natural position, and is exceedingly thick; masses of dirt, larger than most houses, are piled on the sides of these wooden case-mates; the labor performed by Col. Lamar's Battalion is really immense." However, they also found the men to be "ragged and dirty" and out of practice as soldiers since they had had no time to drill but had served rather as laborers for months. According to George Mercer, General Mercer's son, a Confederate officer who recorded the visit in his diary, some weeks would be required before the batteries were complete, but he was skeptical that they would be enough to keep the Yankees out of Brunswick. "Notwithstanding these fine Batteries, which have caused the Government so much expense and the troops so much labor, the harbor of Brunswick can be captured at any moment by any enterprising naval officer; from Jekyl and St. Andrews Sounds to the South, two creeks—Jekyll and Joynters—lead into Brunswick harbor some miles above the Batteries. These are large enough to admit good sized gun boats, and the Yankees have plenty of pilots who know every foot of the way."[48]

Lamar himself was more concerned about the need for batteries at the south end of the island as well as the pressing need for more men. He was keenly aware of his vulnerability at Jekyll: "I will do all I can to keep out of the hands of the Lincolnites, but Everybody knows there are not men enough . . . to protect this Island. Gen'l Wayne said 2000 was necessary. . . . I have less than 500 effective men. . . . I have called Gen'l Mercer's attention to the fact, but he replies, he can get no one to consent to serve on Jekyl since it has been ascertained that there is no way of retreat. I can do nothing to prevent a landing of a force on the South End, nor would I know of it, until attacked by them." He had also requested a boat for the island without any luck, though he noted that the general "has 4 or 5 in

Robert E. Lee personally inspected
the Confederate fortifications at Jekyll
Island in 1862. (Courtesy of the
Library of Congress)

Brunswick . . . and the past 3 weeks, save two or three days, one has been attending exclusively to this Island, but not remaining here a moment after landing the provisions." Because the Jekyll soldiers lacked a boat of their own, they had no control over their schedule: "It frequently happens, that the Boat does not get here until after 12 o'clock, which is the men's dinner hour. They consequently have no meat for dinner, and with the warm weather we have had, it spoils before night—for 3 days, my men had no meat to eat!! I wrote every day making complaint, but no notice has ever been taken of it."

While the construction of the island's fortifications was Lamar's primary concern, the morale of his troops was another. On December 13 he wrote to his father and enclosed two requisitions for whiskey for his men, to be paid by the paymaster, Major Erie Locke, and asked his father to take care of the bill of $21.90 for whiskey and tobacco.[49] Despite efforts to mollify his men with orders of liquor, Lamar's problems at Jekyll continued to mount. Some of the soldiers under his command had begun to show "a mutinous spirit, from the delay in paying them off." Lamar was also concerned that the troops had not been paid and determined that he would advance the money from his own pocket if necessary. When he was away on a brief trip to Savannah, leaving his lieutenant colonel in command, the situation became even more problematic. The officer in charge was judged by George Mercer to be "a man of the most yielding and unmilitary character," one who was "easy . . . temporizing—in a word a politician." Because he dared not wield any true authority over the men, who had the power to elect another officer to replace him, things had gone from bad to worse. At least, Mercer mused, Lamar, "though not an accomplished officer, is a man of great energy, and has kept his men under thorough discipline."[50]

In spite of the problems on Jekyll, Lamar remained optimistic toward the war effort as a whole. He was hoping for help from Great Britain, who in his view "need not land a Soldier—leave the land fighting to the Confederates. Let them sweep the Lincoln vessels from off the sea, & they will be conquered in less than 12 months." Like many others in the South, he judged that "The trade of G[reat] B[ritain] is dependent upon the South, not the North—and I think it high time that they had found it out." The French, too, he believed would come to their aid. "The Emperor of the French will throw his weight to open the ports of the South, as he wants Tobacco as well as Cotton."[51]

Regardless of his complaints and the inconvenience of his task, Lamar took pride in his work and planned to stick it out at least until he had completed his fortifications. "I will leave the strongest and best built sand fortifications on the whole coast—and it will stand as a monument to the working abilities of my men—If they will fight as well, we will be invincible—& they will do it—for all the vessels in Lincoln's Navy cannot batter it down."[52]

On January 31, 1862, Lamar boasted to his wife of both his and General Mercer's satisfaction with his work: "My battery is ready for any kind of a fight and only requires a few finishing touches to make it complete in every part." The general and his staff had come that day for another inspection "and expressed themselves as highly pleased with the appearance of things." Moreover, Lamar had finally convinced General Mercer of the vulnerability of Jekyll's southern shores. "The General has awakened to the importance of doing something to protect the south end of the island. He is to come down tomorrow to look out for a place to locate a battery."[53] A week later he wrote to his wife that he was "at work on the south end of the island, throwing up Earth works for a Battery there. The Genls. are at last convinced that something must be done there." In that same letter he confided to her, "I

Confederate guns were strategically positioned to guard the entrance to
Brunswick harbor. (Courtesy of the Library of Congress)

will hold on for a time to see how things work—but I am getting very tired
of this kind of life."[54]

Even as the work continued on Jekyll, events were developing that were
to make it useless. In spite of the fact that, as Major Edward C. Anderson reported, "the port of Brunswick is continually blockaded by a heavy
side-wheel steamer," the situation was becoming more perilous elsewhere.[55]
Governor Brown had expressed concern as early as November 11, 1861, that
an invasion of Savannah was an imminent danger, and he had begun requesting reinforcements.[56] On February 6, 1862, Commanding General
Robert E. Lee sent a message to the secretary of war expressing similar
concern that "The movements of the enemy for the last week indicate Savannah as the threatened point of attack."[57] He began to discuss with General Wayne the possibility of removing troops from the Brunswick area to

concentrate his strength in Savannah. The governor, although he expressed his desire to hold Brunswick, gave Lee the go-ahead on February 8:

> I have a great desire to see Brunswick remain in the possession of our troops, and should be very reluctant to see it abandoned to the enemy. If, however, it is not reasonably certain that you can with the force at your command, including the State troops, hold both Brunswick and Savannah, I do not hesitate to say that it is important that the whole force be at once concentrated at Savannah. It is the key to the State, and if it falls into the hands of the enemy, Brunswick and the balance of the coast must of course be under their control.[58]

General Lee was having difficulty obtaining a sufficient quantity of large guns to reinforce the entire Georgia coastline. He was thus compelled to make strategic choices and ultimately decided that the defense of Savannah, the most likely point of attack and the more populated area, must come first. Thus, guns intended for Jekyll were diverted to the reinforcement of Savannah. As Lamar noted in a letter to his father on February 8, Lee had "obtained two 32-pound guns for the battery, but he detained them in Savannah to defend the city. He has written for others for this island."[59]

Despite his hard work in building the batteries at Jekyll, Lamar completely understood Lee's decision, for he, too, considered Savannah the more important city to defend. Never in his correspondence do we find the kind of criticism of Robert E. Lee that he had leveled at General Mercer. He wrote to Caro on January 31: "If [Brigadier General A. R.] Lawton does not order me up [to Savannah] I do not think I can stand it down here. I must go to Savannah's assistance. It is my native city and it is my duty to be there in her hour of trial. I am willing to give up position and everything else to protect her."[60] His last letter from Jekyll Island was written to his wife on February 8, 1862. It ended with a postscript asking her to "See General Lawton and ask him to transfer me if he thinks there is any chance for a fight in or around Savannah."[61]

Two days later Robert E. Lee gave General Mercer "discretionary authority to withdraw the troops and guns from the islands to the main, should he, upon a reconsideration of the subject, hold to his opinion as to the inability of the batteries to contend with the enemy's fleet." He also sent Major Edward C. Anderson "to assist in removing the guns," if required. In a letter to the secretary of war, he explained his reasoning in disarming the batteries he had personally inspected and approved only a short time before:

Brunswick is a summer resort for certain planters, and is the terminus of a railroad extending about 60 miles into the interior, where it intersects the Savannah, Albany and Gulf Railroad. There are no inhabitants now in Brunswick, and the planters on the islands have removed their property to the interior; nor is there any population in the vicinity of Brunswick that would seem to warrant jeopardizing the men and guns necessary elsewhere. I would not, therefore, originally have occupied Saint Simon's or Jekyl, but the batteries, though small, are well placed, and the guns well distributed, and I think would defend the channel against ordinary attacks, and I exceedingly dislike to yield an inch of territory to our enemies. They are, however, able to bring such large and powerful batteries to whatever point they please, that it becomes necessary for us to concentrate our strength.[62]

The following Wednesday General Mercer, Major Anderson, and the acting ordnance officer, Mr. Harden, went to Jekyll to oversee "the disarming of the splendid Batteries." The following day the steamboat *Moulton* carried three thirty-two-pound guns to Brunswick. Three more lay on the beach. George Mercer no doubt expressed the sentiments of those present: "A feeling of melancholy came over me when I looked at the massive works we were thus abandoning; Major Barnwell had declared they were the finest on the coast, and Major Anderson pronounced them stronger than Fort Pulaski."[63]

Within the week Lamar received his own orders to withdraw, and on February 16 General Mercer reported that the withdrawal from Jekyll was complete and that the departure from St. Simons was under way. Lee was concerned now that Brunswick was defenseless and that if it fell "into the possession of the enemy, its convenient harbor, salubrious climate, and comfortable buildings might tempt him to hold it for the continuance of the war." For these reasons, he contended, "I propose to destroy it."[64]

Before burning any parts of Brunswick, however, General Lee wanted the acquiescence of the governor of Georgia. Lee informed Governor Brown on February 18 of the withdrawal and relocation of guns and troops from St. Simons and Jekyll and requested permission to destroy the city of Brunswick. He noted, "I am unwilling to order the destruction of the town without the knowledge and approbation of your excellency."

The governor replied three days later, expressing satisfaction "that you have removed the troops from the islands and that you now have the guns

Confederate guns were removed from Jekyll Island to reinforce
the defense of Savannah. (Courtesy of the Library of Congress)

at Savannah." As to the burning of Brunswick, he said, "if my own house
were in Brunswick I would certainly set fire to it, when driven from it by
the enemy, rather than see it used by them as a shelter. We should destroy
whatever the military necessities require."[65] Thus, retreating Confederate
troops, as they prepared to move north to Savannah, set strategic fires in
Brunswick, burning especially sites that could benefit the enemy. The rail-
way station and the docks were still ablaze as Union troops approached the
city on March 10, where they "hoisted the American flag on the Oglethorpe
House."[66]

Federal forces quickly moved a naval division, consisting of three ships,
under the command of S. W. Godon, into the area. The *Mohican*, the
Pocahontas, and the *Potomska* crossed St. Simons Sound on March 8, an-
choring at sundown some two miles from the forts that commanded the
channel. On the following morning Commander Godon discovered that

The New-York Times.

NEW-YORK, TUESDAY, MARCH 11, 1862.

a stream of pure water, and a grist-mill, were near The barracks, with their contents, and large quantities of commissary stores and camp furniture, were fired a few days since, when the rebels heard the coming of Yankee cannon through these mountainous glens. The stables are still standing, and the mill is lading secession wheat and corn for Union troops. sent 100 bloated game cocks, with silver gaffs, are that is left to show that this has been made classic round.

Pierce and his army have industriously reported rough this whole country the wrongs which would inflicted upon the unprotected persons who remained at home, and the consequence has been that th, women and children are fleeing from us as high the angel of destruction were our attendant. few days ago, when our troops entered the town of entonville, the women shrieked and fainted with rror, and would not believe that they would not all butchered at once. We are now waiting for our commissary trains and some reinforcements, when e shall move on ; but all hopes of bagging the man to never retreats are abandoned. By the march of a two armies the country is left in ruin and desolaon.

Bentonville and most of Fayetteville have been laid ashes—the first by our men, because one of their comrades, who had been taken prisoner, was found in sink with his brains dashed out. The latter the enmy have burned, with large quantities of powder nd ammunition.

To-day the weather is like the middle of April in ew-York, although it has been quite cold. The ads are very muddy, and rapid movements will be nnossible without some improvement. No New orker can imagine how we live here. Our bills of Je would astonish, if not disgust some of our episires. Facilities for writing are limited. A report in circulation that one of our commissary trains as been cut off. One of our messengers, with mail nd dispatches, has never been heard from.
ST. LOUIS.

THE REBELS FALLING BACK

Their Lines Along the Potomac Being Withdrawn.

Evacuation of Centreville, Winchester, and Other Important Points.

Their Batteries on the Lower Potomac Deserted.

EVIDENCES OF A GREAT PANIC

Splendid Pieces of Artillery Left in Position.

SPECIAL DISPATCH FROM WASHINGTON.
WASHINGTON, Monday, March 10.

My dispatch last night stated that the appearance of rebel scouts near Vienna was a feint, to cover their retreat. The latter part of the message failed to reach you—why, I know not, as it would have informed you of the great event that to-day convulses Washington—the general abandonment by the rebels of their Potomac line of defences.

From Winchester on the west, to the Cockpit batteries on the east, covering a front of many miles, the rebels have precipitately withdrawn. Their retreat bears many evidences of a panic. Splendid guns were left in position in the Potomac batteries—some of them spiked, some not harmed. Valuable ammunition and stores were left at some places, that came into quiet possession of our troops. It can hardly be doubted that their wary leaders, as usual, obtained full information from traitors among us of the impending advance of our great army, and that they fled to get out of danger.

There seems to be uncertainty enough whether the rebels have evacuated Manassas, but they are certainly gone from Centreville—at all events, after a diligent search in the extensive trenches there, late this afternoon, none were found.

COMMODORE DUPONT'S OPERATIONS IN GEORGIA AND FLORIDA.

Diagram Showing Brunswick, Ga., its Harbor and Channel, and its Relation to the Adjoining Islands and Coast.

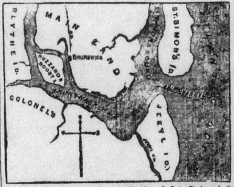

Diagram Showing Fernandina, Fla., the Location of Fort Clinch, and the Character of the Adjoining Coast.

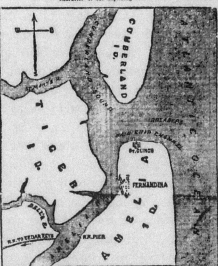

Outline Map Showing the Relations of Brunswick, Ga., and Fernandina, Fla., to Each Other, and to the Contiguous Regions.

OPERATIONS ON THE CO

Brilliant Successes of the Fleet Commodore Dupont.

Capture of Brunswick, Ga. Fernandina, Fla.

Inglorious Flight of the R from Both Places.

Cannon and Munition War Captured.

Old Fort Clinch "Retaken, Hel Possessed."

An Exciting Race Between a G and a Railroad Train.

BALTIMORE, Monday, Mc
The United States steam gunboat A Capt. Lanier, arrived here this morning, fth Fernandina, Fla., bringing Capt. Davis, h Officer of the South Atlantic Squadron, ua dispatches from Commodore Dupont to t Department, announcing the capture of Fe and Brunswick by the fleet under his c

We are indebted to Capt. Davis for an t the operations of the fleet since it left Po about the 1st of March, on what was anno an important expedition, the place of destin ing been held back at the request of the Gov

The first point of the coast approached b was the town of Brunswick, Ga., the enemy ing their works and precipitately flying a proach of the gunboats. It was taken sion of and gunboats left in charge. This Government the control of the whole coast gia from South Carolina to Florida.

Brunswick being disposed of, the fle twenty miles further to Cumberland So entrance to the harbor of Fernandina, fleet entered Cumberland Sound in the order :

The Mohican, Flagship of Com. Dupont.	
The Ottawa.	The James A
The Seminole.	The Florida.
The Pawnee.	The Seneca.
The Flag.	The Huron.
The Bienville.	The Pembina
The Alabama.	

They were followed by the small arm ers Isaac Smith, Potomska, Penguin and Eli came the armed revenue cutter Henrietta, u transports Empire City, Boston, Belvidere, South, George's Creek, and the brig Gen. Wr

When the expedition came in sight Clinch the rebels were discerned mak flight, but they tried two or three o the batterie guns of the fort. The the fleet, however, caused a hasty evacua Fort Clinch was immediately taken posses the flag of the Union raised on an old staf been so long disgraced by traitor colors.

This is the first of the old Southern f Union that has been recovered since the tion of President Lincoln, declaring they restored to the Union.

As the fleet approached the fort a care was observed leaving Fernandina the track runs some three miles shore of the Sound, Commodore Dupon the gunboats in pursuit of her. An exciting place, the steamer throwing shells at the f some of them falling in such close pres the batteries on Jekyll and St. Simons, protecting Brunswick Harbor, like the city itself, had been abandoned. He dispatched three armed boats to take possession of them. Lieutenant Henry W. Miller of the *Mohican* was assigned to seize the batteries on Jekyll Island.

On March 10, exactly one month after Lee's decision to evacuate Jekyll, Miller reported to his commanding officer: "I landed with the rifle company and marines of this vessel and hoisted the flag over the rebel batteries on Jekyl Island, guarding St. Simon's entrance. . . . I dispatched a scouting party to ascertain if possible if any of the enemy remained on the island. A number of log huts on a deserted camp ground were the only sign of the enemy they discovered."[67] In a report dated that same day, Commander Godon elaborated on the findings noted in Lieutenant Miller's dispatch. He described "the fort on Jekyl Island" as "a sand work with five casemates finished, covered with railroad iron, and very well built, and two unfinished casemates, the iron rail ready to be put up." Godon judged that the two forts on St. Simons and Jekyll would have been extremely effective in their defense. "These two forts commanded the channel for a long distance. . . . They would have given a number of vessels severe trouble in getting beyond them."[68] Charlie Lamar would have been proud of the assessment.

Apparently assuming that all Confederate troops had withdrawn, leaving Brunswick completely defenseless, the *Pocahontas* and the *Potomska* moved into the Turtle River without incident. The following day, March 11, the *Pochahontas* returned and anchored outside of town, and the captain sent out sailors in small boats to forage for food, particularly beef, for the men. But some of the Confederates still remained in the area. When the Union troops reached the shore in yawl boats and began to slaughter some of the cattle they found on the shore of Buzzard Island, south of Brunswick, a small contingent of Confederate soldiers opened fire. What followed has been referred to rather gloriously in at least one account as "the Battle of Brunswick." It is in fact more accurately described as "the skirmish of Brunswick." As one young Confederate soldier named Gabriel Farmer wrote to his mother, "We [killed] 5 or 6 of the Yankees and [they] never hurt non[e] of us." The Union troops returned fire with equal vigor, but they had been caught in the open and made as quick a retreat as possible, rowing their small boats with all their might. It was an exciting moment for the young soldier, who wrote, "i be[e]n tel[l] you [it was] live times for a while."[69] The casualties he mentioned were remarkably accurate. According to the official report of Commander Godon, only two men were instantly killed. Two others would eventually die of their wounds, and an additional two received less serious injuries.[70] The Confederates then withdrew and continued their march toward Savannah. It was the only fighting that Brunswick saw during the war.

On March 17 Commander Godon "entered Jekyl Creek and proceeded to Dubignon's place, where I discovered a deserted battery of three guns to command that stream and the remains of a camp of some two hundred men. A considerable quantity of cattle remains on the island, but very wild on our approach."[71] Evidently the concern of George Mercer that the vulnerable point would be Jekyl Creek had at some point been heeded, and Lamar's men had constructed two batteries at the north end, one to command St. Simons Sound and one to protect any backdoor entry to Brunswick Harbor by way of the creek. There is no indication that the Union troops ever discovered the south end batteries, though they soon set to work to destroy those at the north end.[72]

Two days later, on March 19, Commodore Samuel F. Dupont (soon to be an admiral), the flag officer from a newly arrived vessel, the *Wabash,* submitted another report on the fortifications of Jekyll Island, noting that the two batteries he found were "of much greater strength" than those he had seen on St. Simons:

> The one farthest seaward and commanding the main channel was a bomb-proof work, constructed of Palmetto logs, sand-bags, and railroad iron, well supported and braced from the interior with massive timbers. It had mounted three casemated guns, though these, their carriages, and all the ammunition had been removed.
>
> The other battery, 400 yards landward, consisted of two casemates and an earthwork capable of mounting four guns en barbette. A magazine and a hotshot furnace were attached. Both St. Simon's and Jekyl Island had been deserted.[73]

On March 31 Commander Godon ordered Lieutenant George B. Balch, commander of the U.S.S. *Pocahontas,* to assemble "as large a force as you can, [and] at once remove the railroad iron from the bombproof fort of Jekyl Island and place it in some convenient spot above high-water mark for shipment, after which blow up the casemates."[74] The work, carried out in fact under the supervision of Commander Edmund Lanier from the U.S.S.

Officers and members of the crew of the U.S.S. *Pocahontas*.
(Courtesy of the United States Army Military History Institute [USAMHI])

Commodore Samuel F. Dupont, shown here (second from left) aboard the flagship
U.S.S. *Wabash*, was responsible for giving orders to Union sailors to seize Jekyll Island.
(Courtesy of the USAMHI)

The U.S.S. *Wabash* at full sail, painted by Ray Clary.
(Courtesy of the Naval Historical Foundation)

Alabama, had begun by April 10, when Lanier reported that he and his men were at work on Jekyll "getting the railroad iron from the forts to the beach." He estimated there would be "125 tons of this iron."[75] He removed, in all, 960 iron bars from the Jekyll forts.[76] According to some reports, former slaves living in a colony on an abandoned St. Simons plantation did the work of destroying the Confederate fort, but Lanier refers to the workers only as "my men."

Union troops burned what remained of the Jekyll forts on April 21, according to the diary of a naval surgeon, Dr. Jacob Cohen, who visited the island twice. During his second visit on April 29, he describes a leisurely walk on the island:

> Taking a short cut through the brush & underwood we emerged into a military road leading inland from behind the fort. This was a very excellent road and we continued along it for a couple of miles till it brought us to the late encampment of a Georgia regiment commanded by a Col. Lamar of Savannah. . . .
>
> The campground had been selected in a very pleasant and agreeable location. A number of pine trees bordered it in front and along this border were a number of wells of good water. There was a commodious parade ground and in the rear plenty of shade. The quarters were all substantially constructed wooden huts, and the cabins of the officers were furnished with convenient

fireplaces. In the tent of the commanding officer the fireplace was formed with half of an old iron pot and the chimney was built of brick. Every thing seemed to have been complete here. There were cattle pens and slave houses, and all the huts were built of good planking.

We rested here awhile, and then followed a road which within a few hundred yards brought us to an old ruin, formerly the family mansion of the Du-Bignons'[,] the owners of the island. [77]

The road he is describing is Major Horton Road, and the house, as a later visit by another naval officer makes clear, is the old tabby house first built by William Horton and occupied at least for a time by Christophe Poulain du Bignon and his family. Although members of the du Bignon family constructed other dwellings on the island before the Civil War, all have disappeared without a trace.

Jekyll Island continued to be an object of curiosity for the crews of blockading vessels as the war continued, perhaps because of the notoriety it had gained at the time of the *Wanderer* incident. On January 26, 1863, another naval surgeon, Dr. Samuel Pellman Boyer, recorded in his diary, "The Captain and myself in the 1st cutter (Dick Welsh, coxswain) paid a visit to Jakel Island." He made no mention of the batteries that had now been destroyed, but focused instead on

the ruins of an old camping ground. From the inscription on the boxes laying around the camp, I seen that a Rebel company commanded by Capt. Lamar of Savannah, Ga., occupied said ground ere the arrival of our gunboats. The walls of a large building also can be seen on said place. Adjoining said building, say 40 rods from the house is a family graveyard. Therein are buried three persons by the name of Dubignon, one age 70, one 76, and the other 36 years. All three are entombed in fine graves . . . with the tombstones horizontal and consisting of marble. [78]

Those graves can still be seen on Jekyll Island today. His record is important in helping to clarify the approximate location of the Confederate camp on the island.

Upon Lamar's return to Savannah, he requested that two additional companies—one from Tattnall County and one from Bulloch County—be assigned to his regiment. Evidently he did not get the two companies he wanted, for within the next two weeks, he tried to resign his commission "in

consequence of rank in-justice [*sic*] having been done me and my Battalion."
However, as he noted, "my resignation has not been accepted yet, & the
Genls. say wont be," but he indicated his intention to call on the Secretary
of War "unless damages are repaired." At the moment he was serving on
Jackson's staff as a "volunteer aid," with the responsibility of overseeing the
building of a gunboat.[79] He was finally successful in resigning his commission on April 2, 1862. He must have persuaded Confederate officials that he
could better serve the Confederacy as a civilian blockade-runner who would
export southern cotton and import the goods that Georgia so desperately
needed.

Working with his father, Lamar established "a state-subsidized blockade-
running line" that would be known as the Georgia Importing and Ex-
porting Company.[80] By January 9, 1863, he had already contracted with
English shipbuilders for three side-wheel steamers with speeds up to seventeen miles an hour when fully loaded. With these, he would undertake
his blockade-running activities. But he was eager for some official recognition for his activities, and he began at that time to appeal to Governor
Brown, whom he much admired, "requesting an official letter of recommendation." As he explained his intent to General Wayne, "I want no letters of credit. I simply want from an official source, a statement of who
& what I am, and that I am worthy of every confidence."[81] On March 1,
1864, the governor officially appointed Lamar "the Agent of the State of
Georgia, to take charge and conduct said importation and exportation for
the State."[82] Lamar was content with that, for what he had wanted above
all was simply to be employed by the state, "to prevent any interference by
the C[onfederate] S[tates] Gov'mt officials."[83]

With the assistance of Lloyd Bowers of Columbus, Lamar took on the
task "of raising money in England and France, buying, in all, five steamers
fast enough to evade Federal blockaders, and arranging for British agents to
handle the European end of things."[84] All of Lamar's vessels successfully ran
the blockade, most of them more than once. The most successful was the
Little Hattie, which made eight round trips.[85] Blockade-running provided
a new kind of danger and adventure for Lamar, but it was not a role that he
particularly relished. He was already growing weary and homesick, and the
news of repeated battles won by the Union weighed heavily on him.

As the war effort seemed clearly to favor a Union victory, Charlie Lamar
returned to Georgia to rejoin the Confederate Army. He continued to

believe in the inevitability of a southern victory and wrote optimistically to his wife as late as February 14, 1865, "I have no fears of ultimate results. We are bound to triumph in the end." By this time Savannah had already fallen to the Union, and Lamar's father, in an effort to preserve his assets, had taken the oath of allegiance to the Union on January 6, 1865, to Charlie's utter disgust: "He has disgraced the name of Lamar. . . . I would not have taken the oath for all the cotton in the South."[86]

Lamar, who served the final days of the war on the staff of his old adversary, Major General Howell Cobb, made his last visit to Savannah the week of March 16, 1865. The general had assigned him to carry a letter to General Cuvier Grover, commander of the Union forces in Savannah, proposing to negotiate an exchange of prisoners.[87] Even though Lamar's wife was no longer in Savannah but had taken refuge with relatives inland, he was no doubt eager to visit the city. He must have been horrified at what he saw there—Yankees in the fine old houses, including his own, and camped on the magnificent Savannah squares; Confederate prisoners confined at Fort Pulaski; and many buildings reduced to rubble. He returned to Cobb's unit more determined than ever to fight to the very end in an effort to defeat the northern armies that had overrun his state and his home. The one city that had not been touched by Union forces was Columbus. It was there that Cobb's troops would make their final stand.

Even after Robert E. Lee conceded defeat at Appomattox on April 9, 1865, the South could not bring herself to accept the fact that it was over. Incredibly, Jefferson Davis urged the Confederate forces to fight on, and, despite the fact that Lamar's friends encouraged him to go home to his wife, who had just had another daughter, a little girl he would never see, he remained in Columbus to fight what some have called "the last battle of the Civil War." Columbus, which lay on the border between Georgia and Alabama, was a key target in the sights of the Union general James H. Wilson. Factories in Columbus made rifles, revolvers, swords, cannons, saddles, shoes, and textiles, all of which the city had regularly supplied to Confederate troops throughout the war effort. There, southerners from Georgia and Alabama planned to make a "resolute defense."[88]

On the night of April 16, on a bridge across the Chattahoochee River, fighting for a cause that was already lost, Charlie Lamar met his death. His wife received the news that he had been killed and then a second letter saying that he had been seen in Macon, where Cobb and his men had retreated

Fleming Grantland du Bignon, the son
of Charles Joseph du Bignon, married
Caroline Nicoll Lamar, the daughter
of C. A. L. Lamar, in 1874. He had a
distinguished career, becoming president
of the Georgia Senate in 1888.
(Courtesy of Henry Howell)

after the battle of Columbus. It was the sad task of J. O. A. Clark to have to inform Lamar's widow that it was in fact the second letter that was "a mistake. . . . He was killed in the battle of Columbus . . . bravely fighting the enemy."[89]

She received details of his death in a letter from Charlie's aunt Rebecca, with whom, as a boy, he had survived the sinking of the *Pulaski*. Rebecca had learned the news from the wife of Howell Cobb. Charlie had "acted very gallantly," she said, in the confusion of the retreat, and when the Confederates realized that they could not hold out, "he became separated from his friends, was ordered to surrender which he did, ordered to dismount which he did, he was then asked for his side arms and he had just replied that he had none when some foolish fellow shot off a pistol near and the Yankee having his already cocked & supposing that Charles had fired shot him dead."[90]

The name of Charlie Lamar, because of both the *Wanderer* episode and the Confederate occupation, will forever be linked to the history of Jekyll Island. One final event connects the family of C. A. L. Lamar to that of the Jekyll Island du Bignons. Less than a decade after his death, a marriage took place on November 26, 1874, between his daughter, Caroline Nicoll Lamar, and Fleming Grantland du Bignon, the son of Charles Joseph du Bignon and the nephew of John Couper and Henry du Bignon.[91] The

young Fleming du Bignon, said to be "possessed of all the dash of the cavalier that dazzles and fascinates," would go on to a distinguished career as
a lawyer and legislator, serving first as representative and then as senator,
rising to president of the Georgia Senate in 1888.[92] The mingling of the two
bloodlines—Lamar and du Bignon—symbolized the emergence of a new
generation, a veritable phoenix rising from the ashes of the Old South that
would prosper in the new era. Unfortunately, that would not be the case for
the older generations of du Bignons who survived the war.

CHAPTER SEVEN

Aftermath

The South found her jewel in the toad's head
of defeat. The shackles that had held her in
narrow limitations fell forever when the shackles
of the Negro slave were broken.

HENRY GRADY, 1886

HE END OF THE CIVIL WAR had left a devastated South. Unlike many families, the du Bignons of Jekyll Island had lost no close relatives in the conflict, though two of Henri du Bignon's sons, Charles and William, and at least one of his grandsons had served in the Confederate army. How the various family members dealt with the war's aftermath would depend not only on their economic resources but also on their personal adaptability and, to some extent, their generation.

Henri du Bignon, who had been born two years before the French Revolution, survived the war, but not for long. As other Brunswick residents returned to their homes, he too came back with his young family to his home at Ellis Point, between the marshes of Yellow Bluff Creek and what was by then known as du Bignon Creek. But Henri was elderly now and must have realized that he did not have long to live. On October 1, 1866, just two months before his death, he drew up his last will and testament. His signature on the document is unsteady, lacking the assertive assurance of his earlier signings. He was seventy-nine years old. His wife Mary had just turned thirty-six. The provisions of his will left all his possessions to Mary and her children, with a token bequest for her mother, Sarah, and the offspring of his liaison with her. He did not mention in his will any of his children by Amelia Nicolau.

Newton S. Finney (ca. 1863), was the
husband of Henri du Bignon's
granddaughter Josephine. He was but one
of the family members who fought for the
Confederacy during the Civil War.
(Courtesy of Doris Finney Liebrecht)

In all likelihood, that is what they had expected, because in 1863, in the
midst of the Civil War, the children by his first wife had evidently persuaded
their father to deed over to them his property on Jekyll Island. It had been
one of the conditions of his marriage agreement with their mother that their
island property would pass to Henri and Amelia's heirs, and their sons John
and Henry had, after all, taken care of the Jekyll plantation as best they
could for a decade after their father moved away.[1] Just why Henri made the
division of the island at this particular time is uncertain. It seems probable
that the offspring of his first family, alarmed by his growing second legitimate family (he would have at the time of his death fifteen living children),
chose that moment to invoke the prenuptial agreement between their parents. They may have felt that their chances of getting their father to give
them the Jekyll property were greater while the island was still in the hands
of the Union and its fate was, at best, uncertain.

In any case, to his three surviving sons, Charles, John Couper, and Henry,
in consideration of his "natural love and affection," he gave over three major

Charles Joseph du Bignon, one of the
children of Henri du Bignon, to whom
he gave Jekyll Island in 1863.
(Courtesy of Henry Howell)

parcels of the island, reserving a small plot of land for his oldest living and only unmarried daughter, Eliza.[2] To his eldest son, Charles, he deeded the southernmost portion of the island; to his second son, John Couper, he gave the land north of the beach road up to an area known as Rock Bois; to his youngest son and namesake, Henry Charles, he signed over the northern-most extremity of the island north of Rock Bois. Eliza's portion was only a thirty-acre plot known as Bryan's Old Field.[3] Relinquishing the property may have seemed of little consequence to Henri at the time, for when he divided the land on August 3, 1863, the very existence of the nation was at stake, and the island had been deserted by all members of the du Bignon family and abandoned to the Yankees. No one knew what the war would bring or that, at the end of the conflict, all their lives would be irrevocably changed, bringing about a new chapter in the island's unfolding story.

At his death on December 7, 1866, Henri was not brought back to the Jekyll Island cemetery for burial, and his resting place is unknown. He left his widow, Mary, with five minor daughters. Virginia, at fifteen, was the oldest and could provide some help to her mother. Emily, at twelve, was still a playmate for her seven-year-old sister Agnes, while Valeria was only four, and Gertrude, still a toddler, had recently celebrated her second birthday. He also left behind an estate that, in spite of his efforts to make it simple, would inevitably be complicated by his three families of legitimate and il-legitimate children. The complexities would remain for future generations to sort out.

On the surface the estate seemed simple enough. To Mary he left a $150 annuity and to the girls his property at Ellis Point and stock in the Central Rail Road and Banking Company. He set aside $50 for Mary's mother, Sarah (who, on April 19, 1857, had married a man named Willis Reddick), as well as for each of his three children by her, Leonidas, William, and Rosalia.[4] Leonidas and William had lived with Henri and their stepmother and half-sister Mary, and they had taken the name of du Bignon, but Henri referred to them in his will as Leonidas and William Aust, underscoring their illegitimacy.[5] In 1875, nine years after his death, both men changed their last names to Turner, as if to erase the name of their father forever from their lives. In the Turner family Bible, someone has obliterated with a sharp instrument the name of "William du Bignon" and replaced it with that of "William Turner."[6]

The passing of Henri du Bignon, which coincided so closely with the end of the Civil War, was a clear symbol that the Jekyll Island plantation era was ended. The period of Reconstruction that followed the war was a time of painful adjustment for Georgians, black and white alike. The entire dynamic of social and economic relations had changed dramatically, and many formerly wealthy plantation owners, like the du Bignon brothers, found themselves, at least for a time, without land, without workers, and without a livelihood, while for the first time, former slaves tasted the sweetness of freedom.

Abandoned by planters during the war, the coastal islands, Jekyll among them, had been seized by the federal government for the relocation of displaced freedpeople. During the final months of the war, on January 16, 1865, General William Tecumseh Sherman issued his Special Field Order No. 15, allowing the former slaves to settle on the Sea Islands, to the exclusion of their former owners: "in the settlements hereafter to be established, no white person whatever, unless military officers and soldiers, detailed for duty, will be permitted to reside; and the sole and exclusive management of affairs will be left to the freed people themselves, subject only to the United States military authority and the acts of Congress."[7]

Although the colony of freedpeople on St. Simons used Jekyll Island for some of its food supply, digging sweet potatoes from the du Bignon garden and taking advantage of any cattle that may have been left behind by Union soldiers, there is no evidence that any portion of Jekyll land was actually deeded over to former slaves by the Freedmen's Bureau. But it would have mattered little in the long run, for after the assassination of Abra-

Former slaves who lived in a colony on St. Simons, after
they were freed by the Union troops, used Jekyll Island
as a food supply, where they dug sweet potatoes from
the du Bignon garden. (Photo by Rudolf Eickemeyer Jr.,
from *Down South* [New York: R. H. Russell, 1900].
Courtesy of Hargrett Rare Book and Manuscript
Library, University of Georgia Libraries)

ham Lincoln on April 14, 1865, the new president, Andrew Johnson, soon
nullified the Sherman Field Order. The disappointment of the freed men
and women no doubt made the transition even more difficult for Sea Island
plantation owners and their former slaves alike.

When John and Henry du Bignon returned to Jekyll Island after the war,
they found overgrown cotton fields, houses in disrepair, remnants of the old
Confederate bunkers, and perhaps a few stray cattle, now gone wild. The
younger generations of du Bignons who lived on the mainland seemed, for
the most part, to take the postwar changes in stride. Men like John Eugene
du Bignon, the son of their deceased brother Joseph, and Newton Finney,
the husband of their niece Josephine, saw the rebuilding of the postwar
South as an opportunity to restore their fortunes. But for the older generation, reared in a plantation economy, it was harder to adjust. Even Charles

du Bignon, at fifty-nine, the older brother of John and Henry, who had had a successful career as a lawyer and legislator before the war and who had taken over the management of the large plantation in Baldwin County that his wife, Ann Virginia Grantland, had inherited from her father, struggled to survive. John, who was fifty-three, and even Henry, who turned forty the year after the war ended, seemed to have lost heart. They were unable to adapt to the times, and for them only hardship lay ahead. What they wanted above all was a return to their old way of life—but that life was over.

One member of their family describes their reaction: "When they returned to Jekyll everything was in ruins." The "wealth they all had while living there" was but a memory now.[8] They found only devastation on the island. Their land, their slaves, and their plantation, where they had grown Sea Island cotton and raised cattle, had been their primary assets and livelihood. Without workers, the fields lay fallow. They no longer had sufficient laborers to plant, hoe, and pick the cotton, or to renew the land each year by hauling mud from the marshes to renourish the sandy soil that grew the silky long-staple cotton for which the region was known. Even if they could find the workers, they had little means to pay them now. Any monetary benefits they may still have had from the *Wanderer* expedition had been lost as Confederate money and bonds became worthless. Times were particularly difficult for planters on the Sea Islands, where cotton production fell steadily in the coming decades. By 1871 it stood at a mere 20 percent of its 1866 level, and in desperation island planters turned to harvesting timber and depending even more than they had before the war on raising livestock.[9] But neither of these occupations was sufficient for the brothers to keep their land, which continued to require the outlay of annual taxes and, thus, became a financial liability.

For the first time, John and Henry found themselves to be not only part of the senior generation but also veritable relics of an Old South that had ended with the war. Once they were able to return to Jekyll, both men were reluctant to leave the island again and try their hands at something new, and they were perhaps even incapable of doing so. Plantation life was all they knew, and both clung to Jekyll Island as long as possible, for it was their home. The brothers sought ways to try to maintain their lifestyle and status as gentlemen, but without resources it seemed impossible.

One of the last visitors to the island while it was still clearly in the hands of John and Henry was Nathaniel Bishop, who wrote of his visit to Jekyll in

1875 during an odyssey from Quebec to the Gulf of Mexico. He described it as "wild and picturesque Jekyl Island, upon which the two bachelor brothers Dubignon live and hunt the deer, enjoying the free life of lords of the forest. Their old family mansion, once a haven of hospitality, where the northern tourist and shipwrecked sailor shared alike the good things of this life with the kind host, was used for a target by a gunboat during the late war, and is now in ruins." His only other comment about Jekyll Island was to remind his reader that it was there "twenty years ago, at midnight" that the slave ship *Wanderer* landed "her cargo of African Negroes, the capital for the enterprise being supplied by three southern gentlemen, and the execution of the work being intrusted [*sic*], under carefully drawn contracts, to Boston parties."[10] Even though his chronology and facts were not quite accurate, his comments suggest that the memory of the *Wanderer* still clung to Jekyll Island.

While on the surface John and Henry may have seemed "lords of the forest" to a visiting stranger, the realities of the du Bignon brothers were quite otherwise. Without sufficient labor, they could no longer farm the land profitably, and few former slaves seem to have returned to Jekyll Island, as they had to St. Simons and Sapelo, which some of them had never left. Some of the planters on the mainland were able to hire free labor in an effort to restore their fortunes, but on a small island like Jekyll, such arrangements were far more difficult. John and Henry seemed at a total loss for what to do.

One former slave who did return was the freedwoman who had taken the name of Sylvia du Bignon. She came back to the island to live with John Couper du Bignon, whose children she had borne since she was about fifteen and John was in his early thirties. Theirs was a relationship that required the refuge that only the island plantation, cut off from prying eyes and gossipy neighbors, could provide. It endured more than twenty-five years, and together the couple had six children. Whether Sylvia and the children were bound to John by ties of affection or only by those of need is impossible to say, but for a time after the war they all lived together as a family. The older sons, Robert and Joseph, no doubt worked with their father in the fields and did what they could to help.[11] In 1870, as the census record clearly indicates, John and Sylvia were living openly together on Jekyll Island. John du Bignon is listed as the white head of the household, while other members of the household, all mulattos, included Sylvia du Bignon, age 40; Robert du Bignon, age 25; Joseph du Bignon, age 15;

Caroline du Bignon, age 11; Cecelia du Bignon, age 8; Cornelia du Bignon, age 6; and George du Bignon, age 1.[12] Unless John freed his mistress and their children before or during the Civil War—and no record survives to indicate that he did—all but the youngest, George, were born into slavery.

The fact that, although they were free after the war, they chose to return to the island with their former master, as well as the long duration of the relationship between Sylvia and John, suggests that the bond between them was a reasonably committed one. John du Bignon also apparently cared for the children and publicly accepted responsibility for them in a "debenture" drawn up on November 8, 1872, on behalf of their "mother and natural guardian," Sylvia du Bignon, and agreed to by John, in which he expresses his intent to "clothe, Educate, and maintain said children until they are twenty one."[13] All the minor children are listed by name in the document. Only Robert, who was already twenty-seven by this time, was not mentioned. Their mother, Sylvia, signed the debenture agreement with an X. From that point she disappears from public record.

Although John did not openly acknowledge paternity of the children in the debenture, descendents who can trace their ancestry back to the union of John and Sylvia still live in Brunswick today.[14] Former slaves sometimes did apprentice their children to their previous owners if they believed in earnest that the person would provide care that their own position could not afford, but John, in his current financial situation, would not likely take on such a responsibility, especially for the son born after his mother was already free, without some compelling reason for doing so. The relationship suggests an extraordinary degree of commitment to the children and a particular attachment to Sylvia. That same sense of responsibility toward their mistresses or offspring, however limited it may have been, had been manifested in earlier generations by John's father and grandfather. John du Bignon was by no means the first member of the du Bignon family to sire children among their enslaved women. It is almost certain, for example, that Christophe Poulain du Bignon was the father of at least one child by his slave Maria Theresa. In all probability, it was one of the du Bignons' sons who fathered the "free born mulatto child, named Harriot, of about five years of age," for whom Christophe and Marguerite stood as sponsors at her baptism in 1811.[15] We know that Henri also fathered another child, Charlotte, described in the records of the Cathedral of St. John the Baptist as "a free colored person and illegitimate child of Henry Du Bignon."[16]

Charlotte Cooper du Bignon, wife of
John and Sylvia du Bignon's oldest son,
Robert, was the mother of the last
du Bignon children born on Jekyll Island.
(Courtesy of Marian D. Payne)

Although the du Bignon men clearly took advantage of enslaved women, they also seemed to provide a modicum of care for at least some of the children they fathered. Christophe Poulain du Bignon freed his mistress and her child in his will; he and Marguerite saw to the freedom of the child, Harriot; Henri himself apparently saw to the baptism of his freeborn mulatto daughter, Charlotte, whose free status was reiterated in the Catholic Church records; and John accepted, on paper at least, the responsibility for the welfare of his children with Sylvia until they reached adulthood.

The eldest son of this union, Robert du Bignon, was already a married man in his midtwenties by the time the debenture was signed and was thus excluded from the agreement, but, even so, he did not lose touch with John. Even in 1880, after the family had scattered and when John du Bignon, according to the census records of that year, was living alone in his household at Jekyll, Robert remained nearby. He had become a tenant farmer on Jekyll, tilling six acres of land and owning livestock valued at one hundred dollars, the same value as the livestock of his father.[17] In 1867 Robert had married a woman named Charlotte Cooper.[18] The couple already had two children, Frasier (born in 1870) and Randolph (1872), and would go on to have at least four more while they still lived on Jekyll—William (1875), Martha (1876), Dorah (1877), and Mary (1880). On June 5, 1889, Robert purchased from John du Bignon, for a recorded amount of one hundred dollars, Bull Island, one of a cluster of small islands known collectively as Latham Hammock, located between Jekyll and the mainland.[19] According to descendents' records, Robert and his family continued to live on Jekyll until his third son, William, was fifteen years old. His fifteenth birthday would have been on June 26, 1890. The child's grandfather John Couper du Bignon died in late December of that same year.[20] Thus, Robert and Charlotte Cooper du Bignon were the parents of the last du Bignon children born on Jekyll Island, and they remained on the island with Robert's father until his final days.

There can be little question that John's family knew of his long-standing relationship with Sylvia. However, as long as he kept it confined to the island, which could still provide refuge from public censure for such a liaison, they did not seem to object openly. In the wake of the war, John manifested a sense of affection toward his sisters in two property transactions that took place in 1866 and 1867. When lot 54 in Old Town Brunswick was auctioned at a sheriff's sale on December 4, 1866, he purchased it and turned it over to his brother-in-law Tom Bourke, the husband of his sister Sarah, on January 22, 1867, for one dollar. The following day a second transaction was recorded by which he conveyed to another sister, Catherine Amelia Hazelhurst, the western half of lot 305 in Old Town Brunswick "in consideration for the love and affection which I have and bear for my sister."[21] At the time he may still not have realized the extent to which his financial situation had been ruined by the war, or he may have been trying to find a way to maintain his sisters' affection in light of his relationship with Sylvia.

Ultimately, both John and Henry were compelled to mortgage their lands in an effort to survive. In a document that identifies him simply as "John Couper Du Bignon of Jekyl Island," on December 13, 1883, John finally and reluctantly deeded over the portion of the island he had inherited from his father to a Brunswick merchant named Gustavus Friedlander and to Friedlander's lawyer and business partner, William A. O. Anderson. Friedlander was a "tall shrewd-looking" German merchant who had come from New York to Brunswick in 1850 with a sizeable stock of "Yankee notions" to open G. Friedlander and Co., a dry goods store that handled everything from hats and boots to groceries and liquors.[22] The curious sum for which John conveyed to Friedlander his portion of the island, $5,235.76, underscores the fact that the land was given over to pay a debt.[23] No evidence indicates that John du Bignon, still in his early fifties when the war ended, ever took on another profession besides farming.

Even though he sold his portion of the island, he did not leave it. When the entire island was sold again in 1886 to the Jekyll Island Club, John, who

Randolph du Bignon, one of the grandsons
of John Couper and Sylvia du Bignon.
(Courtesy of Marian D. Payne)

was by then seventy-four years old, refused to move away, and club officials granted permission for him to live out his life there. Charlotte Maurice, whose husband was one of the club's original members, remembered him well, noting that he "was so attached to the place where he had spent most of his long life that the Club gave him the right to continue to occupy the little house that he had built in the fields north of the west end of Wylly Road. After his death this tiny and ill kept shack was torn down."[24] John du Bignon finally died of heart failure at the age of seventy-eight on December 31, 1890.[25] Though he had been born to wealth and aristocracy, he ended his days in poverty, surviving on the goodwill of northern millionaires. He lies today in an unmarked grave, crudely outlined with bricks, in Oak Grove Cemetery in Brunswick, one of a small cluster of three graves that also contains the carved tombstones of his brother Henry and his sister Eliza.

What we know about the final days of John's brother, Henry, comes mostly from court records. Younger than his brother John, he seems to have put up more of a fight to keep his land and to have made every effort the legal system could afford to hold onto it. After Henri du Bignon's death, the man named in the will as administrator of the estate, William Audley Couper, the youngest son of John Couper for whom Henri had named his second son, "refused to act in that capacity." No reason is disclosed in the legal documents, but his refusal provided Henry Jr. the opportunity he needed to step forward and petition the court in February 1867 to give him temporary letters of administration. Henri Sr.'s widow, Mary, perhaps caught off guard by the situation, signed an agreement relinquishing her

The graves of the three unmarried children of Henri du Bignon and Amelia Nicolau
in Oak Grove Cemetery in Brunswick, Georgia. They are (left to right) those
of Henry du Bignon, Eliza du Bignon, and John du Bignon, whose grave is
marked only by a brick outline.

rights to administer her husband's estate in favor of her stepson, Henry Jr.
Henry's brother John and his brother-in-law Robert Hazelhurst served as
securities. John and Henry together put up a bond of fourteen thousand
dollars, which represented in all likelihood everything they could possibly
scrape together.[26] The "temporary" role of administrator evolved more or
less into a permanent one. But not long thereafter, Mary came to regret her
decision and began in October 1868 to petition the court for relief, stating
that "Henry du Bignon has hitherto neglected and refused and still does
neglect and refuse to set aside or pay over any thing for the feeding and
clothing of [her] children" and that she has "been compelled to support
them out [of] her limited means."[27]

    The following year she brought suit against her stepson, arguing that her
five minor daughters were entitled to a larger share of their father's estate
than they had received under his administration. She ultimately accused
him of having "mismanaged" the estate and "misappropriated" its assets, a
charge that he vehemently denied. There appears to have been merit to her
case, however, for by 1871, five years after her husband's death, there had still

not been a distribution of the estate, and later court records confirm that Henry did borrow from it certain sums that he had not repaid.[28] Things came to a head in 1873, and in April, Henry petitioned to be discharged as executor of the estate. When ordered before the court on the first Monday in August to give a final accounting, however, he failed to appear. The daughters of Mary Aust du Bignon were reduced to begging Henry for money. Writing from Plymouth, North Carolina, on August 28, 1873, Virginia sent a pleading letter to her half-brother expressing a desperate need for fifty dollars to help her get back home. She underscored her words, *"Please don't disappoint me for I am sick & am more than anxious to get home before cold weather."*[29]

The case of Mary against Henry dragged on for another six months, until finally on January 20, 1874, Henry was notified by the ordinary's court that "the Estate of Henry DuBignon Deceased has been divided and partitioned among the several heirs of said Estate, by virtue of the order in the Superior Court of said County on the Chancery side of said Court: and you are hereby notified and required to be and appear on the third Monday it being the sixteenth day of February 1874 . . . to make a final settlement as administrator as aforesaid."[30] Mary had won her case for her daughters, though it availed her little personally, for she died on June 21, 1876.

Although Henry continued to suffer from a lack of income, his creditors demanded their due and were beginning court proceedings against him. Not only was his father's estate one of those creditors, but he had also borrowed money from various individuals, among them his sister Eliza and the Brunswick merchant who had already acquired his brother John's portion of the island, Gustavus Friedlander. His largest creditors were a Savannah widow named Mary Heisler, from whom he had borrowed $3,100 in 1870; Martin Tufts, a Savannah freight agent for the Central Rail Road and Banking Company, to whom he owed several notes dating from 1873 to 1875 totaling $2,126; and a barkeeper from Tennessee named J. W. Shannon, who had loaned him $1,800. He had even hocked the last vestiges of his family's wealthy past, in the form of a diamond pin and a gold watch, used as collateral for an $80 loan from a Brunswick physician named B. M. Cargyle.[31]

On July 21, 1875, a notice appeared in the *Brunswick Advertiser* stating that a party of gentlemen, including Martin Tufts, was "taking a little pleasure cruise" on the yacht *Sunshine* and "intended stopping some time with Mr.

Henry Du Bignon, on Jekyl. We wish them a happy time."[32] It was in all probability far from a "happy time" for Henry du Bignon, who had recently learned that, in the May term of the Glynn County Superior Court, Mary Heisler had won a lawsuit against him for nonpayment of the loan she had made to him and a judgment for the full amount of the loan plus interest and court costs. Since Henry could not possibly make the payment, the court awarded her all of Henry's property at the north end of Jekyll Island. Martin Tufts, who also knew of the judgment, was working on a deal with Mary Heisler, a neighbor who had recently moved onto his street in Savannah, to get her to sign over her right to the judgment (and hence to the north end of the island) to him—a deal he finalized on December 10, 1877.[33] Tufts seemed already certain that the north end of the island would be his, and he was no doubt coming to inspect the property.

Henry was frantic and immediately began a series of legal maneuvers that dragged on into the 1880s to try to save his land. One of his ploys was to adopt in 1877 a great-nephew, Henry Francis du Bignon, known as Harry, the grandson of his deceased brother Joseph. Claiming himself, after the adoption, to be a head of household, he applied for a homestead exemption, hoping to save his home on Jekyll from his creditors. Not long thereafter he also petitioned for bankruptcy, hoping that his homestead would be spared from his creditors on the basis of the hoped-for exemption.[34]

The adopted child in question, Harry du Bignon, had been born in 1867, not long after his father's return from military service in the Civil War. He was only five years old at the time of the death of his father, Henry Riffault du Bignon, in 1872 and only ten when Henry du Bignon, unmarried and having no heirs, approached his mother, Alice Symons du Bignon, and proposed to adopt the boy. He told her, as she would later testify, that he would "leave everything he had to him" in his will. She declared in a later deposition that she had not wanted to give her consent to the adoption but that, "on the advice of friends and my family," she finally agreed.[35] In spite of it, however, the boy continued to live in her home. According to her testimony, Henry du Bignon contributed nothing to his support and never even asked after the child when he saw her. Henry's motives for adopting little Harry were thus called into question by his adversaries. Tufts argued that Henry had adopted the boy only in order to be able to claim him as a dependent and himself as head of household for the purposes of the homestead exemption. But when the boy's mother

Henry Francis ("Harry") du Bignon,
born in 1867, was adopted by his
great-uncle Henry du Bignon
following the death of the boy's father
in 1872. (Courtesy of Henry Howell)

was asked whether Henry du Bignon adopted her son "for the purpose
of procuring an exception of Homestead," Alice replied, "I know nothing
from Mr. DuBignon of his object in adopting Harry other than stated already."

Alice du Bignon's testimony was not taken as evidence in the case until
1883, as the homestead exemption issue dragged on in the courts. If Henry
won his case, it would allow him to keep his home on Jekyll. Thus, Tufts
argued vociferously that Henry du Bignon was not, in fact, the head of a
family since the boy did not live with him, that he did not contribute to
the child's support, and that the Jekyll Island property Henry was trying to
protect was, in point of law, no longer his to protect since he had already
lost it in a court judgment. Basing his arguments on these issues, he contended that du Bignon was not entitled to a homestead exemption.[36] At
a hearing on June 5, 1883, Tufts claimed that Henry du Bignon had exaggerated his expenses and undervalued his mules and horses, which, in any
case, Tufts, not Henry du Bignon, now owned. Finally, three appraisers
were sent to the island to take a look for themselves. In the end the application for homestead exemption was denied, and Henry had to pay legal
fees and court costs of seventeen dollars for the three appraisers and their
"Passage to Jekle Island and Services." But, despite howls of protest from

(Left to right) Henry Riffault du Bignon (father of Henry Francis du Bignon), John Eugene du Bignon (standing), and W. F. Steuart. (Courtesy of the Jekyll Island Museum Archives)

Tufts, Henry's petition for bankruptcy was granted. Henry had appealed to the court with a personal statement, attesting to the fact that "My inability to pay my debts was caused by losses in my planting," brought about by "caterpillars and by the fall in the price of cotton. I lost from both causes combined—a short crop for which I received a low price." He had also tried planting pine trees, he claimed, but nothing had worked out. Despite the earlier court judgment, he still listed Mary Heisler among his creditors.[37] He simply refused to accept the situation, although illness finally forced him to leave the island.

Before any of these matters could be completely clarified, Henry du Bignon Jr., described as "late of Jekyl Island," died at the age of fifty-nine on January 28, 1885, at the Brunswick home of his older sister Eliza, who was caring for him at the time.[38] (She, too, would die the following year.) He did not keep his promise to will everything to the son of Alice du Bignon, for he died without leaving a will at all. Since Henry had named no administrator, young Harry's uncle, Wilfred F. Symons, stepped forward and applied for letters of administration, noting in his petition that his nephew, "Henry F. du Bignon, a minor [he was seventeen], of said County, . . . was adopted by the deceased and was by proper order of the Superior Court of said County . . . declared to be his adopted child, and made capable of inheriting his estate." In the petition he also noted that the boy's mother had requested him to make this application and that no one else intended to apply for letters of administration. His petition was duly granted on December 1.[39]

Symons valued the estate at five thousand dollars, still including in his assessment the "northern end of Jekyl Island," the portion to which Martin Tufts also laid claim.[40] Included in the property inventory were "a number of wild horses and hogs which are on Jekyl Island in said country, running at-large thereon, that in their present condition with no one to look after and control them . . . are constantly depreciating in value." Symons, estimating the value of the land at thirty-five hundred dollars and that of the livestock and farming implements at fifteen hundred dollars, proposed to resolve the matter by selling the "Equity of Redemption" in the property. Permission for the sale was given by the court on June 22, 1885, and the date was set for an auction "before the Court House Door" on the first Tuesday in December 1885.[41]

The buyer, who acquired the title to the north end of Jekyll Island for only one thousand dollars at the auction, was none other than Henry and John's nephew John Eugene du Bignon, the youngest son of their deceased brother, Joseph. On the surface it looked like a bargain, but in fact it was the second time he had purchased that portion of the island. This time, however, he had acquired "the right, [clear] title and interest or equity of redemption remaining in said estate to the Northern one-third of Jekyl Island."[42] For John Eugene, it was a prize and the final piece of a puzzle. He had kept his eye on it for years, cheering on the efforts of Martin Tufts and occasionally lending his own name to the various protests and court proceedings against Henry du Bignon. The first part of the puzzle, the south end of the island, he had easily acquired in 1879 following the death of his uncle Charles du Bignon. Charles had died bankrupt in 1875, and his widow, Ann V. Grantland, in settlement of a lawsuit and in an effort to restore her financial stability, allowed her husband's Jekyll inheritance, in which she apparently had no interest, to be sold at auction.[43] John Eugene bid it in at forty-five hundred dollars.

His next opportunity had come in 1883, when he persuaded Gustavus Friedlander and William A. O. Anderson to sell him John Couper's middle portion for four thousand dollars, less than the amount of his uncle John's original debt, but it was money in hand for the Brunswick merchant and his partner, who had little use for the island.[44] Finally, on June 13, 1885, he had persuaded his aunt Eliza to deed over to him her thirty acres, promising to pay her one hundred dollars, a promise he had not kept by the time of her death.[45] Now, here at last was the culmination of his dream to own the entire island that had once belonged to his grandfather and great-grandfather. In fact, he thought that he had already purchased the north end when on May 27, 1885, after his uncle Henry's death, he had paid Martin Tufts thirty-five hundred dollars for the property, believing that Tufts already held the clear title. But when the court allowed Symons to claim at least some interest in the property on behalf of his nephew and auction off its "Equity of Redemption," John Eugene made certain to be there to bid it in so that there would be no future problems. In the end, he paid for that north portion of the island the same amount that he had earlier paid for the middle portion that had belonged to his uncle John. In all, he reacquired the free title to all of Jekyll Island for thirteen thousand dollars, excluding the one hundred dollars he never paid to his aunt Eliza. Even in the 1770s the island had been valued at twenty thousand dollars. In short, he had done very well for himself.

Completely unlike John and Henry, who saw no other options for their lives and clung to their land until debt and death took it from them, their nephew John Eugene du Bignon reflected the orientation of a younger generation and was a true entrepreneurial representative of a New South mentality. Involved in efforts to restore the damage that the war had done to Brunswick, John Eugene saw the possibilities of making a fortune from the ruins of the past. Considered a dominant personality and major player in the financial circles of Brunswick, he was a leader in various commercial efforts. In fact, he was involved in almost every major innovation in Brunswick from the late 1870s, when he was a young man just turning thirty, until he retired from active participation in business affairs some forty years later. In the course of his career, John Eugene would serve as president or director of an amazing variety of enterprises, including the Brunswick Savings and Trust Company, the *Times Advertiser* Publishing Company, the Brunswick and Florida Inland Steamboat Company, the Saint Simons Transit Company, the Southern Cement Stone Company, the South Atlantic Towing Company, the Cumberland Route of the Brunswick and South Atlantic Company, and the Brunswick Foundry and Manufacturing Company. He also held a principal interest in the Brunswick and Altamaha Canal project, in the Brunswick Street Railroad, and eventually in the Oglethorpe Hotel.[46]

John Eugene du Bignon saw clearly that the future of the South depended not on the restoration of large plantations but rather on the development of a more diverse economy. He looked to a future when railroads and other forms of transportation, manufacturing, and finance would be increasingly important in the South. He also understood the need to attract northern capital to Georgia. One look at his uncles' situations made it clear to him that they would never be able to revive any expectation of profit on Jekyll Island as an agricultural site. To John Eugene, Jekyll Island represented an immense opportunity in another direction, if only he could pull it off.

At just what point his scheme occurred to him is impossible to determine. But it may have been born with his first opportunity in 1879 to buy the south end of the island. By the time he bought the second portion in 1883, he had already begun to formulate his plan, for the following year he built a house on Jekyll to use as a base of operations. Then, systematically, he set out to acquire the remaining portions that had belonged to his uncle Henry and

John Eugene du Bignon, a New South
entrepreneur, sold Jekyll Island to the
newly founded Jekyll Island Club.
(Courtesy of the Jekyll Island
Museum Archives)

his aunt Eliza for a purpose he had not yet publicly disclosed, but which, no doubt, had begun to take shape in his mind.

Clarification of just what use he could make from the island had come from unexpected places. Northern writers, coming south for the first time since the war, had begun to tout the splendors of the Sea Islands in the national press. *Harper's New Monthly Magazine* ran a lengthy illustrated article in its November 1878 issue that described the "picturesqueness and tender beauty" of the Sea Islands of Georgia, South Carolina, and Florida. One of the most influential accounts that focused particular attention on the Georgia coast was that of Frederick A. Ober in the August 1880 issue of *Lippincott's Magazine*. The article featured adjacent Cumberland Island and the ruins of Dungeness, the magnificent home that had been built by Catharine and Phineas Miller. The article extolled the island as an "Eden-like retreat," an apt analogy given Ober's descriptions of its colorful butterflies and hummingbirds, its abundance of pomegranates and figs, and its sunsets "lighting gloriously the marsh and silver threads of the river." The article portrayed in poetic detail the varieties of seabirds on the islands, and the "shade and coolness beneath the intertwined branches of the live oaks," from whose "limbs hang graceful pennons of Spanish moss, festooned at the sides, waved by every wind, changing in every light."[47]

The temptation of such a paradise would not be resisted. The following year Andrew Carnegie's brother, Thomas, and his wife, Lucy, purchased 4,000 acres of Cumberland for thirty-five thousand dollars, and another 8,240 acres the following year. They would eventually own approximately 90 percent of the island.[48] The description of Cumberland and the Carnegies' interest were no doubt an inspiration to John Eugene, who saw here a golden opportunity to make Jekyll profitable. He would sell it to a New York millionaire.

One of the ways in which he thought to implement his plan was to ally himself with his brother-in-law, Newton Finney, who had recently moved his family to New York. Finney, equally as entrepreneurial as du Bignon, had, like so many other southerners, lost most of his sizeable fortune during the war. But, undaunted, when peace came he turned to the lumber business, which thrived in south Georgia with so much rebuilding to be done. He had left Brunswick in 1871 to go to New York as a representative of the Brunswick City Council in an effort to establish direct steamship communication between the two cities. The following year he moved his wife, Josephine, the sister of John Eugene, and their family to New York. Always on the lookout for financial opportunities and eager to make another fortune, he had become partners by March 1873 with Oliver Kane King in a New York firm called King, Finney and Company, which dealt in railroad bonds and securities.[49] There both he and his partner became members of the ultra elite Union Club.

Finney's membership in the Union Club proved to be John Eugene's entrée into the moneyed world that could afford to buy his island. First, however, he had to acquire the rest of it himself before he could pull off his intention to sell it to a northern millionaire. If four thousand acres on Cumberland were worth thirty-five thousand dollars to a northern millionaire, surely all of Jekyll Island, with the privacy and exclusivity it could afford, would be worth at least as much, if not more. Setting his plans in motion, by 1884 he had built his new house on the island, where he could provide gracious lodging and hospitality to the various northerners he planned to bring down to hunt and show off the property.

He began, with the help of his brother-in-law in New York, to invite to Jekyll for hunting expeditions a series of wealthy northerners, all of whom were in his mind prospective buyers. Among those invited were John Claflin, a wealthy and well-known New York merchant, whose family

This house was built on Jekyll Island by John Eugene du Bignon in 1884 as a place for prospective buyers of the island to stay. A du Bignon house had been indicated on maps at this location as early as the 1860s. (Courtesy of the Georgia Department of Archives and History, Vanishing Georgia Collection, from an original in the Jekyll Island Museum)

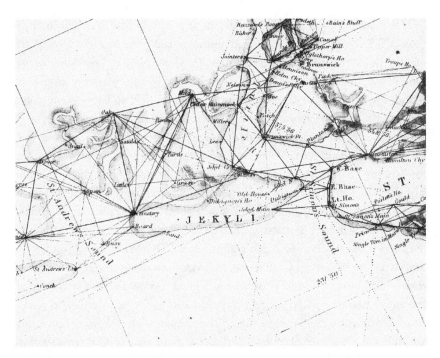

This valuable map (date unknown but pre–Civil War) reveals the location of several du Bignon houses on Jekyll Island. The one identified as "Old House" is most likely the former Horton house. (Courtesy of the Coastal Georgia Historical Society)

owned one of the largest wholesale dry goods business firms in the country, and his cousin, Edward E. Eames. The two came on a hunt to the island in April 1885. Before the end of the year, John Eugene du Bignon would carry off the amazing scheme to reacquire the island, in which John Claflin would play a key role.

On April 25 du Bignon took advantage of his publishing connection with the *Brunswick Advertiser and Appeal* to proclaim Jekyll Island as "the finest hunting ground in Georgia," making certain no doubt that Claflin and Eames noticed the article. He also saw to it that the article included references to the exclusivity of the island and its hunting bounty: "the proprietors of the island having taken special pains to protect their game from the blunderbusses of the average gunmen, they are now able to entertain their friends with a hunt either for deer or turkeys, for the island abounds with both."[50]

The Claflin-Eames visit to Jekyll was immensely fruitful for John Eugene. Claflin, well known for his adventurous spirit (he had in the summer of 1877 trekked through hitherto-unexplored parts of South America by foot, mule, and canoe), was definitely impressed by this relatively unspoiled island. He expressed an interest in purchasing Jekyll if du Bignon could get a clear title, and he agreed to lend him the money to do so.

On June 16, du Bignon recorded three promissory notes to Claflin, one for $350, payable in six months, and two others, one for $350 and the other for $10,000, payable in one year. Jekyll Island, some of which du Bignon still did not own at the time, was used as collateral for the notes. But with the funds Claflin lent him, du Bignon was able to pay off his previous loans and settle any lingering matters, though he apparently overlooked the one hundred dollars he still owed his aunt Eliza. Thus by June 20, only four days after the loan from Claflin was recorded, the *Brunswick Advertiser and Appeal* announced that "Mr. John DuBignon is now the happy owner of the entire island of Jekyll, having purchased recently the middle and north end." Once again the article boasted the virtues of the island: "The lands are rich, the [climate] excellent, and as for game no island in this section can equal it."[51] A later article in the same newspaper boasted of the historic remains on Jekyll, mistakenly attributing them to General Oglethorpe and noting that "the old tabby building he occupied still stands, and the foundation of the old brewery of the same material can still be seen. The old well, too, is there as solid and firm as ever. . . . It is built right on the bank of the creek, and still furnishes most excellent water."[52] Du Bignon never missed an opportunity to display the virtues of his newly acquired island in the press.

Now came the real challenge: to sell the island for a significant profit. Both du Bignon and Finney were well-aware of the sale of Cumberland lands to the Carnegie family. Finney in New York had been talking up Jekyll Island with his Union Club friends and was amazed to find so much interest in it. It occurred to him that he and du Bignon might increase their profit immensely not so much by selling the island to an individual like Claflin, but rather by founding a club in which they could sell shares, thereby controlling the amount the club paid for the island. It was a scheme that Claflin apparently also endorsed, agreeing to become a member of such a club. Thereby was born the idea of the Jekyll Island Club, which was to be from the outset primarily an exclusive hunting club open only to the very

Newton S. Finney organized the Jekyll
Island Club and helped his brother-in-law
John Eugene du Bignon to sell the island
at a significant profit to the club. (Courtesy
of the Jekyll Island Museum Archives)

wealthy and most elite families, primarily from New York and Chicago so-
cieties. It was an ingenious scheme, and one that worked better than either
Finney or du Bignon could possibly have foreseen.

For his part, du Bignon kept his publishing company cranking out favorable publicity both for the island and for the entire Brunswick area, which,
his publications claimed, boasted a climate "as pleasant . . . as can be found.
The winters are never severe, snow being almost unknown and ice a rar-
ity, and our summers are rendered . . . quite pleasant by constant refreshing
breezes."[53] Claflin and Finney, who were both in New York, could attest
to the accuracy of these descriptions. To New Yorkers who from January
through March battled the ice and snow, it sounded like a dream come
true. The recently established direct connection from New York by Mal-
lory Steamship, as well as reasonably convenient overnight railroad routes
that allowed one to go to bed in the snow and wake up to palm trees and
orange groves, made the voyage to Brunswick an easy one. It was even easier,
and certainly more luxurious, in the private railroad cars and yachts that so
many wealthy New Yorkers owned. Thus, the response among Union Club
members was enthusiastic.

It had been Finney's goal to recruit fifty members, each of whom would
own two shares of stock at $600 a share. Before it was all over, he would
recruit fifty-three members. Among these original members were an amaz-

ing array of well-known merchants, business executives, bankers, and rail-road men—the elite of the new industrial wealthy class of the North—men like J. P. Morgan, William K. Vanderbilt, Joseph Pulitzer, Marshall Field, Pierre Lorillard, and Henry B. Hyde. On February 17, 1886, as a representative of the newly chartered club, Finney signed an agreement with du Bignon to purchase Jekyll Island for $125,000, including all improvements, fixtures, and livestock.[54] For du Bignon the profit, no doubt shared with his brother-in-law, was phenomenal. He had turned Jekyll Island from a financial liability, soaking up tax dollars and giving little in return, into an asset that brought him more than a 1,000 percent return.

For Jekyll Island, which still bore vestiges of its Civil War neglect and occupation, it was a fresh start. In this New South, proclaimed so eloquently by Henry Grady in New York the very same year the club was founded (1886), however, Jekyll would no longer be under the control of southerners. Although both Finney (who was himself originally from the North) and du Bignon, the only southerner whose name appears on the original subscription list, were members of the club for a relatively brief time, they would gradually be eased out of club leadership a decade later by the New York and Chicago elite. Jekyll would become their southern refuge from the wintry north, as well as a natural respite from the harried schedules and artificial decors of their daily lives. Thus was founded the famous Jekyll Island Club, a private paradise, a veritable "new Eden" for America's wealthiest families. A spectacular era of the island's history was about to begin.

Notes

ABBREVIATIONS

GCPC   Glynn County Probate Court
GCSC   Glynn County Superior Court
GDAH   Georgia Department of Archives and History
GHS   Georgia Historical Society
NARA   National Archives and Records Administration
ORN   *Official Records of the Union and Confederate Navies in the War
        of the Rebellion*
WR   *War of the Rebellion: A Compilation of Official Records of the Union
        and Confederate Armies*

PREFACE

1. It should be noted that Jekyll Island was spelled "Jekyl" until July 31, 1929, when the General Assembly passed a resolution that altered the traditional spelling of the island's name. Since it had been originally named for Sir Joseph Jekyll, the Assembly declared that "the correct and legal spelling of the name of said island is and shall be Jekyll Island." *Acts and Resolutions of the General Assembly of the State of Georgia, 1929* (Atlanta: Stein Printing Company, 1929), 1505. I will throughout the text use the modern spelling except in quoted materials or titles that use the older spelling.

2. The first printing was "The Legends of Jekyl Island," *The New England Magazine* 8 (1893): 393–99. The editor of a later and much more expanded published version signs his "Postscript by the Editor" with the initials G. B. S. His editorial comments appear on pages 207–8 of the unidentified journal and note, for example, that a writer in the *Christian Advocate* (Michigan) of May 3, 1894, has quoted in all seriousness Head's tale of John Wesley's writing on Jekyll Island a hymn that begins "Lo! On a narrow neck of land I stand." It is, of course, pure invention on Head's part, though he facetiously alleges it to be a "fact," confirming it by a letter supposedly written in 1736 by John Wesley to Lady Dorothy Oglethorpe, whom he names

as the wife of Georgia's founder, James Edward Oglethorpe. In fact, Oglethorpe did not marry until 1744, and his wife's name was Elizabeth Wright, not Dorothy.

3. This copy is in the Margaret Davis Cate Collection, box 60, folder 115, GHS.

4. The entire title of the booklet was *Jekyl Island: Some Historic Notes and Some Legends, Collected by Charlotte Marshall Maurice, and a Brief Outline of the Early Days of the Jekyl Island Club Made by Charles Stewart Maurice*. It was privately printed and bears no date, though correspondence between Charlotte Maurice and various members of the du Bignon family and others that dates from 1905 indicates that she was working on it at that time. See, for example, P. J. Luckie to Charlotte Maurice, February 7, 1905, Maurice Papers, Southern Historical Collection, University of North Carolina.

INTRODUCTION

1. The state legislator Mike Egan sponsored the bill in 1972.

2. See especially McCash and McCash, *Jekyll Island Club*; McCash, *Jekyll Island Cottage Colony*.

3. The story of Christophe Poulain du Bignon is the only part of this history that has been told with exacting detail by Martha Keber in her recent book, *Seas of Gold, Seas of Cotton: Christophe Poulain DuBignon of Jekyll Island*. I should perhaps note at this point that Dr. Keber and I have adopted different ways of spelling the du Bignon name. Both are correct, for "du Bignon" and "DuBignon" were used at various times by members of the family, as were duBignon, Du Bignon, and Dubignon. The earliest French spelling was "du Bignon," and I have chosen to keep this spelling throughout, except in materials that are directly quoted. It was a spelling often used in the 1890s by John Eugene du Bignon (who may have adopted it as an affectation), and it is also the spelling I have used in my earlier books. Thus, I have elected to keep the spelling in this book consistent with those.

I. IN THE BEGINNING

1. On the theory of the land bridge from East Asia, see, for example, Milanich, *Timucua*, 2. For the coastal navigation theory, see Lepper, "Coastal Navigators," 34–35; Dalton, "Coast Road," 10–12.

2. Crook, "Archeological Survey." See also the report "From Colonial Birth," 1. Archaeological visits to Jekyll Island began in the 1950s, when Professor Joseph Caldwell of the University of Georgia and Lewis Larson from the Georgia Historical Commission visited the island. Professor Charles Fairbanks from the University of Florida took charge of the first formal excavations in the mid-1960s. One of his students, Steven D. Ruple, later submitted a master's thesis titled "Archaeology

at Horton House" in 1976. Other studies have been done by Chester DePratter and Donald Cruso, Gordon Macgregor, Morgan R. Cook Jr., and Colin Brooker prior to the most recent report, cited above, prepared by the team from Southern Research.

3. Worth, *Timucuan Missions*. The discovery by Worth in the early 1990s of a cache of documents that had lain forgotten for centuries dramatically changed the interpretation of the early history of Jekyll Island and the entire Georgia coast.

4. "From Colonial Birth," 3. This idea is based on the earlier report by Morgan R. Crook.

5. Coulter, *Georgia: A Short History*, 5. Coulter incorrectly suggests that the Cherokees were Muskogean-speaking Creeks, while John R. Swanton correctly lists the Cherokees as being of Iroquoian, not Muskogean, stock. See Table 1: "Classification of the Southeastern Tribes" in Swanton, *Indians*, between pages 10 and 11.

6. Grant D. Jones, "Ethnohistory of the Guale Coast," 178. See, for example, Swanton, who suggested that the Guale territory extended "from St. Andrews Sound [at the southern tip of Jekyll Island] to the Savannah River" (*Indians*, 135).

7. See Worth, *Struggle for the Georgia Coast*, 4. In this volume, Worth has conveniently assembled and translated many of these documents. He is still bringing others to light. See his more recent two-volume work, *Timucuan Chiefdoms*.

8. Bushnell, *Situado and Sabana*, 134. Bushnell is following the division made in 1978 by the anthropologist Grant D. Jones, "Ethnohistory of the Guale Coast," 178–210. The *auto* is in the "Audiencia de Santo Domingo," contained in the Archivo General de Indias.

9. For a comprehensive recent look at the French role in *La Florida*, see McGrath, *French in Early Florida*.

10. The location of their short-lived colony, San Miguel de Gualdape, is still disputed. Most historians place it on Sapelo Sound, but Douglas Peck has recently suggested that the geographical description of the area better fits the Savannah River at Tybee Road. In any case, it is interesting to note that it was this little band of Spaniards who brought the first black slaves to Georgia. For a recent assessment of this first Spanish colony, see Peck, "Lucas Vásquez," 183–98. See also Hoffman, *New Andalucia*, 60–83.

11. It is difficult to understand why so many of the early attempts to establish colonies on the Georgia coast, the first by Ayllón and the second by Ribault and Laudonnière, suffered from famine when the forests were filled year round with deer, wild turkeys, and many other animals that they commonly ate in Europe and when the sea and estuaries were brimming with fish and shellfish. Nonetheless, this was a stated problem for both of these early groups, and they relied on Native Americans to provide them with food.

12. Cited by Peck, "Lucas Vásquez," 195, from E. L. Stevenson, "Early Spanish

Cartography of the New World with Special Reference to the Wolfenbuttal-Spanish Map and the Work of Diego Ribero," *Proceedings of the American Antiquarian Society* 19 (1909): 394.

13. Ponce de Leon's Florida landing was outside Timucuan domains. While Pánfilo de Narvárez and Hernando de Soto had some contact with western Timucua, they did not visit the coastal regions of Georgia. Finally, the establishment of the tiny colony of Allyón was farther north, outside of Timucuan territory. See Hann, *History of the Timucua Indians*, 27–41.

14. See McGrath, *French in Early Florida*, 74.

15. Laudonnière, *Three Voyages*, 20.

16. Ribaut, *Whole and True Discouerye*, 76. This enthusiastic account of the first voyage by Ribault (sometimes spelled Ribaut, though the sixteenth-century spelling, which I am using, was Ribault) represents the original English account published in 1563. Although, according to its second English publisher, Richard Hakluyt, who reprinted the text in 1583, the work was "extant in printe both in Frenche and Englishe" (48), the French version has been lost. Suzanne Lussagnet has included a retranslation of the text into French in her book *Les Français en Amérique pendant la deuxième moitié du XVIe siècle*, vol. 2, *Les Français en Floride* (Paris: Presses Universitaires de France, 1958), 1–26. I have chosen to use the English account, which is at least an authentic version from the sixteenth century, in preference to one that has undergone translation into English and back into French. To make the text easier to read and understand, I have very lightly modernized the spelling, the punctuation, and occasionally the wording, where it was particularly awkward.

17. Laudonnière, *Three Voyages*, 18; Hulton, *Work of Jacques Le Moyne*, 1:120. Although the Ayllón expedition met with some hostility from the Guale, it was only after some of their men helped themselves to the Natives' food supplies. Even then, the Guale allowed the Spaniards to feast on their food for several days before the Indians finally had enough and killed them all. See Peck, "Lucas Vásquez," 194.

18. Another Frenchman on the expedition, Robert Meleneche, agreed, noting that they were "good people" with a "pleasant disposition." Later captured by the Spanish, he gave a deposition in which he described his experiences and answered specific questions put to him by the Spanish. A copy of this deposition is in the Woodbury Lowery manuscripts, Library of Congress. It is cited in Bennett, *Laudonnière and Fort Caroline*, 90.

19. Ribaut, *Whole and True Discouerye*, 82, 72, 84.

20. Laudonnière, *Three Voyages*, 22.

21. Ribaut, *Whole and True Discouerye*, 88.

22. Laudonnière, *Three Voyages*, 67; Hann contends that this chief was probably Tacatacuru, *History of the Timucua Indians*, 40.

23. Laudonnière, *Three Voyages*, 139–40.

24. Hulton, *Work of Jacques Le Moyne*, 1:119. "This assignment," he claims, "I carried out as faithfully as I could." We can judge the skill and accuracy of Le Moyne's work by his careful portrayals in his collections of nature drawings. For centuries art historians believed that all of Le Moyne's works had been lost. But a volume of fifty-seven plant drawings came to light in 1922 and is now in the Victoria and Albert Museum, while another album of fifty watercolor images of fruits and flowers, not discovered until 1961, is now in the British Museum. Both are remarkable for their accuracy of detail and care of execution.

25. De Bry, *America, part II*. Various scholars have issued words of caution concerning de Bry's work, noting that "there is no indication how many of the details of de Bry's engravings were drawn from Le Moyne's work and how many derived from de Bry's imagination or from other sources" (Hann, *History of the Timucua Indians*, 20). However, the comparison of the image that corresponds with the only surviving Le Moyne drawing of the Timucua, a miniature discovered in 1900, suggests an amazing accuracy in the copy. Although Le Moyne's images were based primarily on the Saturiwa group, with those relating to warfare based on the Outina, it is not likely that the Natives on Jekyll, who were of the same people and general linguistic group, would have lived in a significantly different way. See Hulton, *Work of Jacques Le Moyne*, 1:10. It is also significant that the English editor Richard Hakluyt, in a letter to his (and Le Moyne's) patron, Sir Walter Raleigh, commented in 1587 that Le Moyne "hath put downe in writing many singularities which are not mentioned in this treatise: which he meaneth to publish together with the purtraitures before it be long, if it may stand with your good pleasure & liking." Cited in Hulton, *Work of Jacques Le Moyne*, 1:11. The "purtraitures" to which he refers appear to be the drawings of Le Moyne himself, rather than the de Bry engravings, which did not yet exist. Le Moyne did not meet de Bry until 1587, and the engraver was unable to obtain copies of the artist's work until after the latter's death in 1588, when he purchased them from Le Moyne's widow.

26. Hulton, *Work of Jacques Le Moyne*, 1:15.

27. This estimate comes from Jerald T. Milanich, "The Timucua Indians of Northern Florida and Southern Georgia," in *Indians of the Greater Southeast*, ed. Bonnie G. McEwan, 1. Kathleen A. Deagan gives what she terms a "conservative" estimate of fifteen to twenty thousand for the entire Timucuan population ("Cultures in Transition: Fusion and Assimilation among the Eastern Timucua," in *Tacachale*, ed. Milanich and Proctor, 94).

28. See Bennett, *Settlement of Florida*, "The Narrative of Le Moyne," 102. See also Laudonnière, *Three Voyages*, 66 and 78, where the word is given as "Thimogona."

29. On various terms used for chiefs and other officials, as well as for a more complete look at the political structure, see Milanich, "Timucua Indians," 6–7.

30. Laudonnière, *Three Voyages*, 11.

31. Hann, "1630 Memorial," 95–96.

32. Laudonnière, *Three Voyages*, 9, 11, 93. Le Challeux adds that they "tucked [it] up neatly around their head" (Lussagnet, *Les Francais en Amérique*, 211).

33. Hulton, *Work of Jacques Le Moyne*, 1:145, 147.

34. Ibid., 120.

35. Ibid., 151.

36. Ibid.

37. Ibid., 120.

38. Ibid., 151.

39. Hann, *History of the Timucua Indians*, 101–2.

40. Hulton, *Work of Jacques Le Moyne*, 1:150.

41. Laudonnière, *Three Voyages*, 13.

42. Hulton, *Work of Jacques Le Moyne*, 1:150.

43. Hann, *History of the Timucua Indians*, 90.

44. Méndez de Canzo to the King of Spain, September 22, 1602, in Archivo General de Indias, Seville. Quoted in Hann, *History of the Timucua Indians*, 90.

45. For an in-depth look at cassina, see Hudson, *Black Drink*. See also Hann, *History of the Timucua Indians*, 96–97.

46. Lussagnet, *Les Français en Amérique*, 18.

47. Hann, "1630 Memorial," 93–94.

48. See Hulton, *Work of Jacques Le Moyne*, 1:146–47, 120, 148.

49. See Swanton, *Indians*, 135. Lewis Larson, writing in 1978, reiterated that the Guale controlled "the area between St. Andrews and St. Catherines sounds" ("Historic Guale Indians of the Georgia Coast and the Impact of the Spanish Mission Effort," in *Tacachale*, ed. Milanich and Proctor, 120).

50. Genaro García, *Dos antiguas relaciones de la Florida* (Mexico City: J. Aguilar vera y Comp. [S. en C.], 1902), 2.

51. Laudonnière, *Three Voyages*, 14.

52. Larson, "Historic Guale Indians," 124.

53. Cited in Rebecca Saunders, "The Guale Indians of the Lower Atlantic Coast: Change and Continuity," in *Indians of the Greater Southeast*, ed. McEwan, 34. Much of the information concerning the Guale was derived from this article.

54. Cited in Larson, "Historic Guale Indians," 129. The eyewitness in question was a Spaniard named San Miguel. It is Larson who suggests that it resembles a game called "chunkee," common among the Creeks.

55. Larson, "Historic Guale Indians," 136.

56. Genaro García, *Dos antiguas relaciones*, 194.

57. Oré, *Martyrs of Florida*, 43–44. Also cited in Larson, "Historic Guale Indians," 131.

58. Most scholars still consider Guale a Muskogean language; however, this assumption has recently been questioned by William C. Sturtevant, "Misconnection of Guale and Yamasee," 139–48.

59. See Hann, *History of the Timucua Indians*, 122–36.

60. Swanton, *Indians*, 135.

61. According to the Southern Research study in 2002, Morgan R. Crook Jr., an archaeologist from West Georgia College, exposed the remains of a council house on Jekyll Island during a recent dig (12). He has to date not published his findings.

62. On the Ribault colony, see Grant D. Jones, "Ethnohistory of the Guale Coast," 181. Laudonnière wrote his *Histoire notable de la Floride* in 1586. It was translated by Richard Hakluyt under the title *A Notable Historie Containing Foure Voyages Made by Certayne French Captaynes into Florida in 1587*. More recently Charles E. Bennett has translated it under the title *Three Voyages*. The fourth account referred to in the Hakluyt translation was written by Dominique de Gourgues. It was included in Bennett's translation titled *Settlement of Florida*, which contained all four accounts as well as the de Bry engravings of the drawings of Le Moyne. There can be no doubt of Menéndez's hatred of Protestants, for he wrote to King Philip II in the aftermath of this episode: "because they are Lutherans, and that so wicked a sect should not remain alive in these parts, I shall do everything in my power . . . so that, within five or six months, not one of them shall remain alive" (cited in McGrath, *French in Early Florida*, 154). For an excellent analysis of the sources of this incident, see McGrath, *French in Early Florida*, 171–84.

63. "La Reprinse de la Floride par le capitaine Gourgues," in M. M. Basanier, *L'Histoire notable de la Floride* (Paris: 1586); translated by Jeannette Thurber Connor and reproduced in Bennett, *Settlement of Florida*, as "The Revenge of Captain Gourgues," 204.

64. "Revenge of Captain Gourgues," 210.

65. Menéndez ordered that Tacatacuru be hunted down and killed in retaliation. We do not know how Tacatacuru died or whether the Spanish soldiers were successful.

66. Jerald T. Milanich titled his most recent book *Laboring in the Fields of the Lord: Spanish Missions and Southeastern Indians*.

67. For earlier works that place Guadalquini on Jekyll, see, for example, the writings of Swanton, *Early History*; David Hurst Thomas, *Archeology of Mission Santa Catalina*; Hann, "Twilight," 1–24; and Bushnell, *Situado and Sabana*, see 61.

68. Bolton and Ross, *Arredondo's Historical Proof*.

69. This suggestion was first made by Worth, *Struggle for the Georgia Coast*, 181 n. 8.

70. Ibid., 176. For locations of these missions, see ibid., 181 n. 8.

71. See ibid., 58, 176. Although Worth notes this possibility (see note 69), he suggests elsewhere that Jekyll was uninhabited, 196.

72. See Hann, *History of the Timucua Indians*, 139–44.

73. Hann notes that they generally obeyed the Franciscan Fray Lopéz, who had come to instruct them, but that in 1598 Juan grew angry with the friar for telling his people that they should not work on a holy day.

74. David Hurst Thomas, *Archaeology of Mission Santa Catalina*, 13.

75. Hann, *History of the Timucua Indians*, 175.

76. Bolton and Ross, *Arredondo's Historical Proof*, 38, 41; Worth, *Struggle for the Georgia Coast*, 41–42, 127–45; Hann, *History of the Timucua Indians*, 271.

77. The writer was Luis Jerónimo de Oré, who was translated by Maynard Geiger, *Martyrs of Florida*. Cited in Deagan, "Cultures in Transition," 114; see also Maynard J. Geiger, *The Franciscan Conquest of Florida, 1573–1618* (Washington: The Catholic University of America Press, 1937), 13.

78. Hann, *History of the Timucua Indians*, 191.

79. Alonso del Moral et al., letter to the king, September 10, 1657, in "Visitations and Revolts in Florida, 1656–1659," *Florida Archaeology* 7 (1993): 7, 11.

80. Del Moral et al., letter to the king, 14. This letter represents a strong complaint from the religious community of Santa Elena to the king, citing Don Diego's "misgovernment, lack of experience, and rejection of advice" (7).

81. Hann, *History of the Timucua Indians*, 200–220.

82. Ibid., 245.

83. This information comes from ibid., 322. Deagan, writing in 1978, almost twenty years earlier, notes that "Indian slave raids had reduced the Timucua to fifteen men and eight women, and these Indians for their own security moved to within a cannon's shot of the fort [at St. Augustine]. They were struck by a pestilence, however, and only the cacique survived" ("Cultures in Transition," 115). Her source is Bishop Gerónimo Valdez, "Letter from the Bishop of Cuba to the Spanish Crown," 1729, Archivo General de Indias, Seville, Spain, 58–2–16/25. Hann, however, used later documents, notably a 1752 list by Franciscan friars of the Natives who resided in the village of Palica.

84. Hann, *History of the Timucua Indians*, 323.

2. WILLIAM HORTON AND THE TRUSTEES' COLONY

1. Bolton and Ross, *Debatable Land*.

2. Arnade, *Siege of St. Augustine*, 1.

3. Ibid., 2.

4. *Colonial Records*, 36:316.

5. The assessment of Walpole comes from Phinizy Spalding, "Georgians and the War," 461. The "imagination of the people" comes from page 463.

6. John T. Juricek, *Georgia Treaties, 1733–1763*, vol. 11 (1989) of *Early American Indian Documents*, ed. Vaughan; Vaughan, *Early American Indian Documents*, 15–17.

7. Moore, *Voyage to Georgia*, 1:121–22, 124. On Tomochichi's trip to England, the most recent account is by Sweet, "Bearing Feathers of the Eagle," 339–71; the oldest biographical study of the Yamacraw chief was that by Charles C. Jones Jr., *Historical Sketch*.

8. Lane, *General Oglethorpe's Georgia*, 2:346.

9. In a recent report prepared for the Jekyll Island Museum, Colin Brooker cites research undertaken by the Reverend Stanley C. Dedman, the former librarian of Salisbury Cathedral, who would seem to have impeccable credentials, attesting that "Horton was not a Herefordshire man" (Brooker report, 3). Rev. Dedman is, however, in error, as the information contained within this chapter will clearly show.

10. I take the spelling of her name, which is variously rendered (Phillip, Philip, Philipp), from her first husband's will.

11. Records of the Hereford St. Nicholas Parish in Herefordshire, England. Thomas Horton, William's older brother, was baptized two years earlier on August 29, 1706. He was buried on April 7, 1707. His sister Catherine was baptized on September 27, 1707, and his sister Mary on June 5, 1710. Four years later to the day, William Horton's father was buried. Three years later his mother married Richard Butler of Hereford St. Owen.

12. I am grateful to Irene Cordell, William Horton's descendent, who graciously shared with me information compiled by her nephew, Thomas Wilkins. Information on the will of William Horton comes from the Prerogative Court of Canterbury, where the will was probated in July 1714. He was buried in Hereford Cathedral in an enclosure between the Lady Chapel and the southeast transept, where his tomb bears this simple inscription: "Here lyeth the body of William Horton of this city, gent."

13. It is interesting to note that Richard Butler was very proud of his heritage, and in his will he requested that on his gravestone should be inscribed, "Here Lyeth the body of Mr Richard Butler, second son to the Lord Viscount Mountgarrett, with my Age, and the time of my decease." The first Richard Butler, the second son of Pierce Butler, first Earl of Ossory and eighth Earl of Ormonde, was created Viscount Montgarrett of the kingdom of Ireland on October 23, 1550. In short, Richard Butler, William Horton's stepfather, was descended from the same family as Pierce Butler of Butler Plantation near Darien, Georgia.

14. It is possible that there was a third son, Nicholas, but records are not clear on this point.

15. Moore, *Voyage to Georgia*, 85–86; McPherson, *Journal of the Earl of Egmont*, 114–20.

16. Moore, *Voyage to Georgia*, 81.

17. McPherson, *Journal of the Earl of Egmont*, 107, 109; Coleman, *Colonial Georgia*, 122.

18. *Colonial Records*, November 19, 1735, 21:46; Moore, *Voyage to Georgia*, 80.

19. Curnock, *Journal of the Rev. John Wesley*, 1:121.

20. Ibid., 1:123, 262, 286; Horton to Causton, May 7, 1737, in Lane, *General Oglethorpe's Georgia*, 1:310. Horton's diatribe against John Wesley is recorded in Curnock, *Journal of the Rev. John Wesley*, 1:234.

21. Moore, *Voyage to Georgia*, 87; McPherson, *Journal of the Earl of Egmont*, 120, gives the date of departure as December 8.

22. Only once was punishment meted out, when a boy was whipped for stealing turnips. See Moore, *Voyage to Georgia*, 87–88.

23. Brownfield to Trustees, February 11, 1736, in *Colonial Records*, 21:112; Brownfield to Trustees, March 6, 1736, in Lane, *General Oglethorpe's Georgia*, 1:247; Moore, *Voyage to Georgia*, 91.

24. Moore, *Voyage to Georgia*, 103–4.

25. Lane, *General Oglethorpe's Georgia*, 1:239; Moore, *Voyage to Georgia*, 103–4.

26. Moore, *Voyage to Georgia*, 108–9, 118; Lane, *General Oglethorpe's Georgia*, 1:239.

27. Moore, *Voyage to Georgia*, 114.

28. Lane, *General Oglethorpe's Georgia*, 1:258.

29. Oglethorpe to Trustees, March 28, 1736, in *Colonial Records*, 21:124. See also the anonymous letter of April 12, 1736, in Lane, *General Oglethorpe's Georgia*, 1:262; Moore, *Voyage to Georgia*, 122–27.

30. Moore, *Voyage to Georgia*, 130–31.

31. Stewart, *"What Nature Suffers to Groe,"* 67.

32. Moore, *Voyage to Georgia*, 130–31.

33. Ibid., 147–48.

34. Lane, *General Oglethorpe's Georgia*, 1:269.

35. Moore, *Voyage to Georgia*, 146. For accounts of Horton's adventures as a prisoner, see 132–33, 137–39, 146–49; Lane, *General Oglethorpe's Georgia*, 1:269–71; McPherson, *Journal of the Earl of Egmont*, 150.

36. Moore, *Voyage to Georgia*, 150–51; Lane, *General Oglethorpe's Georgia*, 1:271–72.

37. Ivers, *British Drums*, 63–64.

38. Ibid., 78; Phinizy Spalding, *Oglethorpe in America*, 100; McPherson, *Journal of the Earl of Egmont*, 218.

39. McPherson, *Journal of the Earl of Egmont*, 246.

40. Hawkins to Trustees, June 24, 1737, in *Colonial Records*, 21:486; see also Elisha Dobree to Trustees, December 17, 1736, in ibid., 21:283–86.

41. Ibid., 21:459.

42. Horton to Causton, May 7, 1737, in Lane, *General Oglethorpe's Georgia*, 1:309–10.

43. Moore, *Voyage to Georgia*, 96.

44. Horton to Causton, May 7, 1737, in Lane, *General Oglethorpe's Georgia*, 1:309–10.

45. According to the Earl of Egmont, the words are those of one who had previously "fomented underhand" and contributed to the divisiveness at Frederica, who was now writing to assure Oglethorpe that Horton's orders were being obeyed "with pleasure." See Thomas Hird to Oglethorpe, December 5, 1737, in *Colonial Records*, 22:pt. 1, 121.

46. Ibid., 24:265.

47. *Journal of William Stephens*, December 13, 1737, in ibid., 4:49; Stephens to Trustees, December 20, 1737, in ibid., 22:pt. 1, 50.

48. Ruple, "Archeology of the Horton House," 20; J. Everett Fauber, "Captain Horton's House on Jekyll Island, Georgia: Research Report and a Proposal for Restoration," prepared for the Jekyll Island State Park Authority, April 10, 1967, 8, 10, copy in the Jekyll Island Museum.

49. Ruple, "Archeology of the Horton House," 106.

50. *Colonial Records*, 4:72–75, 669.

51. Lane, *General Oglethorpe's Georgia*, 2:344.

52. Ibid., 2:574, 346.

53. Ibid., 2:350; *Colonial Records*, 22:pt. 1, 275–76. Horton was later reimbursed for his generosity. See *Colonial Records*, 2:270.

54. Lane, *General Oglethorpe's Georgia*, 2:343–44.

55. *Colonial Records*, 4:345.

56. Lane, *General Oglethorpe's Georgia*, 2:346.

57. Ivers, *British Drums*, 80–82.

58. For references to Horton's character, see *Colonial Records*, 4:50; 5:425. See also ibid., 22:pt. 1, 275–76.

59. Ibid., 4:227–28, 247, 249, 327.

60. Ibid., 39:312–13.

61. Coleman, *Colonial Georgia*, 63–66; Lane, *General Oglethorpe's Georgia*, 2:451.

62. *Colonial Records*, 22:pt. 2, 284–85.

63. Ibid., 4:503, 538. It is possible that Rebecca Horton and her sons had already come to Georgia aboard one of the five ships that brought Oglethorpe's Forty-second Regiment of Foot and families to Frederica. That expedition included approximately three hundred women and children, who arrived at St. Simons on September 18, 1738.

64. Ibid., 5:347, 348, 351, 355.

65. Ibid., 5:347, 427, 426; the "Planters' Lobby" and Stephens are discussed at length in Taylor, *Georgia Plan*, 169–81.

66. *Colonial Records*, 5:356, 362.

67. Ibid., 5:385, 425; for Horton's changing views on slavery, see 5:48 and 25:347–51.

68. Ibid., 2:338; 5:355, 512, 591; Ivers, *British Drums*, 136.

69. The passenger list for his crossing on the *Symond* is extant, and his family was not with him on this earlier crossing.

70. Francis Moore to Harman Verelst, July 3, 1742, in Lane, *General Oglethorpe's Georgia*, 2:616.

71. Lane, *General Oglethorpe's Georgia*, 2:619; *Journal of William Stephens*, 1741–43, 103; Ivers, *British Drums*, 154.

72. Ivers, *British Drums*, 151–67. The English took prisoners during the battle, and William Logan records meeting one of them during his visit to Frederica in 1745: "Dined at Patrick Hewstons in Comp. with several Gent. Officers & a Spanish Captain, Prisoner who has been detailed here since the Spanish Invasion" ("William Logan's Journal," 171). Judging from Logan's comment, the Spanish captain was well treated by the English and even dined with their officers.

73. James Oglethorpe to the Duke of Newcastle, enclosure, July 30, 1742, in Lane, *General Oglethorpe's Georgia*, 2:622.

74. Ibid., 2:623; Ivers, *British Drums*, 170–71.

75. *Journal of William Stephens*, 226. It was not until February 10, 1763, with the Treaty of Paris, that the Seven Years' War (called the French and Indian War in America) ended and Spain finally ceded the entire area to Great Britain.

76. Scott, "Frederica Homefront," 506.

77. *Journal of William Stephens*, 6.

78. Lane, *General Oglethorpe's Georgia*, 2:568.

79. Ruple, "Archeology of the Horton House," 29–50.

80. Keber, *Seas of Gold*, 192.

81. *Colonial Records*, 25:248–49.

82. Ibid., 4:138.

83. *Journal of William Stephens*, 71; Coleman, *Colonial Georgia*, 116–17; *Colonial Records*, 31:27.

84. "William Logan's Journal," 177–78; see also 172.

85. *Colonial Records*, 25:249.

86. Ibid., 25:97.

87. It is not unlikely that Horton knew Eliza and Charles Pinckney, who lived near Charleston, where Horton had business dealings with Henry Laurens. Horton was even elected in 1747 to represent St. Helena Parish in the South Carolina Commons House of Assembly, even though he was a Georgia resident. Wood and Bullard, *Journal of a Visit*, 79 n. 84.

88. Ruple, "Archeology of the Horton House," 82, 107–8; Club Prospectus (1887), 27, Jekyll Island Museum; *New York Times*, April 9, 1892; *Brunswick Journal*, March 16, 1908, p. 3; *Colonial Records*, 25:248–49.

89. Wood and Bullard, *Journal of a Visit*, 25.

90. *Colonial Records*, 6:214–15, 219, 224.

91. See Elizabeth Evans Kilbourne, *Savannah, Georgia, Newspaper Clippings*, vol. 3 (Savannah: Elizabeth Evans Kilbourne, 1999), 127.

92. *Journal of William Stephens*, 112, 115, 149.

93. Ibid., 214–15, 217, 232–40, 247.

94. *Colonial Records*, 25:236, 244.

95. McCall, *History of Georgia*, quoted on 1:146; *Colonial Records*, 25:365. In *Our Todays and Yesterdays*, Margaret Davis Cate gives the date of Horton's death as January 23, 1748 (p. 45); however, she provides no source for this date and it is virtually certain that he was still alive toward the end of the year. His burial place was on the right-hand side as one entered the church, according to Levi Sheftall.

96. British Pension Register Indexes 8221, 8227, 8229, abstracts in Horton file in the Hartridge Collection, GHS. In 1800 Rebecca's pension is marked "d.d." (discharged deceased); *Colonial Records*, 6:214–15, 219, 224; Pat Bryant, compiler, Entry of Claims for Georgia Landholders, 1733–55, p. 127. William Aldworth Horton evidently did not survive to adulthood.

3. FROM ROYAL COLONY TO REVOLUTION

1. Ivers, *British Drums*, 214.

2. Harman Verelst to president and assistants in Georgia, January 2, 1749, *Colonial Records*, 31:113.

3. Ibid.

4. The original plans by John Thomas are located today at Fort Frederica.

5. *Colonial Records*, 26:210.

6. Patrick Demere, "Deméré of Georgia: The Story of the Family of Huguenot Redcoat Captains, Raymond and Paul Demeré," copy of typescript provided to me by Patrick Demere (2000), 7. The Demeré brothers' parents were Isaac Deméré and his wife, Marie La Chapelle, and they had two sisters, Catherine and Marguerite (or Margaret). Arthur Collins, *The Peerage of England* (London: W. Strahan, 1779), 54–57. The spelling of the Demeré name is, most commonly in America, written without any accents. The original French spelling included two accent marks— "Deméré." In using the spelling "Demeré," I am following the lead of Patrick Demere, for it most closely approximates the pronunciation of the name (Demray or Demry) in the St. Simons area.

7. Public Record Office, Kew, England, WO 25/89. It is interesting to note that

the famous missionary George Whitefield arrived on the same voyage as Raymond Demeré.

8. Manuel de Montiano to the governor of Havana, April 3, 1739, in East Florida Spanish Papers, Library of Congress, *Correspondence of the Governor of Florida with the Governor of Havana, 1737–1741*, vol. 37, folios 156–59. I used a transcription of this letter in the Cate Collection at the Georgia Historical Society. Details are taken from this account. One week after this incident, on April 11, 1739, Raymond and Paul Demeré's father died in Nérac.

9. Ivers, *British Drums*, 82.

10. For details on the siege at St. Augustine, see ibid., 105–24.

11. Ibid., 166.

12. William L. McDowell Jr., *The Colonial Records of South Carolina: Documents Relating to Indian Affairs, 1754–1765* (Columbia: South Carolina Department of Archives and History, 1970), 119.

13. See Coleman, *Colonial Georgia*, 174.

14. See ibid., 175–77.

15. *Colonial Records*, 6:227.

16. Ibid., 8:229, 355. Demeré also requested and was granted land at Newport, in Frederica, 530 acres in St. Andrew's Parish. See 8:202, 241, 246, 342, 769, 770–71.

17. Hawes, *Collections*, 1:274; cited in Wood and Bullard, *Journal of a Visit*, 76 n. 79.

18. "William Logan's Journal," 171. On October 13, as well as on many other occasions, he "dined at Capt. Demmerys in Co. with Capt Horton & other Gent & spent the afternoon in overlooking our Workman, supped at Capt Demmerys in Co. with the same Gentlemen that we dined with, it being Demmery's Clubb night" (172).

19. *Colonial Records*, 6:428. Captain Raymond Demeré received on February 8, 1754, a receipt for provisions for troops under his command in these locations from June 25 to December 23, 1753.

20. Wood and Bullard, *Journal of a Visit*, 24.

21. Ibid., 25, 27.

22. *Colonial Records*, 6:440; see also 9:376.

23. While the treaty ended the threats of France and Spain against the colony of Georgia, it would be a factor in the American Revolution. In the wake of the treaty, British subjects were prohibited by the Proclamation of 1763 from living west of the Appalachians, a stipulation designed to minimize conflict and placate all parties, including Native Americans. However, colonists considered it too restrictive and a clear indication that the British king did not understand their needs and interests.

24. Watkins and Watkins, *Digest of the Laws*, 114.

25. Information on the lawsuit involving his grandmother's estate comes from

Testamentary Lawsuit PROB 18/74/5 (1763), *Demeré versus Bourdillon and others. Proceedings of the Huguenot Society of Great Britain*, 24:1938–88. Miscellanea III: Huguenot Evidence in Testamentary Lawsuits, 158. Demeré's sisters Marguerite (called Margaret in English) and Catherine, now living in England, were also named as plaintiffs in the lawsuit.

26. *Colonial Records*, 9:376.

27. Ibid., 572. Information concerning the land in St. John's Parish comes from the *Georgia Gazette*, October 26, 1768, 2:2, where all of the lands except for Jekyll and the lot in Savannah were announced for sale at the Exchange in Savannah on the following November 25.

28. References to him in this capacity in the 1750s appear in the *Saint Christopher Register*, located in the National Archives of St. Kitts. Many records, including deeds, wills, court transcripts, and land transfer records, were lost in a courthouse fire in Basseterre in the early 1980s. Only a partial index, itself in poor condition, survives. Civil registration, recording births, marriages, and deaths, did not begin until 1855. Thus, information Clement Martin's early life and family is sparse.

29. *Colonial Records*, 6:443. At the same time Clement Martin Jr. requested lands on behalf of William Martin, including five hundred acres adjacent to his own. The council approved. Elizabeth de St. Julian is referred to as a widow in another land grant, ibid., 7:304. In his will, however, Clement Martin Jr. acknowledges all his children to be by a woman named Elizabeth Jackson and implies that they were born out of wedlock. It is also possible that Elizabeth Jackson was his former wife, who had remarried. Whether this is the same Elizabeth is impossible to ascertain on the basis of currently available records.

30. Ibid., 27:23.

31. Ibid., 73.

32. Ibid., 27:22; 7:89, 174. Martin had also been elected to represent the town of Ebenezer (along with George Cuthbert and James De Vaux) in the assembly. He was then chosen with De Vaux "to attend the Governor in the Council Chamber" and inform him of the elections. Ibid., 13:7.

33. Memorial of Alexander Kellet to the Board of Trade, July 7, 1756, in ibid., 27:117.

34. Ibid., 7:254. The accusations against Little are outlined in the council's letter to the governor, 251–54. His response begins on p. 255.

35. John Reynolds to the Board of Trade, September 22, 1755, in ibid., 27:73–74.

36. See ibid., 7:174, 264, 265; for additional details on the Little affair, see Abbot, *Royal Governors of Georgia*, 45–54.

37. William Little to Governor John Reynolds, September 12, 1755, in ibid., 7:255–61.

38. Memorial of Alexander Kellet to the Board of Trade, July 7, 1756, in ibid., 27:117.

39. Ibid., 28:pt. 1, 180.

40. James Wright to Board of Trade, February 20, 1761, in ibid., 28:pt. 1, 304.

41. See, for example, Davis, *Fledgling Province*, 147 n. 72, 162.

42. The 1906 edition of *Colonial Records*, 7:328, specifies only "Clement Martin Esqr" as the recipient of both grants. However, the 1977 publication of the original papers of Governor John Reynolds, published by Coleman and Ready in *Colonial Records*, 27:136, expands on the nature of the grant and specifies that one of the Newport grants was for "Clement Martin Senr. Esqr.," while the other one was for "Clement Martin Junr. Esqr." However, there is no question that Clement Martin Sr. was still at St. Kitts in 1761, for records of at least two deeds indicate his presence, both from June 1761 at the National Archives of St. Kitts, Record Book A2, 6637 and 6638.

43. *Colonial Records*, 7:175.

44. Ibid., 7:328, 330; 27:136.

45. Ibid., 7:782.

46. Ibid., 6:443. William Martin is not listed in Clement Martin Sr.'s will. Thus, if he was a son, he must have died or fallen from favor before 1775. He may have been a cousin or an uncle. It is interesting to note that Clement Jr. named one of his sons William.

47. Ibid., 9:40.

48. Ibid., 9:380.

49. *Georgia Gazette*, July 8, 1767. See also Hawes, *Georgia Historical Society*, 10:26.

50. Penson, *Colonial Agents*, 6. The information on dates of Clement Martin Sr.'s birth and marriage and other genealogical information were provided by his descendent Robert Cronk. The public records of St. Martins (not St. Kitts) indicate that a Clement Martin, who was married to a woman named Elizabeth, lived there. If these were one and the same, Jane Edwards would have been his second wife, and their marriage date considerably later. However, this Clement Martin, which can be either a British or French name, could very well be another person entirely. The name Clement (or Clément) was fairly common in the eighteenth century, and certainly Martin is not a rare surname in either English or French.

51. These children are all mentioned in Clement Martin's will, though Susannah receives only a token bequest, provoking speculation that she may have been illegitimate.

52. A series of letters from Thomas Mills dating from 1752 and 1753 makes it clear that Captain Clement Martin had become a merchant, but at least two of the letters refer to his shipments of sugar, which may suggest that he was also a sugar planter.

See D. W. Thomas, *West India Merchants and Planters in the Mid-eighteenth Century with Special Reference to St. Kitts*, master's thesis, University of Kent at Canterbury, England, February 1967.

53. Penson, *Colonial Agents*, 11.

54. Captain Thomas Southey, *Chronological History of the West Indies*, vol. 3 (1827; reprint, London: Frank Cass, 1968), 237, 319.

55. Ibid., 343.

56. Roger Sheridan, *The Development of the Plantations to 1750: An Era of West Indian Prosperity, 1750–1755* (Barbados: Caribbean Universities Press, 1970), 86.

57. See Ward, *British West Indian Slavery*, 38–40.

58. *Colonial Records*, 9:12–13.

59. Ibid., 9:402–3.

60. Ibid., 9:571–72; Office of the Secretary of State of Georgia, Register of Grants, Book G, p. 78. The island was surveyed in two tracts by George McKintosh, the first on March 10, 1765 (presumably the Clement Martin Jr. tract) and the second on February 18, 1768, Colonial Plats, Book C, 266.

61. *Colonial Records*, 10:434.

62. July 1, 1766, ibid., 9:571.

63. Ibid., 11:271.

64. We know that Demeré had ten white servants and eleven Negroes whom he planned to use in cultivating 1,150 acres on the Newport River. See ibid., 7:186. We also know that he had at least five Negro slaves at Frederica (four men and one woman) who were seized as valuable property by the Frederica constable, William Abbot, in a lawsuit brought against Demeré by Captain Caleb Davis pursuant to a dispute that began in 1747. See Raymond Demere Papers, Duke University.

65. See *Georgia Gazette*, February 24, 1768. Clement Martin Jr. was also a justice of the quorum. Button Gwinnett was, like John Martin, a justice of the peace from the parish of St. John, and both men were closely associated with Sunbury, where Martin was posted during his military service in the British Army.

66. Clement Sr. recognized the child of his late daughter in his will, which was drawn up in 1771. John Simpson applied on May 2, 1776, for permission to depart the province. He may have taken the child and returned to England. However, in 1783 a John Simpson was given the right to ship ten barrels of rice to east Florida "in order to pay for a negroe [*sic*] taken from him on the 9th January 1779." See Candler, *Revolutionary Records*, April 16, 1783, 2:493. It is uncertain whether this is the same John Simpson.

67. Coleman, *Georgia History in Outline*, 17.

68. James Wright to Henry Seymour Conway, March 15, 1766, in *Colonial Records*, 37:123. The Sons of Liberty held their first meeting on October 28. The first time

the term "Liberty Boys" was used in the Georgia press was in the *Georgia Gazette*, November 7, 1765.

69. *Colonial Records*, 12:421; *Georgia Gazette*, October 11, 1771. Yamacraw was a settlement on the outskirts of Savannah overlooking the Savannah River.

70. See Misc. Bonds Book R, 435–37, GDAH.

71. Will of Clement Martin Sr., Colonial Will Book AA, 212, GDAH.

72. Colonial Will Book, AA, 212, GDAH. The will was made on September 9, 1771. A copy of the will made by Charles Spalding Wylly is in the Jekyll Island Museum.

73. Will of Clement Martin Jr., Colonial Will Book AA, 190–93, GDAH.

74. Davis, *Fledgling Province*, 162. He cites as evidence a conveyance of Clement Martin Jr. to Elizabeth Jackson, July 7, 1755, Misc. Bonds Book R, 205, GDAH.

75. *Georgia Gazette*, December 20, 1775, 2:1.

76. Candler, *Revolutionary Records*, 1:207.

77. Ibid., 1:207–8.

78. Ibid., 1:146.

79. Agreement signed July 14, 1779, by Lewis Johnston, George Baillie, Richard Leake, and John Martin. Leake Papers, box 1, folder 1, University of North Carolina.

80. Cited in Coleman, *American Revolution in Georgia*, 48.

81. Killion and Waller, *Georgia and the Revolution*, 131.

82. Candler, *Revolutionary Records*, 1:146.

83. Ibid., 1:146, 207, 380; 2:443. Ironically, Clement Sr.'s son John bore the same name as the John Martin who became governor of Georgia after the Whigs took control. There were, in fact, at least three John Martins in the colony, which makes land records uncertain. I have thus been extremely cautious in attributing grants to this son of Clement Martin Sr., mentioning only those that were made at the time another family member also requested land.

84. Ibid., 1:380, 387.

85. See Robert S. Lambert, "The Repossession of Georgia, 1782–1784," *The Proceedings of the South Carolina Historical Association* (1957), 14–25; Horatio Marbury and William H. Crawford, *Digest of the Laws of the State of Georgia* (Savannah: Seymour, Wookhopter and Stebbins, 1802), 62–63.

86. He was named to the post on December 24, 1768. See *Colonial Records*, 9:107.

87. Candler, *Revolutionary Records*, 3:168.

88. See ibid., 3:136; 1:548. Among those whose lands he purchased was the late James Spalding, buying two hundred acres for £220. The will of Clement Martin Sr. was witnessed by George Houston, William Moore, and John B. Randall.

89. The letter of mark was granted on November 13, 1782. Ibid., 2:393. See Glynn County Archives, Records ABEF, 55 ff.

90. Jekyll Island was sold as a five-hundred-acre plot, which may have consisted only of what the state considered John Martin's portion. Or the county may have considered that to be the only arable land on the island. Sheriff's deed, dated June 30, 1784, recorded November 18, 1785, in the Office of the Clerk, Superior Court, Liberty County, Georgia. See also Liberty County, Deed Book A, 48.

91. See GHS, Colonial Dames of America Collection, 965, box 11, folder 124, titled "Thomas Spalding Family." A document (item 13) in this folder sets the 1784 price of Jekyll Island at thirty-four pounds eleven shillings. However, Liberty County documents make it clear that Leake paid five hundred pounds for the island at auction. This discrepancy is explained by a document drawn up at the time for Richard Leake, "The Commissioners of Confiscated Estates supposing that some lands which are really part of the Estate of the said Clement Martin [Sr.] to be the property of the said John Martin advertised them for sale." For details, see the Leake Papers, University of North Carolina.

92. Thomas Spalding, "Observations on the Introduction," 189–90. In his address before the 1860 Cotton Planters Convention of Georgia, Dr. Joseph Jones notes that "Previous to the year 1788, cotton was not cultivated in Georgia as an article of commerce; in this year, Richard Leake made an extensive and successful experiment in this new staple." See Joseph Jones, M.D., *Agricultural Resources of Georgia. Address before the Cotton Planters Convention of Georgia at Macon, December 13, 1860* (Augusta, Ga.: Steam Press of Chronicle and Sentinel, 1861), 8. See also Coulter, *Thomas Spalding*, 67–68.

93. Leake Plantation Book, box 11, folder 124, GHS.

94. *Georgia Gazette*, December 20, 1792; see also Leake Plantation Book.

95. Receipt from Francis Washington [?] to Richard Leake, Jekyll Island, May 7, 1789. Leake Papers, University of North Carolina.

96. *Georgia Gazette*, November 12, 1795. Leake also owned a plantation on St. Simons at Gascoigne Bluff, which James Hamilton purchased from him in 1793. See Sullivan, *Early Days*, 97.

97. On Leake's death, see the *Georgia Gazette*, March 18, 1802.

98. Concerning the price paid for the island, Martha Keber contends that the true asking price and the price Dumoussay paid was only one thousand pounds, but that for some reason Dumoussay deliberately inflated the island's price on the warranty deed to state the purchase price at two thousand pounds (*Seas of Gold*, 158–59). Articles of Agreement between Dumoussay and Leake, February 11, 1791, Howell Collection; Indenture of Lease, February 14, 1791, Glynn County Deed Book ABEF, pp. 53–55; Warranty Deed, February 15, 1791, Glynn County Deed Book ABEF, 55–60. See also Leake Plantation Book for Leake's comments about the sale.

4. THE LAND OF LIBERTY

1. See the State Constitution of Georgia, February 5, 1777, Watkins and Watkins, *Digest of Georgia Laws*, 8; see also Act 415 of the General Assembly of the State of Georgia, approved December 20, 1789, in ibid., 386. Jekyll was not specifically mentioned in this enactment, but it was clearly located in the designated area. Jekyll Island was added to St. James's Parish on March 25, 1765 (ibid., 114). Despite this change, deed books and legal records of 1791 still describe the island as being in Liberty County. See, for example, the deed by which Richard and Jane Leake sold the island to Dumoussay, February 14, 1791, recorded July 2, 1791, in Glynn County Deed Book A, 70. The warranty deed is on p. 72.

2. Documents relating to his birth and baptism are found in a private collection of Doris Finney Liebrecht under the title "Christophe-Anne Poulain Du Bignon: A Compilation of Information on His Life, on His Ancestors, the Poulains of Brittany; and on a Few of His Descendants." The originals of the documents relating to his birth and baptism are located in the Mairie of Lamballe, Côtes du Nord, France. The spelling of Henri du Bignon's name varies, as names often did in eighteenth-century France, and it is frequently written "Henry."

3. The company was established by Colbert in 1664 as La Compagnie des Indes Orientales but reorganized in 1719 as the Compagnie des Indes.

4. A record of du Bignon's career with the Compagnie des Indes is contained in a dossier at the Archives Nationales, côte Marine C⁷ 257. For a detailed account of Christophe's seafaring career and later life, see Keber, *Seas of Gold*.

5. She had been previously married to Lieutenant Jean Paschal Du Jong de Boisquenay. Her father was François Guillaume Lossieux de Fontenay, who had died in 1761. For a look at their relationships, see Keber, *Seas of Gold*, 79–82.

6. See ibid., 147.

7. See Liberty County Court House, Superior Court, Deed Book C (1793–95), p. 25. This document records the agreement between Poulain du Bignon and Dumoussay signed at St.-Brieuc, France, on October 5, 1790, and recorded in Liberty County on March 29, 1793. The sale of the island from John McQueen to Dumoussay is recorded in the same office, Book B, 170–71.

8. The other investors in the Sapelo property were Charles Pierre César Picot de Boisfeuillet, Nicholas François Magon (sometimes given as Mazon) de la Villehuchet, and Pierre Jacques Grandclos Meslé, who were the original investors, with Chappedelaine purchasing one of the shares of Sapelo in 1792. See Vanstory, *Georgia's Land*, 56–57.

9. Chappedelaine to George Washington, January 9, 1791, "Papers of George Washington, vol. 284," Floyd Collection, box 37, folder 459, GHS.

10. Concerning Washington's Savannah visit, see *Georgia Gazette*, May 12, 1791. Washington's diaries also recall his earlier visit from "the marquis de Chappedelaine," during which the two men rode and hunted together. See John C. Fitzpatrick, ed., *George Washington Diaries*, vol. 3 (Boston: Houghton Mifflin Company, 1925), 304, entries for February 13–15, 1788. For more detailed information on the Sapelo Company, see Kenneth H. Thomas Jr., "Sapelo Company," 37–64. See also Keber, "Refuge and Ruin," 173–200. All other references are to Keber, *Seas of Gold*, where she also discusses the Sapelo Company (169–91).

11. GCSC, Deed Book A, 60.

12. Tax Collector's Deed, GCSC, Deed Book K, 112. Keber (*Seas of Gold*, 175) gives the date as April 17, 1791, but the aforementioned legal record as well as others all give the date as 1792.

13. Keber, *Seas of Gold*, 159.

14. Ibid., 232. Thomas Dechenaux would be a good and loyal friend to du Bignon, handling many business matters for him in Savannah, witnessing various agreements, from the reestablishment of the lost agreement concerning land transfers to the baptism of his granddaughter, Maria Louisa, for whom Dechenaux's wife stood as godmother.

15. See Sullivan, *Early Days*, 763. See also Keber, *Seas of Gold*, 156.

16. See Liberty County Superior Court, Deed Book C (1793–95), 25.

17. Richard K. Murdoch, "Correspondence of the French Consuls in Charleston, 1793–1797," *South Carolina Historical Magazine* 74 (1973): 7.

18. See Keber, *Seas of Gold*, 179.

19. Quoted from Act 53 of the General Assembly, the "Act to relieve the heirs of Francis Marie Loys Dumousay de la Vaue [*sic*], the heirs of Hyacinth de Chapedelane [*sic*] and Christopher Poulain Dubignon," February 19, 1796, Watkins and Watkins, *Digest of Georgia Laws*, 592–93. See also Deposition of Dechenaux and du Bignon, GCSC, Deed Book C, 226.

20. Dumoussay tried almost immediately to unload du Bignon's share, advertising in the *Georgia Gazette* on June 19, 1794, "one divided Fifth Part of Sapelo Island, containing two thousand two or three hundred acres, formerly the property of M. Poulain Dubignon at the Hermitage Plantation upon Tea Kettle Creek." See Liberty County Court House, Superior Court, Deed Book C (1793–95), 25. The other one-fourth of Jekyll belonged jointly to Villehuchet and Grandclos Meslé.

21. For details on his problems with the Revolution and his subsequent execution, see Keber, *Seas of Gold*, 189.

22. See ibid., 186–87.

23. *Georgia Gazette*, September 25, 1794. See "Skeletons of the History of the Jemison and Boisfeuillet Families," compiled by Mamie Jemison Chestney, 1964,

GHS. See also the Sacramental Register no. 1, 1786–1816, Cathedral of St. John the Baptist, where the date is recorded as August 13, 1800.

24. Act 553 of the General Assembly of the State of Georgia. See Watkins and Watkins, *Digest of Georgia Laws*, 592.

25. Dechenaux's depositions are recorded in GCSC, Deed Book C, 217, 220, 223, and 226.

26. GCSC, Deeds and Mortgages 1765–1800, 82, box 33, 300–301; see also 199–201.

27. This sale was never officially recorded, but the document attesting to it remains in the hands of the du Bignon family. See Keber, *Seas of Gold*, 188–89.

28. Christophe Poulain du Bignon to René Peltier, March 1, 1798, Fonds Revel, 58J, Archives Départementales des Côtes d'Armor. Cited in Keber, *Seas of Gold*, 9.

29. Dumoussay sold the southern half of St. Catherines to du Bignon's friend Thomas Dechenaux in June 1794.

30. Keber, *Seas of Gold*, 199.

31. For the names of the servants, see ibid., 183.

32. Mark Van Doren, ed., *Travels of William Bartram*, 75, 77–78.

33. John McQueen to Eliza Ann, May 31, 1799. Du Bignon Correspondence, Jekyll Island Museum. Walter C. Hartridge, ed., *The Letters of Don Juan McQueen to His Family* (Columbia, S.C.: Georgia Society of the Colonial Dames of America, 1943), 52.

34. See *Republican and Savannah Evening Ledger*, May 21, 1812, 3:4.

35. See Aaron Burr to Theodosia, August 31, 1804, in Matthew L. Davis, ed., *Memoirs of Aaron Burr*, vol. 2 (1836; reprint, Freeport, N.Y.: Books for Libraries Press, 1970), 334. The editor transcribed Amelia Nicolau's name as "Mademoiselle Nicholson." I have taken the liberty of correcting it.

36. Maurice and Maurice, *Jekyl Island*, 7. Charlotte Maurice, whose account is based on personal recollections from members of the du Bignon family several generations removed from the incident, says she was staying with the James Hamilton Coupers, but in 1804, James Hamilton Couper was but a ten-year-old boy. Without question, the host was John Couper, who was renowned for his hospitality at his plantation, Cannon's Point.

37. Keber, *Seas of Gold*, 220–21.

38. The civil marriage may have taken place shortly after the signing of the prenuptial agreement, but the Catholic priest made his rounds infrequently, and it was not uncommon for the religious marriage to be performed somewhat later than the legal marriage. The prenuptial agreement, dated April 30, 1807, is recorded on June 20, 1808, in GCSC, Deed Book F, folio 37–39 and in the current Book ABEF, 530–31. The record of the marriage itself is in the Sacramental Register, no. 1, Archives of the Diocese of Savannah.

39. Letter from Grand Dutreuilh to "ma très chère et bonne maman," June 14, 1802, Port Républicain, Grand Dutreuilh Family Papers, GDAH. The young man's full name was Louis Claude Jean-Baptiste Jerome Grand Dutreuilh, son of Jean Baptiste Jerome Grand Dutreuilh and his wife, Marie Anne Félicité Rossignol Belleanse Grand Dutreuilh.

40. Grand Dutreuilh to "ma chère maman," Vendredi à 1 heure après-midi [n.d.], Frederica, Grand Dutreuilh Family Papers, GDAH.

41. Grand Dutreuilh to "ma chère maman," January 12, 1809, Grand Dutreuilh Family Papers, GDAH.

42. The record of Anne Georgienne Goupy's baptism on July 16, 1801, the day before Henri du Bignon's baptism, affirms that she was born on Jekyll Island on October 22, 1800. See Sacramental Register, no. 1, 1786–1816, Cathedral of St. John the Baptist. The information concerning the slave sale is from a list compiled by Martha Keber, based on records in the Glynn County Court House, and contained in the Jekyll Island Museum.

43. Louis Grand Dutreuilh to his mother, January 12, 1809, Grand Dutreuilh Family Papers, GDAH. Concerning the life of Pierre Bernardey, see Bullard, *Pierre Bernardey*, 108, 134–38. See also Bullard, *Robert Stafford*, 82–83.

44. Another non-French farmer who rented lands on Jekyll was John W. Gray. Like Pierre Bernardey, he purchased a five-hundred-acre tract on Cumberland, the Springs Plantation, and moved there with his slaves in 1825. See Bullard, *Cumberland Island*, 134.

45. Keber, *Seas of Gold*, 231.

46. According to a document contained in the Margaret Davis Cate Collection, box 16, folder 377, GHS, the information about the three Wylly children born on Jekyll Island was copied by Margaret C. Stiles directly from the Wylly family Bible, which was owned at the time by the late Thomas S. Wylly. The children born on Jekyll included Margaret Matilda Wylly, February 19, 1804; John Armstrong Wylly, October 29, 1805; and Heriot Louisa Baillie Wylly, April 1, 1808. They apparently left Jekyll shortly thereafter (some sources give the date 1809, others 1810 for their departure), because the Wyllys' eleventh child, Caroline Georgia Wylly, was born at the family's new residence of St. Clair on St. Simons on May 24, 1811.

47. M. H. [Mary Houston] to Mother [Elizabeth T. Houston], December 24, 1957, Wylly Papers. Houston, who was from Marengo Plantation, was visiting the Wyllys for the wedding of Caroline Wylly to James Hamilton Couper, which took place December 25, 1827, at The Village. See also M. H. to Mother, January 4, 1828, Wylly Papers, for additional details about Susan and a description of Captain Wylly, whom Mary considered "a warm hearted hospitable gentleman—courtesy itself to all in or of his household, but you can feel that to him life has brought many

and bitter disappointments." Susan Wylly died in October 1829, the year after this last letter was written. She is buried at Christ Church, St. Simons.

48. Susan Wylly to Louisa du Bignon, June 26, 1824, Liebrecht Collection.

49. Keber, *Seas of Gold*, 206.

50. Roswell King to Pierce Butler, October 30, 1814, no. 1447, series II, A, box 2, folder 25, Butler Papers, Historical Society of Pennsylvania, Philadelphia. Cited in Keber, *Seas of Gold*, 213.

51. See Keber, *Seas of Gold*, 214.

52. War of 1812, Claims under Treaty of Ghent, Record Group 76, Entry 190, Claim 137, National Archives, Washington, D.C.

53. Although the Treaty of Ghent was signed on December 24, 1814, it was not ratified by the Congress and president and finally proclaimed until the following February 18. However, by the time of the second invasion of Jekyll, there was no doubt that the British knew that the war had ended. See du Bignon's deposition, July 16, 1821, War of 1812, Claims under the Treaty of Ghent, Record Group 76, Entry 190, Claim 137, National Archives, Washington, D.C.

54. Ibid., December 24, 1814.

55. Miscellaneous Treasury Account 52518, August 25, 1827, National Archives, Washington, D.C. See also Keber, *Seas of Gold*, 219.

56. See Keber, *Seas of Gold*, 212; Bell, *Major Butler's Legacy*, 111.

57. The story is recounted in *Jekyll's Golden Islander*, April 2, 1980. See the deposition of John Couper, October 16, 1827, Record Group 76, Entry 190, Claim 137, National Archives, Washington, D.C.

58. *Georgia Gazette*, July 31, 1794, 2:2.

59. *Columbian Museum and Savannah Advertiser*, July 12, 1808.

60. See GCPC Wills and Appraisals, Book D, 153. The values were appraised on December 31, 1825.

61. The original of this document is in the GCPC, Wills and Appraisals, Book D, 153. Being a free person of color in Georgia was not yet as dangerous as it would be in the years just prior to the Civil War, but it was never a comfortable position in antebellum Georgia. Unfortunately, we do not know what happened to Maria Theresa after du Bignon's death.

62. For Louis Jerome's seafaring career, see Keber, *Seas of Gold*, 82, 84, 122, 128–29, 225–26.

63. Keber argues that du Bignon would not have objected to this marriage on the issue of consanguinity, for "marriages between an uncle and niece were rare but not held to be incestuous" (*Seas of Gold*, 238). While that may have been true in terms of public opinion, it was certainly not true of the Catholic Church. Marriage was forbidden between an uncle and niece, whether of full or half blood, and, according

to Church law, would require a special dispensation, of which we have no evidence. As a Catholic as well as a father, du Bignon must have had qualms about the relationship. Although consanguinity may not have been his primary objection to the marriage, it was no doubt a factor. See Humphrey J. Desmond, *The Church and the Law, with Special Reference to Ecclesiastical Law in the United States* (Chicago: Callaghan, 1898), C.x.

64. Their marriage license, dated October 27, 1819, is recorded in Chatham County Marriage Records, 1805–52, compiled by Mabel F. LaFar, 1939, no. 654. Clémence's name is given in this typewritten record as "Clemence D. Borgrias," an apparent misreading of Clémence [Du Jong] de Boisquenay. Joseph apparently died in about 1830. He is no longer listed in the 1830 census record, which lists only "Mrs. Joseph DuBignon." However, it was not until April 20, 1831 (*Savannah Daily Georgian*, 2:6) that his brother Henri applied for letters of administration on Joseph's estate.

65. The ad suggested that interested parties could apply to "Poulain Dubignon, Esq. at his residence on the island, or in Savannah to Richard Leake." *Savannah Daily Georgian*, November 16, 1819, 3:3.

66. Keber, *Seas of Gold*, 243.

67. Ibid., 237.

68. Henry du Bignon to M. Peltier, February 9, 1828. 58J, Archives départementales des Côtes d'Armor.

5. BITTER HARVEST

1. On December 31, 1825, James Gould, James B. Wright, and John W. Gray appraised the estate of Christophe Poulain du Bignon. Their appraisal is recorded in Glynn County Estate Records, Inventories, Appraisements, 1810–53, drawer 82, box 4. The will is recorded in book D, file 155, February 18, 1826; see also Glynn County Wills and Deeds 1825, 153.

2. Robert Stafford, for example, in 1830 had 148 slaves to work only 1,360 acres. Du Bignon owned fewer than half that number in 1826. By 1850 Stafford had 348 slaves, while du Bignon's never increased to more than 57.

3. This entire process is described in detail in Rosengarten, *Tombee*, 70–74. Moting was a part of the process whereby ginned cotton was laid out on a frame, before baling, for one final cleaning by hand to remove any debris, specks, or yellow cotton that might have escaped the "assorting" phase of preparation.

4. Keber, *Seas of Gold*, 235.

5. Henry du Bignon to M. Peltier, May 31, 1827, Archives départementales des Côtes d'Armor.

6. See Southern Historical Association, *Memoirs of Georgia*, 1:263.

7. See James C. Bonner, *Milledgeville: Georgia's Antebellum Capital* (Athens: University of Georgia Press, 1978), 164.

8. See Anna Maria Green Cook, *History of Baldwin County, Georgia* (1895; reprint, Spartanburg, S.C.: Southern Historical Association, 1978), 311, 384–85. Concerning Charles and Ann du Bignon, see also *Biographical Souvenir of the States of Georgia and Florida* (Chicago: Battey, 1889), 247–48.

9. Copy of a letter in the Liebrecht Collection, Ref. 28. Joseph Nicolau was also the cousin of Joseph du Bignon's bride, Félicité. His father was Bernard Nicolau, the brother of Joseph's mother, while his mother was "Treyette" Grand Dutreuilh, sister of Félicité's mother.

10. *Brunswick Advocate*, December 27, 1838.

11. Anne Amelia Nicolau du Bignon to Eliza du Bignon, July 14, 1845, Liebrecht Collection.

12. A letter from W. Bourke to John du Bignon, written on July 17, 1855, while he was evidently still serving in the legislature, concerns the nomination of a Mr. King. Bourke is writing to solicit John's vote, without which, he argued, Mr. Burnett and Mr. Houston will "rule the county." He speaks of the "rascality of this party." From the tone of the letter, he seems to think that John is indifferent to the issue. Liebrecht Collection.

13. Letter contained in the Liebrecht Collection.

14. Fanny Nicolau to Eliza du Bignon, January 29 (no year), Du Bignon letters, Jekyll Island Museum. This is one of a collection of sixteen letters written between 1824 and 1860 that were acquired by Dr. Jacob Solis Cohen during the Union occupation of Jekyll Island in 1862. His descendent Charles L. Rosenthal returned them to the Jekyll Island Museum, with copies to du Bignon family members in August 1985.

15. Military Records, 1808–29, microfilm, box 16, drawer 40, GDAH. See also the *Savannah Georgian*, March 6, 1828, and February 2, 1830.

16. *Republican and Savannah Evening Ledger*, December 27, 1809.

17. This statement by Roswell King is cited in Stewart, *"What Nature Suffers to Groe,"* 185.

18. See, for example, the Charles Rinaldo Floyd Diary entries for February 21–23, 1834; August 24, 1834; October 18, 19, 30, 31, 1834; and January 13–14, 1836; Floyd Collection, GHS. He records visits to Jekyll on December 1 and 6, 1834.

19. See, for example, ibid., July 27, 1838.

20. Ibid., January 12, 1836.

21. Coulter, "Boating as a Sport," 237.

22. *Brunswick Advocate*, June 8, 1837.

23. Ibid., November 2, 1837, p. 3.

24. Coulter, "Boating as a Sport," 244.

25. The article, originally appearing in the *Savannah Georgian*, was reprinted in the *Brunswick Advocate* on May 10, 1838, p. 2. Julia Floyd Smith mentions this race in her book *Slavery and Rice Culture*, 168.

26. *Brunswick Advocate*, January 18, 1838, p. 2.

27. Ibid., May 3, 1838; see also Coulter, "Boating as a Sport," 231–47.

28. *Weekly Georgian*, February 9, 1840.

29. *Daily Georgian*, April 23, 1849. Cited in Coulter, "Boating as a Sport," 246.

30. See Floyd Diary, September 28, 1833.

31. The duel was reported in the *Georgian*, October 9, 1833, 2:1. See Floyd Diary, entry for June 30, 1833; September 27–28, 1833. This was the same spot where another well-known duel took place between Charles Spalding and Thomas Butler King in January 1845, also recorded in the Floyd Diary on January 6, 1845.

32. Eighteen months later Henri du Bignon witnessed another such shooting, when Dr. Thomas E. Hazzard killed John Wylly at the Oglethorpe House in early December 1838. See *Brunswick Advocate*, December 6, 1838, p. 3.

33. Holmes, *"Dr. Bullie's" Notes*, 107–9. The editor of this edition erroneously identifies the "Col. du Bignon" in question as Charles Joseph du Bignon. This identification is clearly not correct. Charles Joseph, who was only twenty-eight at the time of the incident, had not risen to the rank of colonel in any military position, nor had he earned any such honorary title. At the time, however, his father, commonly referred to as "Col. du Bignon," was well-known in the area, a good friend of General Charles R. Floyd, and a cosecretary of the Aquatic Club of Georgia. No evidence places Charles Joseph du Bignon at the Oglethorpe House on this occasion, though Henri du Bignon was present without question.

34. Floyd Diary, February 20, 1837.

35. Ibid., March 7, 1834. Selecting the seed was a much-valued process that determined the quality of the future cotton yields.

36. Julia's recollections are contained in *Slave Narratives, Georgia*, vol. 12, part 3 (1936; reprint, St. Clair Shores, Mich.: Scholarly Press, 1976). Her story is also collected in *The American Slave: A Composite Autobiography*, vol. 13, pt. 3 (Westport, Conn.: Greenwood Publishing Company, 1941), 229–31.

37. Eugenia's husband, Archibald Burke, would not release Julia from her bondage even after the Civil War, according to this account. It states that Julia tried repeatedly to escape and finally succeeded, moving to another part of the state, where she married. On the relationships between masters and their female slaves as well as between the master's wife and his slave mistress, see Fox-Genovese, *Within the Plantation Household*, especially 192–241.

38. Will of Christophe Poulain du Bignon, Glynn County Wills, Inventories, and Appraisements, 1825.

39. Some area planters were even more lenient than du Bignon. James Hamilton Couper, the son of John Couper, for example, was considered "the epitome of the benevolent master," according to his biographer, James Bagwell (*Rice Gold*, 119). Although in many respects his treatment of his slaves followed patterns similar to those of du Bignon's plantation, Bagwell describes somewhat more lenient workdays, rations that included pork (though still supplemented by vegetables from the slaves' gardens), and an even more generous clothing allotment, whereby adult slaves received two pairs of shoes a year (123–25).

40. On the vicissitudes of cotton growing, see Rosengarten, *Tombee*, 74–75. Such diversification as that in which Henri du Bignon engaged was not unusual. Ralph Betts Flanders notes that "many slave owners and planters were not primarily interested in augmenting their fortunes by their planting interests, but looked to other investments for their major profits. The ownership of slaves constituted a badge of honor and membership in a select group" (*Plantation Slavery in Georgia*, 225).

41. Du Bignon also owned Central Rail Road and Banking stock.

42. *Brunswick Advocate*, November 1, 1838, p. 3.

43. See Bullard, *Robert Stafford*, 97.

44. She is listed among the island residents in the 1840 census record.

45. The marriage between Sarah Ann Maccaw and George Butler Aust is recorded in W. Bruce Bannerman and Major W. Bruce Bannerman, eds., *The Registers of St. Stephen's, Walbrook, and of St. Benet Sherehog, London*, pt. 2 (London: 1920), 269. They were married January 16, 1830, and are noted as being of St. Mary, Newington, London. I am grateful to E. Lynn McLarty, who provided this information and copies of the register entries. Additional information comes from the "Index of West Palmetto Cemetery, Brunswick, Georgia," Three Rivers Library, Brunswick, 57–58.

46. A notice of George Aust's death appeared in the *Brunswick Advocate*, January 25, 1838. It states that he was "in the 38th year of his age." Aust had recently been a candidate for county surveyor. In the election held in early January 1838, he was defeated by John M. Tisou. See ibid., December 7, 1837, and January 4, 1838. The following curious statement appeared with the announcement of his death: "He is now beyond the reach of friendship or of hatred; nor can his ashes be affected by censure, or by praise. May he rest in peace; and if charity and good nature open not the benevolent lip, let the finger of silence rest on the tongues of malevolence and detraction."

47. Baptisms, Marriages, Deaths, 1816–38, Mss, Cathedral of St. John the Baptist. See also Charles Spalding Wylly, *Memories* (Brunswick: 1916); Julia Floyd Smith, *Slavery and Rice Culture*, 158.

48. Amelia du Bignon to Eliza du Bignon, July 14, 1845, Liebrecht Collection.

49. Maurice and Maurice, *Jekyl Island*, 7–8. Although Charlotte Maurice was not herself an eyewitness to the event, she made an effort to gather information from people who were. Thus, in all probability the account is reasonably accurate.

50. The marriage of Henri and Mary is recorded in the Marriage Record Book A, in GCSC.

6. FROM THE *WANDERER* TO WAR

1. Wells, *Slave Ship Wanderer*, 24.

2. Assessments of the number of Africans who survived the *Wanderer* vary considerably from as few as 70 to as many as 700. The number 409 is given as the best and most credible assessment in ibid., 31.

3. The theoretical capacity of the vessel was 380. Both the fact that the Africans were loaded "spoon fashion" into the vessel and the fact that most of them were young allowed the captors to expand the number, thus providing what must have been almost unbearable conditions to the captives. The record on which the original 487 number of passengers is based was a notebook introduced into evidence during legal proceedings. The handwriting was that of William Corrie, one of Lamar's co-owners of the *Wanderer* and also its captain. See ibid., 30. Despite the fact that the *Augusta Dispatch* reported, "We learn on good authority that the original cargo consisted of 420, and that not one of them died or was seriously ill on the passage" (quoted in *Savannah Daily Morning News*, December 17, 1858), both the documentary evidence and the various court testimony, which estimated losses between 60 and 80, make it clear that 12 to 16 percent of the Africans lost their lives en route.

4. On the capacity of the slave ship, see Wells, *Slave Ship Wanderer*, 30.

5. The *Wanderer* was not the last shipload of Africans brought to America as slaves, as many have contended, but rather the last documented (and successful) ship to have brought such large numbers. In July 1859 a vessel called the *Clothilde* brought 116 captives (out of an original 175) to Mobile Bay. Reports of others exist but cannot be clearly and indisputably documented. On such attempts to revive the African slave trade, see Wish, "Revival," 569–88.

6. Montgomery, "Survivors from the Cargo," 611–27. One of the recently arrived was a baby born on the *Wanderer,* who was given the name Clementine. She lived in the Brunswick area, where she was known as "Mom Clem" or "Steamboat." A notice of her death appeared in the *Brunswick Advocate*, January 20, 1923. Information concerning her birth during the voyage is reported in a statement by Maria C. Blain contained in the Margaret Davis Cate Collection, GHS.

7. Wells, *Slave Ship Wanderer*, 28.

8. Ibid.

9. Ibid., 29. Information concerning Sophia Tillman's purchase of the *Wanderer* slaves is from Francis Butler Simkins, *Pitchfork Ben Tillman: South Carolinian* (Baton Rouge: Louisiana State University Press, 1944), 30.

10. Mrs. Hugh McLeod (Rebecca Lamar), "The Loss of the Steamer Pulaski," *Georgia Historical Quarterly* 3 (1919): 63–95. According to her account of the 131 passengers aboard the *Pulaski*, 77 were lost. Thomas Lamar, one of the younger brothers of Charles, survived the wreckage but died of hunger, thirst, and exposure, like many of the others, while they were waiting to be rescued.

11. Wells, *Slave Ship Wanderer*, 3. The second description is taken from Winfield Thompson, "Slave Ship Wanderer," 54. The third quotation comes from Bancroft, *Slave Trading*, 359. The Thompson article also gives a physical description of Lamar as "of medium build, with sandy hair and mustache, rather florid complexion and blue eyes" (54).

12. This quotation is from Lamar's pamphlet, *The Reply of C. A. L. Lamar of Savannah, Georgia, to the Letter of Hon. Howell Cobb, Secretary of the Treasury of the United States, Refusing a Clearance to the Ship Richard Cobden* (Charleston: 1858), 1.

13. *Savannah Daily Morning News*, August 14, 1858.

14. These are the views expressed in "Slave-Trader's Letter-Book," 449. The letter-book is allegedly that of Charlie Lamar. Tom Henderson Wells concurs that it has the style and tone of Lamar's letters. Unfortunately, the original is lost. See Wells, *Slave Ship Wanderer*, 5, 97–98.

15. Winfield Thompson, "Slave Ship Wanderer," 54.

16. The *Wanderer* was built in 1856–57 in Fort Jefferson, New York, a construction supervised by its sailing master, Captain Thomas Brewster Hawkins. It was designed and built by W. J. Rowland of Setauket.

17. Charles Lamar to Caro Lamar, January 10, 1858, Lamar Papers, GDAH. A letter from W. D. Duncan to Godfrey Barnsley (curiously dated January 8, 1858, a date clearly in error) notes that the ball entered "about an inch under the eye." Godfrey Barnsley Papers, Duke University.

18. See the *Georgian*, October 9, 1833, 2:1.

19. [C. A. L. Lamar] to L. Viana, December 26, 1857, quoted in "Slave-Trader's Letter Book," 452.

20. *Savannah Daily Morning News*, December 28, 1858.

21. *New York Times*, March 28, 1859, 4:5; April 22, 1859, 2:1.

22. *Savannah Republican*, quoted in the *New York Times*, April 22, 1859, 2:1.

23. *New York Times*, April 1, 1859; *New York Tribune*, April 1, 1859.

24. *New York Times*, April 22, 1859, 4:3.

25. [C. A. L. Lamar] to J. S. Thrasher, February 25, 1855, quoted in "Slave-Trader's Letter-Book," 449.

26. Wells, *Slave Ship Wanderer*, 45, 58–59. See also Minutes of the Sixth Circuit Court, Savannah, NARA. Doris Finney Liebrecht, a du Bignon descendent, writes that the notoriety gained in the *Wanderer* incident had a devastating effect on Henry du Bignon. Although he was not found guilty of any crime and his case was dismissed, the "whole episode broke his spirit. He became a recluse and lived in a 'shack' on Jekyll alone. He never married" (Liebrecht Collection). It was, in fact, John Couper du Bignon who lived alone in the shack on Jekyll. Henry du Bignon died in 1885. John du Bignon survived in his solitude until 1890.

27. Wells, *Slave Ship Wanderer*, 47.

28. Louella Styles Vincent, "From Chapter IV of 'My Mary and Others,' a story of the Old South," a typewritten document in the Carey W. Styles Papers, Emory University. See also Wells, *Slave Ship Wanderer*, 70.

29. *Savannah Republican*, quoted in *Charleston Courier*, May 30, 1860.

30. Even the churches of the South, many of which had split from their northern counterparts in 1844, refused to accept the idea that slavery was immoral. In fact, many preached that it was a Christian duty to help the "savages" by bringing them to work and to worship in a Christian world.

31. *Savannah Daily Morning News*, December 14, 1858.

32. T. R. R. Cobb to Howell Cobb, March 4, 1860, Howell Cobb Collection, University of Georgia.

33. Wells, *Slave Ship Wanderer*, 68.

34. See Lincoln's First Inaugural address.

35. Paul Angle, ed., *Created Equal? The Complete Lincoln-Douglas Debates of 1858* (Chicago: University of Chicago Press, 1958), 17.

36. C. A. L. Lamar to Father, November 26, 1860, Lamar Papers, Emory University. On the du Bignon family's sentiments toward the war, see McCash and McCash, *Jekyll Island Club*, 3–4.

37. Diary of George A. Mercer, January 19, 1861, original in the Southern Historical Collection, Wilson Library, University of North Carolina; typescript copy in the Mercer Papers, GHS. I am grateful to both Henry Howell and Martha Keber for alerting me to this diary.

38. Ibid., 148.

39. Most Glynn County residents who evacuated went into adjacent Brantley, Wayne, and Ware counties.

40. Bell, *Major Butler's Legacy*, 358.

41. Mercer Diary, December 22, 1861.

42. WR, ser. 1, vol. 6, p. 305. See also C. A. L. Lamar to Henry C. Wayne, December 5, 1861, Civil War Mss. Collection, GDAH. A few of the officers, including Lamar, had brought slaves with them to the island, which may account for the discrepancy in the numbers.

43. C. A. L. Lamar to Father, November 5, 1860, Lamar Papers, Emory University.

44. C. A. L. Lamar to Adj. Gen. Henry C. Wayne, May 23, 1861, Civil War Mss. Collection, GDAH.

45. C. A. L. Lamar to Father, December 22, 1861, Lamar Papers, GDAH.

46. C. A. L. Lamar to Father, December 18, 1861, ibid.

47. C. A. L. Lamar to Father, December 22, 1861; C. A. L. Lamar to Father, December 26, 1861, ibid.

48. Mercer Diary, January 12, 1862.

49. C. A. L. Lamar to Father, December 13, 1861, Lamar Papers, GDAH.

50. Mercer Diary, January 4, 1861.

51. C. A. L. Lamar to Father, December 22, 1861, Lamar Papers, GDAH.

52. C. A. L. Lamar to Father, December 22, 1861, ibid.

53. C. A. L. Lamar to Caro [Lamar], January 31, 1862, ibid.

54. Charlie [C. A. L. Lamar] to Caro [Lamar], February 8, 1862, ibid. Two heavy gun carriages were discovered in April 1965 on the south end of the island. Ross Hopkins, a historian at Frederica National Monument, judged them to be of 1860 vintage, equipped to mount both one-hundred-pounder and two-hundred-pounder Parrott muzzle-loading seacoast artillery. However, he believed they had been erected during the island's fortification for the Spanish-American War in 1898. *Brunswick News*, April 27, 1965.

55. WR, ser. 1, vol. 6, p. 368.

56. Ibid., 315.

57. Robert E. Lee to Hon. J. P. Benjamin, February 6, 1862, ibid., 376.

58. Ibid., 377.

59. C. A. L. Lamar to Father, February 8, 1862, Lamar Papers, GDAH.

60. C. A. L. Lamar to Caro [Lamar], January 31, 1862, ibid.

61. Charlie [C. A. L. Lamar] to Caro [Lamar], February 8, 1862, ibid.

62. R. E. Lee to Joseph E. Brown, February 10, 1862, and R. E. Lee to J. P. Benjamin, February 10, 1862, WR, ser. 1, vol. 6, pp. 379–80.

63. Mercer Diary, February 14, 1862.

64. Robert E. Lee to General S. Cooper, February 18, 1862, WR, ser. 1, vol. 6, p. 390.

65. Joseph E. Brown to R. E. Lee, February 21, 1862, ibid., 396.

66. See the account given by the Union commander S. W. Godon, ORN, ser. 1, vol. 12, p. 608, in which he reports that "The fire we noticed was the work of retiring soldiers and proved to be the railroad depot and wharf."

67. Ibid., 592.

68. Ibid., 592.

69. Gabriel Farmer to Mother, March 14, 1862, Gabriel Farmer Family Civil War Papers, folder 2, GDAH.

70. ORN, ser. 1, vol. 12, pp. 610–11.

71. He made his report on March 30, 1862. Ibid., 633.

72. A gun emplacement, minus the gun, remains on the south end of the island today, still hidden among the dunes that have grown wider since 1862. See note 54.

73. ORN, ser. 1, vol. 12, p. 689.

74. Ibid.

75. Ibid., 727.

76. E. Lanier to Samuel F. Du Pont, April 18, 1862, ibid., 756.

77. Jacob Solis Cohen Diary, in the possession of Charles L. Rosenthal; copies in the possession of Doris Liebrecht and the Jekyll Island Museum.

78. Elinor Barnes and James A. Barnes, eds., *Naval Surgeon: The Diary of Dr. Samuel Pellman Boyer* (Bloomington: Indiana University Press, 1963), 1:51–52.

79. C. A. L. Lamar to Gen. Wayne, March 28, 1862, Civil War Mss. Collection, GDAH.

80. See C. A. L. Lamar to Gen. Wayne, March 10, 1862, ibid.; Wells, "Charles Augustus Lafayette Lamar," 166.

81. C. A. L. Lamar to Gen. Henry C. Wayne, June 8, 1863, Civil War Mss. Collection, GDAH.

82. Joseph E. Brown, March 1, 1864, in Allen D. Candler, ed., *The Confederate Records of the State of Georgia* (Atlanta: 1909), 2:581.

83. C. A. L. Lamar to Gen. Wayne, January 15, 1864, Civil War Mss. Collection., GDAH.

84. Wells, "Charles Augustus Lafayette Lamar," 166. The blockade-running vessels in the fleet were the *Little Ada*, the *Mary Bowen*, the *Lillian*, the *Little Hattie*, and the *Florie*. The *Susan Brown* was added to the fleet late in 1864. See Thomas R. Hay, "Gazaway Bugg Lamar, Confederate Banker and Business Man," *Georgia Historical Quarterly* 37 (1953): 120.

85. See Hay, "Gazaway Bugg Lamar," 120. Tom Wells reported that the vessel was alleged to have made sixty successful trips, though such a figure is clearly inflated. See his "Charles Augustus Lafayette Lamar," 166. During one of his trips, Lamar encountered Trowbridge, one of the *Wanderer* conspirators, in Halifax, Nova Scotia, as he was en route to London, Charlie [C. A. L. Lamar] to Caro [Lamar], [1863], Lamar Papers, GDAH.

86. Charlie [C. A. L. Lamar] to Caro [Lamar], February 14, 1865, ibid.

87. WR, ser. 2, vol. 8, p. 403.

88. See the *Columbus Daily Sun*, April 15, 1865.

89. J. O. A. Clark to Mrs. Lamar, Wednesday afternoon in April 1865, Lamar Papers, GDAH.

90. R[ebecca] J. McLeod to G. B. Lamar, May 1, 1865, Gazaway Bugg Lamar Papers, Hargrett Library Special Collections, University of Georgia.

91. Of the surviving sons of Henri du Bignon, Charles had been the most successful. For details on his life, see *Georgia: Comprising Sketches of Counties, Towns, Events, Institutions, and Persons, Arranged in Cyclopedic Form*, vol. 1 (Atlanta: State Historical Association, 1906), 629–31. This work is commonly referred to as *Cyclopedia of Georgia*.

92. On the career of Fleming Grantland du Bignon, see Southern Historical Association, *Memoirs of Georgia*, 2:384–86.

7. AFTERMATH

1. The marriage agreement states, "all the property that may devolve to the said Charles Henry duBignon or Ann Amelia Nicolau . . . shall not undergo any alienation . . . without the express consent of the aforesaid Christopher Poulain du-Bignon, Bernard Nicolau and John Couper." GCSC, Deed Book F, 37–39.

2. GCSC, Deeds and Bonds, Book C, 1859–69, 437–38.

3. These deeds of gift are dated August 3, 1863, GCSC Deeds, Book N, 381–87.

4. GCPC, Wills, Inventories, and Appraisals, Book G, 353.

5. Loose document in the du Bignon file, GCPC.

6. This Bible is in the possession of E. Lynn McLarty and his wife, Miriam, who is a descendent of William Turner. The reasons for the name change are a matter of speculation, and Superior Court Records for the November 1875 term are not currently available in the Glynn County Court House. According to a handwritten entry in the Bible, it was at this term that the name change was legally granted.

7. War Department Archives, General Sherman's Special Field Order No. 15, Savannah, Georgia, January 16, 1865; included in Fleming, *Documentary History*, 1:350.

8. Letter from Mrs. A. H. Brown, whose great-grandfather was Henri du Bignon's son Joseph, to Alice, December 23, 1963. At the time of my research a copy was in the possession of the late Mrs. Malcolm Kitchens of St. Simons.

9. Clara Mildred Thompson, *Reconstruction in Georgia*, 303 n. 1.

10. Bishop, *Geographical Journey*, 307. Evidence suggests that, even during the time of Richard Leake and probably earlier, timber was a commodity on Jekyll. See the Leake Papers, University of North Carolina.

11. See the 1870 census record of Glynn County.

12. The census record gives his age as fifty-one, when in reality he was fifty-eight, having been born in 1812. However, no other white John du Bignon lived on the island, so there is no question that this is John Couper du Bignon. The slave schedule from Glynn County of 1860 lists John Couper du Bignon as owning eighteen slaves, nine blacks and nine mulattos. Of the latter there is one female, age twenty-five, who is probably Sylvia. Considering the fact that the census missed John's age by approximately seven years, Sylvia's age may be mistaken as well. However, there is no certainty that she is the mulatto slave of the 1860 schedule, since the schedule does not include names, as earlier lists do. Two other mulattos' ages and sexes correspond exactly with two of the children in question. One male, age fifteen, is in all probability Robert, and the five-year-old mulatto male is most likely Joseph. The only other child who could have been born by the time of the 1860 schedule is Caroline. However, if she was born after August 8, the date of record, she would not have been included.

13. GCPC, Estates, du Bignon files; see also Keber, *Seas of Gold*, 222. In the late 1980s I saw in the same file as the debenture a document that referred to Sylvia and her children as John du Bignon's "family." That document has since disappeared.

14. Among the Brunswick descendents of William du Bignon, son of Robert and Charlotte, are his daughter, Willie Mae du Bignon Washington, whom I first encountered at the dedication of the newly restored du Bignon Cottage in 1989 and who is now buried in Greenwood Cemetery in Brunswick, and her daughter Marian D. Payne, who has graciously provided me with information and photographs.

15. Baptismal Record, July 16, 1811, Sacramental Register No. 1, Cathedral of St. John the Baptist. Although other whites were living on Jekyll Island at the time, Martha Keber argues (*Seas of Gold*, 222) that the special interest that Christophe and Marguerite took in the child, making certain that her baptism was inserted into the record and that she be recorded as "free born," implies that she may indeed have been their first grandchild.

16. Ibid., Sacramental Register No. 2, 1816–38.

17. See Agricultural Census, Schedule 2, June 1880, NARA.

18. Robert and Charlotte du Bignon were married in Brunswick on November 4, 1867. GCPC records. I am grateful to E. Lynn McLarty for providing me with a copy of this certificate.

19. See GCSC Deed Book UU, 240. On Robert's family, see the 1880 census record of Glynn County, Georgia.

20. Information that William was born on Jekyll and lived there until he was fifteen years old comes from both his obituary in the *Brunswick News* (June 30, 1975) and information provided by his granddaughter Marian D. Payne. He died on June 26, just two months shy of his one hundredth birthday on August 28. The

date of his death is from family records, though the *Brunswick News* gives it as June 25. He is buried in Greenwood Cemetery, Brunswick.

21. GCSC, Deeds and Bonds, Book C, 67–68 (1859–69).

22. *Brunswick Advertiser*, March 24, 1875, p. 4. He was well settled in Brunswick by 1853, when Joseph Smith recounts their meeting there. Friedlander died about 1889. See Joseph W. Smith, *Visits to Brunswick*, 16, 38, 104. Smith notes that Friedlander arrived in Brunswick in the early 1850s. Since he is listed in the 1850 census, living in a boarding house owned by Ann C. Clark, we must conclude that he arrived that year.

23. See GCSC Deed Book W, 77. Friedlander would also be a creditor in a later bankruptcy case involving John's nephew, John Eugene du Bignon. See bankruptcy case no. 1333 involving du Bignon and Beck, NARA.

24. Maurice and Maurice, *Jekyll Island*, 9.

25. The date of John Couper du Bignon's death is contained in the Glynn County Mortuary Book, Glynn County Health Department. I am grateful to Sarah K. Johnson, registrar, for helping me locate this record.

26. See documents signed on February 13 and April 1, 1867, GCPC, du Bignon file. William Audley Couper's refusal to serve as Henri's administrator is puzzling, particularly since the will had been drawn up so recently. Apparently early in his own marriage, Couper had had some indiscretions, not unlike those of Henri, but he had "confessed his sins & implored [his wife's] pardon" and subsequently changed his ways. (See Fox-Genovese, *Within the Plantation Household*, 238–39.) His wife may have objected because of Henri's reputation in the community, or, as some Turner descendents believe, his refusal may have come at the request of the children of Henri's first family.

27. GCPC, loose documents in the du Bignon file, October 5, 1868.

28. See the document dated April 7, 1873, signed by Mary, Agnes, and Emily du Bignon. See also the document dated February 6, 1873, in the du Bignon file, GCPC. The record of Henry's borrowing from the estate is contained in case no. 1546, "Henry DuBignon Bankrupt," NARA.

29. Letter filed with the GCPC, loose document in the du Bignon file.

30. Document dated January 20, 1874, GCPC, du Bignon file.

31. All debts are recorded, as noted above, in his bankruptcy file at NARA. Mary Ann Heisler's last name is variously spelled in the legal records, all of which are hand-written, as Heuisler, Haesler, Hensler, and Henisler. I have elected to use the spelling that appears in Henry du Bignon's bankruptcy records.

32. *Brunswick Advertiser*, July 21, 1875, p. 4.

33. See the documents in GCPC, Accounts of Estates, 1870–95, 196–99. A copy is in the Church of the Latter Day Saints Roll no. 0202336, section 2. I am grateful

to E. Lynn McLarty for calling this to my attention. In a motion filed by Tufts's lawyer, H. H. Cunningham, to the U.S. District Court, South District of Georgia, on March 25, 1878, as part of Henry du Bignon's bankruptcy case no. 1546, NARA records, he claims that the judgment was assigned to Martin Tufts on March 2, 1874. However, other records do not bear this out. This may have been the date that he and Mary Heisler made the agreement between themselves, but legal records indicate that it was not finalized until 1877. An inventory of Henry's property, signed by Martin Tufts on February 18, 1877, and contained in the records of Henry's bankruptcy case, includes not only the land but also twenty-seven marsh ponies, three old mules, twenty head of wild cattle, sixty head of wild hogs, one hundred "gentle hogs," three plows, one wagon, one double-barrel shot gun, wearing apparel, and the diamond pin and gold watch he had used as collateral for a loan. The inventory notes that the pin and watch are "in the hands of Cargile [*sic*] for money loaned."

34. The name of the boy that Henry adopted is given as Henry F. du Bignon in the homestead exemption petition as well in the Administrator's Deed, dated December 1, 1885, GCPC Deed Book Z, 391. Curiously, it appears in Henry's bankruptcy records as Frank J. du Bignon. However, no child by that name is listed among any du Bignon descendents of the time. The name, Frank, was likely derived from the child's middle name, Francis.

35. The responses to the Interrogatories presented to Alice Symons du Bignon, excerpts of which are quoted here, were filed with the court May 7, 1883. GCPC, du Bignon file. In this document W. J. Williams is named as attorney for the applicant, Henry du Bignon.

36. GCPC, du Bignon file, document filed April 30, 1883.

37. Document submitted to the District Court of the United States for the Southern District of Georgia, May 14, 1880, case no. 1546, as part of Henry's petition for a final discharge of the bankruptcy (NARA).

38. The date of Henry du Bignon's death is provided by the du Bignon papers filed in the GCPC and entered into the minutes, 339. See also Deed Book Z, 391.

39. Administrator's Deed, December 1, 1885, recorded January 30, 1886, GCPC Deed Book Z, 391. Henry F. du Bignon would go on to become clerk of the Glynn County Superior Court, serving for fifty-four years, before his death on June 29, 1957. He was said at the time of his death to be "better known than any Brunswick resident" (*Brunswick News*, July 1, 1957).

40. Documents dated February 12, 1885, in GCPC, du Bignon file. Also recorded in Administration and Guardiancy Book 65; entered into minutes on p. 239.

41. Document signed by E. P. Dart, Ordinary, GCPC, du Bignon file.

42. Administrator's Deed, December 1, 1885, GCPC Deed Book Z, 391.

43. See bankruptcy records of the District Court of the United States Southern District, case no. 736, NARA. See Commissioner's Deed, July 1, 1879, Glynn County Deed Book T, 11. On that same date the court recorded a mortgage contracted by John E. du Bignon to his aunt, Ann V. [Grantland] du Bignon, representing a lien of one thousand dollars on the southern end of Jekyll Island. The note was marked paid on September 11, 1881.

44. Warranty Deed, June 16, 1885, GCSC Deed Book Y, 303.

45. Eliza du Bignon, who died October 16, 1886, left to her sisters Catherine A. Hazelhurst and Sarah B. Berryman "all my interest in and right to the unpaid purchase money due me for thirty (30) acres more or less of land lying upon Jekyl Island . . . heretofore conveyed by me to John E. duBignon." GCPC, loose papers in the du Bignon file, February 4, 1886.

46. See McCash, *Jekyll Island Cottage Colony*, 26–29.

47. Ober, "Dungeness," 241–49.

48. Harris, *Deep Souths*, 45; Nightingale, "Dungeness," 369–83.

49. See R. G. Dun Collection, vol. 347, 800H, Harvard University. Many details about the life of Newton Finney have been carefully assembled by his descendent Doris Finney Liebrecht. A copy is contained in the Finney file at the Jekyll Island Museum.

50. *Brunswick Advertiser and Appeal*, April 25, 1885. See McCash, *Jekyll Island Cottage Colony*, 28.

51. *Brunswick Advertiser and Appeal*, June 20, 1885.

52. Ibid., August 22, 1885.

53. *Brunswick—the City by the Sea*, 9, 21.

54. For additional details on the founding of the Jekyll Island Club and its history, see McCash and McCash, *Jekyll Island Club*, 1–13. During his 1901 visit to Brunswick, Joseph Smith took special notice of the change in Jekyll Island. Although he had unfortunately not described his earlier visit, he stated: "Jekyl Island, which I had visited years before, had been purchased by influential citizens of New York who had spent much money in beautifying the island. A fine steam yacht plies between Jekyl Island and Brunswick" (*Visits to Brunswick*, 105).

Selected Bibliography

ARCHIVAL SOURCES

Duke University, Perkins Library Special Collections, Durham, North Carolina
  Godfrey Barnsley Papers
  Raymond Demere Papers
Emory University, Woodruff Library Special Collections, Atlanta, Georgia
  Lamar Papers
  Carey W. Styles Papers
  Wanderer Log
Georgia Department of Archives and History, Morrow, Georgia
  Civil War Manuscripts Collection
  Gabriel Farmer Family Civil War Papers
  Grand Dutreuilh Family Papers
  Lamar Papers
Georgia Historical Society, Savannah, Georgia
  Margaret Davis Cate Collection
  Floyd Collection
  Hartridge Collection
  Leake Plantation Book
  Mercer Papers
Harvard University, Baker Library, Cambridge, Massachusetts
  R. G. Dun Collection
Jekyll Island Museum, Jekyll Island, Georgia
  Jacob Solis Cohen Diary
  Du Bignon Papers
Museum of Coastal Georgia History, St. Simons, Georgia
  Couper Collection
  Lamar Papers
  Wylly Papers

National Archives and Record Administration, Southeast Region, East Point, Georgia
Admiralty Court Records
Bankruptcy Court Records
Census Records
Private Collections
Cordell Collection
Demere Collection
Howell Collection (formerly McDowell Collection)
Liebrecht Collection
McLarty Collection
University of Georgia, Hargrett Library Special Collections, Athens, Georgia
Howell Cobb Collection
Gazaway Bugg Lamar Papers
University of North Carolina, Southern Historical Collection, Chapel Hill,
North Carolina
Leake Papers
Maurice Papers
Other Public Archives Used
Archives départementales des Côtes d'Armor, St.-Brieuc, France
Chatham County Superior and Probate Court Records, Savannah, Georgia
Glynn County Superior and Probate Court Records, Brunswick, Georgia
Liberty County Superior and Probate Court Records, Hinesville, Georgia
Library of Congress, Washington, D.C.
Mauritius Archives, Petite-Rivière, Mauritius
National Archives, Washington, D.C.
National Archives of St. Kitts, Basseterre, West Indies
Public Record Office, Kew, England
Sacramental Registers, Cathedral of St. John the Baptist, Savannah, Georgia
Saint Christopher Heritage Society, St. Kitts, West Indies

NEWSPAPERS

Atlanta Constitution
Augusta Dispatch
Brunswick Advertiser and Appeal
Brunswick Advocate
Brunswick News
Charleston Courier
Columbian Museum and Savannah Advertiser
Columbus Daily Sun

Daily Georgian
Georgia Gazette
New York Herald
New York Times
New York Tribune
Republican and Savannah Evening Ledger
Savannah Daily Morning News
Savannah Daily Republican
Savannah Georgian
Savannah National Republican
Savannah Press
Savannah Republican
Weekly Georgian

BOOKS, ARTICLES, AND OTHER WRITINGS

Abbot, W. W. *The Royal Governors of Georgia, 1754–1775*. Chapel Hill: University of North Carolina Press, 1959.

Arnade, Charles W. *The Siege of St. Augustine in 1702*. Gainesville: University of Florida Press, 1959.

Bagwell, James. *Rice Gold: James Hamilton Couper and Plantation Life on the Georgia Coast*. Macon, Ga.: Mercer University Press, 2000.

Bancroft, Frederic. *Slave Trading in the Old South*. Baltimore: J. H. Furst, 1931.

Bell, Malcolm Jr. *Major Butler's Legacy: Five Generations of a Slaveholding Family*. Athens: University of Georgia Press, 1987.

Bennett, Charles E. *Laudonnière and Fort Caroline: History and Documents*. Gainesville: University of Florida Press, 1964.

———. *Settlement of Florida*. Gainesville: University of Florida Press, 1968.

Bishop, Nathaniel. *Voyage of the Paper Canoe: A Geographical Journey of 2500 Miles from Quebec to the Gulf of Mexico, during the Years 1874–5*. Boston: Lee and Shepard, 1878.

Bolton, Herbert E., and Mary Ross. *The Debatable Land: A Sketch of the Anglo-Spanish Contest for the Georgia Country*. 1925. Reprint, New York: Russell and Russell, 1968.

———, trans. and eds. *Arredondo's Historical Proof of Spain's Title to Georgia*. Berkeley: University of California Press, 1925.

Brunswick—the City by the Sea: A Pamphlet Descriptive of Brunswick and Glynn County Georgia. Brunswick: Published by the Advertiser and Appeal, 1885.

Bullard, Mary R. *Cumberland Island: A History*. Athens: University of Georgia Press, 2003.

————. *Pierre Bernardey of Cumberland Island.* S. Dartmouth, Mass.: National Park Service, 1984.

————. *Robert Stafford of Cumberland Island: Growth of a Planter.* Athens: University of Georgia Press, 1995.

Bushnell, Amy. *Situado and Sabana: Spain's Support System for the Presidio and Mission Provinces of Florida.* Athens, Ga.: American Museum of Natural History, 1994; distributed by University of Georgia Press.

Candler, Allen D., ed. *The Confederate Records of the State of Georgia.* Atlanta: 1909.

————. *Revolutionary Records of the State of Georgia.* Atlanta: Franklin-Turner, 1908.

Cashin, Edward J. *William Bartram and the American Revolution on the Southern Frontier.* Columbia: University of South Carolina Press, 2000.

Cate, Margaret Davis. *Our Todays and Yeserdays: A Story of Brunswick and the Coastal Islands.* Brunswick: Glover Bros., 1930.

Coleman, Kenneth. *The American Revolution in Georgia, 1763–1789.* Athens: University of Georgia Press, 1958.

————. *Colonial Georgia: A History.* New York: Scribner, 1976.

————. *Georgia History in Outline.* Athens: University of Georgia Press, 1960.

Colonial Records of the State of Georgia. Vols. 1–19 and 21–26 edited by Allen D. Candler; vols. 20 and 27–32 edited by Kenneth Coleman and Milton Ready; vols. 22–26 revised and edited by Lucian Lamar Knight. Athens: University of Georgia Press.

Coulter, E. Merton. "Boating as a Sport in the Old South." *Georgia Historical Quarterly* 27 (1943): 231–47.

————. *Georgia: A Short History.* Chapel Hill: University of North Carolina Press, 1947.

————. *Thomas Spalding of Sapelo.* Baton Rouge: Louisiana State University Press, 1940.

————, ed. *Journal of William Stephens, 1743–1745.* Athens: University of Georgia Press, 1959.

Crook, Morgan R., Jr. "An Archeological Survey of Jekyll Island, Georgia." Report prepared for the Jekyll Island Authority, June 20, 1985.

Curnock, Nehemiah, ed. *Journal of the Rev. John Wesley, A.M.* Vol. 1. London: Epworth Press, 1938.

Dalton, Rex. "The Coast Road." *Nature* 422 (March 6, 2003): 10–12.

Davis, Harold E. *The Fledgling Province: Social and Cultural Life in Colonial Georgia, 1733–1776.* Chapel Hill: University of North Carolina Press, 1976.

De Bry, Theodore. *America, part II. Brevis narratio eorum quae in Florida Americae prouincia Gallis acciderunt.* Frankfurt, 1591.

Flanders, Ralph Betts. *Plantation Slavery in Georgia*. Cos Cob, Conn.: John E. Edwards, 1967.

Fleming, Walter L. *Documentary History of Reconstruction: Political, Military, Social, Religious, Educational, and Industrial, 1865 to the Present Time*. Cleveland: A. H. Clark, 1906–7.

Fox-Genovese, Elizabeth. *Within the Plantation Household: Black and White Women of the Old South*. Chapel Hill: University of North Carolina Press, 1988.

"From Colonial Birth to Civil War Rebellion: Archaeological Investigation of 125 Years of Occupation at Horton House, Jekyll Island, Georgia." Report prepared for the Jekyll Island Authority by Rita Folse Elliott, Virginia A. Pierce, and Daniel J. Elliott of Southern Research, August 2002. Jekyll Island Museum.

Hann, John H. *A History of the Timucua Indians and Missions*. Gainesville: University Press of Florida, 1996.

———. "Twilight of the Mocama and Guale Aborigines as Portrayed in the 1695 Spanish Visitation." *Florida Historical Quarterly* 66 (1987): 1–24.

———. "1630 Memorial of Fray Francisco Alonso de Jesús on Spanish Florida's Missions and Natives." *The Americas* 50 (1993): 85–105.

Harris, J. William. *Deep Souths: Delta, Piedmont, and Sea Island Society in the Age of Segregation*. Baltimore: The Johns Hopkins University Press, 2001.

Hawes, Lilla M., ed. *Collections of the Georgia Historical Society*. Vol. 10, *The Proceedings and Minutes of the Governor and Council of Georgia*. Savannah: Georgia Historical Society, 1952.

Head, Franklin Harvey. "The Legends of Jekyl Island." *The New England Magazine* 8 (1893): 393–99.

Hoffman, Paul E. *A New Andalucia and a Way to the Orient: The American Southeast during the Sixeenth Century*. Baton Rouge: Louisiana State University Press, 1990.

Holmes, James. *"Dr. Bullie's" Notes*. Edited by Delma Eugene Presley. Atlanta: Cherokee Publishing Company, 1976.

Hudson, Charles M. *Black Drink: A Native American Tea*. Athens: University of Georgia Press, 1979.

Hulton, Paul. *The Work of Jacques Le Moyne de Morgues: A Huguenot Artist in France, Florida, and England*. 2 vols. London: British Museum, 1977.

Ivers, Larry. *British Drums on the Southern Frontier: The Military Colonization of Georgia, 1733–1749*. Chapel Hill: University of North Carolina Press, 1974.

Jones, Charles C. Jr. *Historical Sketch of Tomo-Chi-Chi, Mico of the Yamacraws*. Albany, N.Y.: Joel Munsell, 1868.

Jones, Grant D. "The Ethnohistory of the Guale Coast through 1684." In *The An-*

thropology of St. Catherines Island, edited by David Hurst Thomas et al. New York: American Museum of Natural History, 1978.

Keber, Martha L. "Refuge and Ruin: The French Sapelo Company." *Georgia Historical Quarterly* 86 (2002): 173–200.

———. *Seas of Gold, Seas of Cotton: Christophe Poulain DuBignon of Jekyll Island.* Athens: University of Georgia Press, 2002.

Killion, Ronald G., and Charles T. Waller. *Georgia and the Revolution.* Atlanta: Cherokee Press, 1975.

Lane, Mills, ed. *General Oglethorpe's Georgia: Colonial Letters, 1733–1743.* Savannah: Beehive Press, 1975.

Laudonnière, René. *Three Voyages.* Translated by Charles E. Bennett. Tuscaloosa: University of Alabama Press, 2001.

Lepper, Brad. "Coastal Navigators: The First Americans May Have Come by Water." *Scientific American Discovering Archaeology* (February 2000): 34–35.

Martin, C. Brenden, and June Hall McCash. "From Millionaires to the Masses: Tourism at Jekyll Island, Georgia." In *Southern Journeys: Tourism, History, and Culture in the Modern South,* edited by Richard D. Starnes, 154–76. Tuscaloosa: University of Alabama Press, 2003.

Maurice, Charlotte, and Charles Stewart Maurice. *Jekyl Island: Some Historic Notes and Some Legends.* Privately printed, [1926].

McCall, Hugh. *The History of Georgia, Containing Brief Sketches of the Most Remarkable Events up to the Present Day.* 2 vols. 1811–16. Reprint, Atlanta: A. B. Caldwell, 1909.

McCash, June Hall. *The Jekyll Island Cottage Colony.* Athens: University of Georgia Press, 1998.

McCash, William Barton, and June Hall McCash. *The Jekyll Island Club: Southern Haven for America's Millionaires.* Athens: University of Georgia Press, 1989.

McEwan, Bonnie G., ed. *Indians of the Greater Southeast: Historical Archaeology and Ethnohistory.* Gainesville: University Press of Florida, 2000.

McGrath, John T. *The French in Early Florida: In the Eye of the Hurricane.* Gainesville: University Press of Florida, 2000.

McLeod, Mrs. Hugh (Rebecca Lamar). "The Loss of the Steamer Pulaski." *Georgia Historical Quarterly* 3 (1919): 63–95.

McPherson, Robert G., ed. *Journal of the Earl of Egmont: Abstract of the Trustees' Proceedings for Establishing the Colony of Georgia.* Athens: University of Georgia Press, 1962.

Milanich, Jerald T. *Laboring in the Fields of the Lord: Spanish Missions and Southeastern Indians.* Washington, D.C.: Smithsonian Institution Press, 1999.

———. *The Timucua.* Oxford: Blackwells, 1996.

Milanich, Jerald, and Samuel Proctor, eds. *Tacachale: Essays on the Indians of Florida and Southeastern Georgia during the Historic Period.* Gainesville: University Presses of Florida, 1978.

Montgomery, Charles J. "Survivors from the Cargo of the Negro Slave Yacht Wanderer." *American Anthropologist*, n.s., 10 (1908): 611–27.

Moore, Francis. *A Voyage to Georgia, Begun in the Year 1735.* London, 1744. Reprinted in *Collections of the Georgia Historical Society*, vol. 1. Savannah, Ga., 1840.

Nightingale, B. N. "Dungeness." *Georgia Historical Quarterly* 22 (1938): 369–83.

Ober, Frederick. "Dungeness, General Greene's Sea Island Plantation." *Lippincott's Magazine of Popular Literature and Science* (1880): 241–49.

Official Records of the Union and Confederate Navies in the War of the Rebellion. 30 vols. Washington, D.C.: Government Printing Office, 1894–1922.

Oré, Luis Jerónimo de. *The Martyrs of Florida (1513–1616).* Translated by Maynard Geiger. New York: J. F. Wagner, 1936.

Peck, Douglas T. "Lucas Vásquez de Ayllón's Doomed Colony of San Miguel de Gualdape." *Georgia Historical Quarterly* 85 (2001): 183–98.

Penson, Lillian M. *The Colonial Agents of the British West Indies: A Study in Colonial Administration, Mainly in the Eighteenth Century.* 1824. Reprint, London: Frank Cass, 1971.

Ribaut, Jean. *The Whole and True Discouerye of Terra Florida.* Gainesville: University of Florida Press, 1964.

Rosengarten, Theodore. *Tombee: Portrait of a Cotton Planter.* New York: Morrow, 1986.

Ruple, Steven D. "Archeology of the Horton House." Master's thesis, University of Florida, 1976.

Scott, J. T. "The Frederica Homefront in 1742." *Georgia Historical Quarterly* 78 (1994): 493–508.

Sheridan, Richard B. *The Development of the Plantations to 1750: An Era of West Indian Prosperity, 1750–1775.* Barbados: Caribbean Universities Press, 1970.

"Slave-Trader's Letter-Book." *The North American Review* 143 (1886): 447–61.

Smith, Joseph W. *Visits to Brunswick, Georgia, and Travels South.* Boston: Adison C. Getchell and Son, 1907.

Smith, Julia Floyd. *Slavery and Rice Culture in Low Country Georgia, 1750–1860.* Knoxville: University of Tennessee Press, 1985.

The Southern Historical Association. *Memoirs of Georgia: Containing Historical Accounts of the State's Civil, Military, Industrial and Professional Interests, and Personal Sketches of Many of Its People.* 2 vols. Atlanta: The Southern Historical Association, 1895.

Spalding, Phinizy. "Georgians and the War of Jenkins' Ear: Oglethorpe, Georgia, and the Spanish Threat." *Georgia Historical Quarterly* 78 (1994): 461–70.

———. *Oglethorpe in America.* Chicago: University of Chicago Press, 1977.

Spalding, Thomas. "Observations on the Introduction of Long Staple Cotton into Georgia." *Southern Agriculturist* 5 (1832): 189–90.

Stewart, Mart A. *"What Nature Suffers to Groe": Life, Labor, and Landscape on the Georgia Coast, 1680–1920*. Athens: University of Georgia Press, 1996.

Sturtevant, William C. "The Misconnection of Guale and Yamasee with Muskogean." *International Journal of American Linguistics* 60 (1994): 139–48.

Sullivan, Buddy. *Early Days on the Georgia Tidewater*. 5th ed. Darien, Ga.: Darien Printing, 1997.

———. *Georgia: A State History*. Charleston: Arcadia, 2003.

Swanton, John R. *Early History of the Creek Indians and Their Neighbors*. 1922. Reprint, New York: Johnson Reprint, 1970.

———. *The Indians of the Southeastern United States*. New York: Greenwood Press, 1969.

Sweet, Julie Ann. "Bearing Feathers of the Eagle: Tomochichi's Trip to England." *Georgia Historical Quarterly* 86 (2002): 339–71.

Taylor, Paul S. *Georgia Plan: 1732–1752*. Berkeley: University of California Press, 1972.

Thomas, David Hurst, et al. *The Archaeology of Mission Santa Catalina de Guale: 1. Search and Discovery*. Anthropological Papers 63, pt. 2. New York: American Museum of Natural History, 1987.

Thomas, David Hurst, et al., eds. *The Anthropology of St. Catherines Island*. Anthropological Papers 55, pt. 2. New York: American Museum of Natural History, 1978.

Thomas, Kenneth H. Jr. "The Sapelo Company: Five Frenchmen on the Georgia Coast, 1789–1794." *The Proceedings and Papers of the Georgia Association of Historians* 10 (1989): 37–64.

Thompson, Clara Mildred. *Reconstruction in Georgia, Economic, Social, Political, 1865–1872*. New York: Columbia University Press, 1915.

Thompson, Winfield. "The Slave Ship Wanderer." *The Rudder* 15 (1904): 51–61, 114–22, 238–43.

Vanstory, Burnette. *Georgia's Land of the Golden Isles*. Athens: University of Georgia Press, 1956.

Vaughan, Alden T., ed. *Early American Indian Documents: Treaties and Laws, 1607–1789*. Frederick, Md.: University Publications of America, 1989.

Ward, J. R. *British West Indian Slavery, 1750–1834: The Process of Amelioration*. Oxford: Clarendon Press, 1988.

War of the Rebellion: A Compilation of Official Records of the Union and Confederate Armies. 70 vols. Washington, D.C.: Government Printing Office, 1880–1901.

Watkins, Robert, and George Watkins. *A Digest of the Laws of the State of Georgia*, pt. 1. Philadelphia: R. Aitken, 1800.

Wells, Tom Henderson. "Charles Augustus Lafayette Lamar: Gentleman Slave Trader." *Georgia Historical Quarterly* 47 (1963): 158–68.

———. *The Slave Ship Wanderer.* Athens: University of Georgia Press, 1968.

"William Logan's Journal of a Journey to Georgia, 1745." *Pennsylvania Magazine of History and Biography* 36 (1912): 1–16, 162–86.

Wish, Harvey. "The Revival of the African Slave Trade in the United States, 1856–1860." *Mississippi Valley Historical Review* 27 (1908): 569–88.

Wood, Virginia Steele, and Mary R. Bullard, eds. *Journal of a Visit to the Georgia Islands of St. Catherines, Green, Ossabaw, Sapelo, St. Simons, Jekyll, and Cumberland, with Comments on the Florida Islands of Amelia, Talbot, and St. George, in 1753.* Macon, Ga.: Mercer University Press, 1996.

Worth, John E. *The Struggle for the Georgia Coast: An Eighteenth-Century Spanish Retrospective on Guale and Mocama.* Anthropological Papers 75. New York: American Museum of Natural History, 1995.

———. *The Timucuan Chiefdoms of Spanish Florida.* 2 vols. Gainesville: University Press of Florida, 1998.

———. *The Timucuan Missions of Spanish Florida and the Rebellion of 1656.* PhD diss., University of Florida, 1992.

Index

Wanderer (slave ship), 152–69 passim, 187, 194, 243 (nn. 5–6), 244 (n. 9), 245 (n. 26), 247 (n. 85); auction of, 164; building of, 244 (n. 16); landing of, at Jekyll Island, 152, 154, 156; notoriety of, 165, 166, 184, 195; original owner of, 160; passenger capacity of, 243 (nn. 2–4); slaves of, 154, 155, 163, 243 (n. 6); William Corrie as captain of, 163, 243 (n. 3). *See also* Lamar, Charles Augustus Lafayette
War of 1812, 3, 119, 120
War of Jenkins' Ear, 60, 69, 74
War of Spanish Succession, 40
Washington, George, 105, 235 (n. 10)
Wassaw Island, 119
Waycross, Ga., 168
Wayne, Anthony, 97, 98
Wayne, Henry C., 169, 172, 175
Waynesville, Ga., 168
Wesley, Charles, 47
Wesley, John, 47, 49, 55, 224 (n. 20)
West Indies, 93, 98, 125, 215 (n. 2); St. Kitts, 82, 86, 87, 88. *See also* Martin, Clement, Jr.; Martin, Clement, Sr.
Whitefield, George, ix, 228 (n. 7)
Williams, Uster (Mabiala), 154, 155
Wilson, James H., 186

Wood, John, 96
Woodville Plantation, 132, 194
World War II, 4
Wright, James, 84–86, 97
Wylly, Alexander Campbell, 110, 237–38 (n. 47); marriage of, to Margaret Armstrong, 116; and refuge on Jekyll Island, 116; and service in the King's Rangers, 116
Wylly, Caroline Georgia, 237 (nn. 46–47); marriage of, to James Hamilton Couper, 237 (n. 47)
Wylly, Heriot Louisa, 237 (n. 46)
Wylly, John Armstrong, 237 (n. 46)
Wylly, Margaret Armstrong, 117; marriage of, to Alexander Campbell Wylly, 116
Wylly, Margaret Matilda, 237 (n. 46)
Wylly, Susan, 116–17, 237 (n. 47); death of, 238 (n. 47)

Yamacraw, 7, 41, 43, 223 (n. 7), 232 (n. 69). *See also* Creeks
Yamasee, 37
Yamasee War, 40
Yellow Bluff Creek, 150, 189

Zow Uncola (*Wanderer* slave), 155